AMONG THE TROLLS

Marianna Spring is the BBC's first disinformation and social media correspondent and an award-winning journalist. She presents podcasts and documentaries investigating disinformation and social media for BBC Radio 4, as well as for BBC *Panorama* and BBC Three. She is also one of the presenters of the BBC's *Americast* podcast. She has been named the British Press Guild's Audio Presenter of the Year and Royal Television Society Innovation winner.

AMONG THE TROLLS

My Journey Through Conspiracyland

Marianna Spring

Atlantic Books
London

First published in hardback in Great Britain in 2024 by Atlantic Books, an imprint of Atlantic Books Ltd.

Copyright © Marianna Spring, 2024

The moral right of Marianna Spring to be identified as the author of this work has been asserted by her in accordance with the Copyright, Designs and Patents Act of 1988.

All rights reserved. No part of this publication may be reproduced, stored in a retrieval system, or transmitted in any form or by any means, electronic, mechanical, photocopying, recording, or otherwise, without the prior permission of both the copyright owner and the above publisher of this book.

Every effort has been made to trace or contact all copyright holders. The publishers will be pleased to make good any omissions or rectify any mistakes brought to their attention at the earliest opportunity.

10 9 8 7 6 5 4 3 2

A CIP catalogue record for this book is available from the British Library.

Hardback ISBN: 978 1 83895 523 6
Trade paperback ISBN: 978 1 83895 524 3
E-book ISBN: 978 1 83895 525 0

Printed and bound by CPI (UK) Ltd, Croydon CR0 4YY

Atlantic Books
An imprint of Atlantic Books Ltd
Ormond House
26–27 Boswell Street
London
WC1N 3JZ

www.atlantic-books.co.uk

MIX
Paper | Supporting
responsible forestry
FSC
www.fsc.org   FSC® C171272

To Mum, Dad, and everyone I love
but can't name because of the trolls.

CONTENTS

CONTENTS

INTRODUCTION

I was five years old when hijackers flew planes into the Twin Towers in New York on 11 September 2001. My mum collected me from school and told my teacher what a terrible day it was. As we walked home, I asked her what had happened. She explained how these aeroplanes had been flown into the towers on purpose. I kept asking her – was it an accident? To which she would reply 'no'. I couldn't get my head around how something like that could happen deliberately. It was terrifying.

In the weeks and months that followed the attack, conspiracy theories about 9/11 proved very popular. Rather than spreading like wildfire on social media, they unfolded in chatrooms and on websites, via DVDs and talks. I often think back to that moment. Partly because it explains a lot of why I wanted to become a journalist – I wanted to understand why bad things happen and reveal it to other people. And partly because it was my entry point into the world of conspiracy theories, somewhere I'm going to call Conspiracyland.

We all to some degree want to make sense of the chaos around us. We want to be able to predict when people could cause harm. We want to be one step ahead of them. The way my five-year-old brain couldn't understand the attack in some ways mirrors the mentality of the people who deny it ever happened, in spite of the evidence. We all find it difficult to make sense of. Except the explanations spun by conspiracy theorists about 9/11 were much more complicated and much less innocent than my 'well, maybe they didn't mean to'.

The people who believed and pushed these conspiracy theories were the founding fathers of Conspiracyland. It isn't a real place, of course. The only way inside is by falling down the rabbit hole. Not quite in the same way as in Lewis Carroll's *Alice's Adventures in Wonderland*, where Alice chases after a flustered white rabbit with a pocket watch and finds herself in a whole new universe. You just have to venture into certain parts of the online world, and you'll find yourself tumbling very quickly.

I've spent a lot of time exploring the UK's Conspiracyland in particular. Sometimes, I've heard or read as many as ten impossible things before breakfast. You'd be mistaken in thinking this is a universe limited to social media. It's a parallel world where everything is topsy-turvy. It has its own leaders, its own holiday retreats, its own protests, its own festivals – and its own media, from video channels to conspiracy theory newspapers. Everything you think you know – well, in Conspiracyland it's the opposite. The beliefs some of its members hold extend far beyond legitimate concerns, fears and questions of wrongdoing. Real examples of corruption and conspiracy are extrapolated and used to declare that almost everything is staged – from global pandemics and climate change to wars and terror attacks.

2

Some of the inhabitants of Conspiracyland are fluent in hate and blame. In modern-day Britain, a committed minority calls for the execution of journalists, politicians, nurses and doctors, based on an unflinching belief in disinformation stating that these people are complicit in sinister plots to harm people. But there's no evidence to back up these grand plans, and even the most powerful people in the world would struggle to pull them off.

As the BBC's disinformation and social media correspondent, I spend my days investigating this strange new world. And I frequently come face-to-face with people who really don't like me very much. Between January and June 2023, I received 11,771 of the 14,488 abusive messages escalated in the BBC's own system designed to detect hate. Conspiracyland is not limited to one place in Britain, either. It's infected towns up and down the country. Anywhere with an internet connection, you'll likely be able to venture into it.

It might seem a faraway place for some of us. But all of our social media feeds can distort the world around us. We can be constantly exposed to subjective and polarized online worlds, and pushed more and more of what we want to see by automated computer systems – algorithms. They use the hundreds of clues we give them every day to figure out who we are and what we like. They drive us to places and people we otherwise might not have found. They push us further to the extremes. Politicians and influencers and anyone else chasing likes and power weaponize that fact. Nuance and moderate viewpoints can be rare in this universe. No one is immune to these powers, and the consequences are far from fringe and inconsequential – for individuals, communities and societies.

At the most extreme end, there have been conspiracy-theory-driven riots at the US Capitol and a coup attempt foiled in Germany. Disinformation and hate have driven apart local communities. Victims of war have been targeted by ruthless propaganda campaigns waged by governments. Survivors of terror attacks have been told their injuries were faked. Healthcare workers, reporters and politicians have had their lives threatened by those in the online world just for doing their jobs – myself included. Lies about illnesses and vaccines have caused people to lose their lives. Families have been fractured by one person's belief in conspiracy theories, isolating them from those they love the most. Elections in Brazil and Ethiopia have been plagued with mistruths. There are threats with real-world consequences. More so than ever, what's happening on social media is bleeding into all of our lives – and it's having a huge impact.

I don't reside in an ivory tower. I go out and meet the conspiracy theorists, the trolls and their victims, and everyone else affected. I travel all over the UK, and across the world, so I can uncover for myself what's happening. My focus is primarily on the disinformation war waged on British soil, but that connects up with the one being waged everywhere.

I've eaten fruit in an anti-vaxxer's kitchen with a blind cat, doorstepped a disaster troll at a market stall in a Welsh town and unearthed the conspiracy underbelly swelling in the picturesque town of Shrewsbury. I've been called a bitch while attending conspiracy theory rallies in Devon by a protester who claimed that's not what they were doing, confronted my own trolls and quizzed the editor of a conspiracy theory newspaper in a pub with multiple cameras rolling.

I've cried with a grieving mum as I stood in the bedroom she still hoovers for her son, and I've had cups of tea with people who've been told that the worst day of their life never happened. I've met social media insiders in mysterious hotel rooms and had one of the world's most powerful social media bosses tweet a picture of my face. I've gone on car journeys with true crime TikTokers. I've interviewed people caught up in wars accused of acting, and I've wandered around French towns looking at looted shops and smashed windows, the flames of violence fanned by social media.

I've huddled in my bedroom with five phones featuring fake characters I created to enter subjective social media worlds, and then flown with those same phones to Washington and Milwaukee to match up what these characters were seeing online to the experiences of real people. I've spoken to the bravest truth-tellers in the Philippines targeted by the worst online abuse, doctors who are the recipients of death threats, and journalists attacked in Germany by people who seemed to believe disinformation.

It became clear to me early on that this was so much more than bots – inauthentic accounts used to manipulate online conversations. I wanted to understand the real people caught up in this world, who are often there at great risk to themselves and others. Through their stories, I want to show who really believes this stuff, how this problem manifests – and how it's shaping the world around us. From podcasts and investigative documentaries to online, digital, radio and TV news bulletins, my hope has been to report on this for everyone.

Before we get started, let me introduce you to the language of Conspiracyland and how some of the terms I'll be using interact with each other. Let's begin with the basics.

What's a *conspiracy theory*? It's defined as the explanation for an event that relies on a belief in a conspiracy being carried out by powerful groups – when other explanations are actually a lot more likely. Conspiracy theories are characterized by a lack of evidence, and are often more about feelings and suspicions than cold, hard facts. In this book, the conspiracy theories I'll be explaining aren't the quirky ones we often like to indulge. They're not fantasies with little or no consequence – for example the idea that the moon landings were staged, or that aliens exist.

Instead, they are more sinister theories that suggest global events affecting all of us are staged in some way as part of a plot. Think of anything bad that's happened over the past few years, and someone in Conspiracyland thinks the government and powerful people faked it. These theories are often all at once totally unwieldy and too complex to follow and also very black-and-white. This politician has lied before and is accused of corruption (true) and therefore they are part of a plot to kill us all with vaccines but are pretending they are not (not true). Conspiracy theories can come true, of course – and it's important to underline early on that the extreme theories being shared online have somewhat undermined the interrogation of real allegations of plots and wrongdoing.

These conspiracy theories sit adjacent to misinformation and disinformation. The difficulty with conspiracy theories is that, since they often rely on allegations of complicated, sinister plots for which there isn't any evidence, it's harder to categorically disprove them. Rather, they're characterized by an absence of evidence – and their improbability.

Misinformation is the catch-all term used to describe the spread of misleading claims. Crucially, intention isn't required. *Disinformation*, however, refers to the deliberate dissemination of false information. Take, for example, the Russian government claiming that someone caught up in an attack they've waged in Ukraine is really a paid actor who is just trying to make Russia look bad. When talking about disinformation, it's important to think about its purpose. It's usually about deliberately undermining the truth because it's beneficial to the person lying; whether that's because it convinces a population that their government hasn't hurt civilians with bombs, or – on a smaller scale – because the person spreading this mistruth can make money and grow a following out of it.

Trolling has become a weapon for those who disseminate disinformation or promote conspiracy theories. Very aptly, the term itself seems to derive from language about hunting, and less so from fairy tales about trolls living under bridges. The old French term *troller* means 'to wander around looking for something to kill' or 'to go hunting for game with no specific purpose'.[1] Trolling is in its essence sending out provocative and mean messages purely for a reaction. It's all about getting a rise out of someone.

These days, trolling is much more synonymous with inflammatory and offensive comments online. Those caught up in false allegations or implicated in these conspiracy theories about shady plots can find themselves prime targets for hate. That's how this works. It's about finding someone specific to blame for what's going wrong. Only, instead of being righteous, the anger is often misplaced. You're not just disagreeing with someone; you're going as far as threatening them. You're targeting who they are rather than what they've done, and it can all get very nasty.

This beat didn't exist when I was born – but it is now crucial to understanding the modern world and where we're all headed. Conspiracyland ultimately poses a threat to the fabric of our society. After all, the democracies we live in are built on the concept of a shared reality, a universal truth. You and I can both look up at the sky and agree that it's blue. I might like that it's blue and you might hate the colour, but ultimately we agree it exists. But if you don't think the sky is there at all, we can't have any kind of rational conversation about it. When the objective truth is out of our reach, we're in trouble.

In the past, the world of conspiracy theories and hate was

very different. As recently as a decade ago, you might have thought of online trolls as lonely basement-dwellers posting inconsequential, nasty remarks on internet forums. While disinformation has always plagued our society, it was spread in a different way – via the front pages of specific newspapers, and the mouths of certain politicians. Spin is nothing new, and it is true that politicians and powerful people lie and have always done so. Think of the ruins in Pompeii, where propaganda is scrawled on the walls. As journalists, it's our job to investigate and hold the powerful to account for their mistruths. Rumour is not new, either. Gather a group of human beings in one space for any period of time, and whispers will begin to spread.

But before, the speed at which this propaganda, speculation and disinformation could spread was just a lot slower. Conspiracy theories, too, weren't quite so widespread or pervasive. They were used to explain events that had happened a while ago, whether that be the death of the Roman emperor Nero or the assassination of the US President John F. Kennedy. They didn't apply to day-to-day life or explain the present in quite the same way they do now.[2]

Social media has just made it a whole lot easier for everyone who believes these ideas to connect with one another – and to reach other people who are vulnerable to some of these beliefs and behaviours.

The online world is now impossible to untangle from reality, and therefore the disinformation and hate that proliferates can affect everything: the leaders we elect, the way our economy works, the quality of public debate, the way we conduct our relationships, the jobs we choose. This didn't happen overnight – all of the elements involved have been present to varying degrees for a long time. But it's in recent years they've blended together and become turbocharged. We are all living through a golden age for misinformation and hate, and to some extent we're all taking part.

After all, the rise of social media has fundamentally shifted how our world works. All of us have the power to post and share and comment and connect with others online in a way that wasn't possible before. Social media feeds constantly update us on everything from friends to politics to disasters, and for some it's increasingly the only place they turn to in order to figure out what's happening.

Data from the UK's media regulator Ofcom has shown how younger people turn less to the news on the TV and radio as their first port of call to figure out what's going on. Less than two-thirds of 16- to 24-year-olds in Britain get their news from the TV. Instead, they rely on the online world, and social media feeds play a key part in that.[3] There's a myth that misleading and hateful content online affects older people who are less native to social media, but this kind of evidence suggests it's also younger people who are hyper-exposed to all of this.

Loss of trust in traditional media has contributed to the boom in conspiracy theories. Without a doubt, journalists are guilty of getting it wrong. Those deeply immersed in Conspiracyland, however, now disbelieve almost everything that what they call the 'mainstream media' say, even when it's backed up by evidence.

To some extent, I also think that's because some traditional media outlets have been squeamish about investigating the darker corners of social media, ones that our readers, viewers and listeners are likely to have encountered. There are fears about amplifying the people who promote harmful ideas and giving them a platform. I'm driven by exposing disinformation, hate and polarization that cause serious harm and often reach a significant number of people. We can't pretend this is not fundamentally affecting society, and we can't be passive observers either.

Only now are conversations about regulation and moderation of the major social media sites really beginning. These companies wield as much power over society as many governments. Even then, spiky debates over free speech – ironically turbocharged by the hyper-polarized forums that social media creates – infect discussion about how to better protect users online. I'm not a campaigner, I'm an investigative reporter. It's not my job to come up with solutions, but I can hold companies to account and expose what's happening. Increasingly, social media insiders are agreeing to speak to me and reveal the impact these sites can have. We're the guinea pigs, and their insights can tell us so much about how this could be changing each and every one of us.

This isn't just about social media, either. There are various different ingredients required for Conspiracyland to exist and flourish. Political upheaval and major global events play a role in creating uncertainty, anxiety, fear and questions. Everything from the Brexit referendum to the Covid-19 pandemic, war breaking out in countries like Syria and Ukraine, climate change and the cost-of-living crisis, has exacerbated division and distrust. A tidal wave of falsehoods and conspiracy theories has accompanied these kinds of events. And when disinformation is legitimized and fuelled by politicians and leaders, that plays a part, too.

Right now, it feels like we're at a crossroads. Everyone is waking up to this problem and asking, 'Where's the accountability?' I've covered several cases, both in the UK and internationally, where people targeted by disinformation and hate are turning to the courts for justice against the conspiracy theorists targeting them.

In the US in 2022, alt-right conspiracy theorist radio host Alex Jones sat in court in front of a mum and dad who'd lost their six-year-old son, Jesse Lewis, in the Sandy Hook Elementary School shooting in Connecticut in 2012. Jones had spent years suggesting this attack was staged in some way, during which time his online following grew significantly. The victims' families described the hate they had faced as a result of the conspiracy theories. *We are real*, they told him. *He was our son.* He had to admit in that courtroom that the shooting was real – and he was ordered to pay almost $1.5 billion in damages to those families.

Survivors of the 2017 Manchester Arena attack also decided to take action against a conspiracy theorist in the UK who was attempting to deny what they lived through, and a woman in Dublin took a conspiracy theory newspaper to court which had used a photo of her son to suggest his death could be linked to the Covid-19 vaccine when it wasn't.

These people are taking matters into their own hands. They no longer want to rely on social media sites or policymakers to tackle the disinformation and trolling they face. Instead, they are choosing to hit conspiracy theorists where it hurts most – through legal action targeting their wallets. Maybe that is the best way to deter and even stop the individuals doing this. After all, the conspiracy industry to some extent thrives on the money and power these theories can generate. But it comes at a cost for those taking action too, as they can find themselves on the receiving end of even more hate as – like me – they call out and uncover what's happening.

Although this book doesn't pretend to offer all the solutions, it will at least show how the problem manifests. Because we're all living among the trolls now – and just by recognizing the scale of the problem, we can play a part in defending against the harm it causes.

1

TRUE BELIEVERS

I spend a lot of time down rabbit holes – the secret worlds inhabited by people with polarized beliefs where fiction trumps fact. How did they end up down there? The descent often starts with real fear, a legitimate question, a worry. Once you begin to tumble, it's very hard to stop. Your view of the world fundamentally shifts. Everything is part of a sinister plot and everyone is against you.

Over the centuries, disasters, floods, poisonous algae, wars, famine – you name it – have been explained by conspiracy theories and folk tales. It's an understandable way to make sense of catastrophe when conclusive explanations are scarce. Only, back then social media wasn't around to amplify these ideas to millions and connect those looking for answers, who are then drawn to alternative explanations.

The Covid-19 pandemic seemed to suck in more believers than ever before, and we shouldn't really be surprised at all. Psychologists have pointed to catastrophe as a key trigger for conspiracy theories – professor of social psychology Dr Karen Douglas states that they 'tend to prosper in times of crisis as people look for ways to cope with difficult and uncertain circumstances'.[4]

As the pandemic progressed, fault lines began to emerge. Not necessarily between political parties, but rather between people who believe and trust in the fundamentals of democracy, in health officials and doctors, in institutions, and those who don't. There are lots of reasons to distrust the powerful – politicians and governments – but this went beyond that. For some, there was a total loss of faith in what we rely on to coexist in a functioning society where we can speak freely and all agree on the objective truth.

As the pandemic eased, the fault lines deepened. Those who had become embroiled in this world didn't turn around and admit to having lost sight of the truth. They didn't untangle their legitimate concerns and questions from the extreme conspiracy theories declaring that Covid-19 was a hoax. Instead, they doubled down. That's why I want to start with the pandemic, and the anti-vaccine conspiracy theories that proliferated.

An important question is undoubtedly why people believe conspiracy theories in the first place – and that was at the forefront of my mind when I covered two different protests during the pandemic: an anti-lockdown march in Sussex and a so-called freedom rally in Devon.

* * * *

The sunny coastline of Brighton is decorated with a gaggle of conspiracy-believing Santas. The people gathered together are dressed up in whatever festive attire they could get their hands on, many with Father Christmas hats. It's a chilly December morning in 2020, and Covid-19 cases are rising in the UK. Having paraded through Brighton's Lanes alongside this bunch, I've returned to its original starting point, the Peace Statue in Hove. The group begins to disband, still decorated with tinsel and Christmas decorations.

You'd be forgiven for thinking this was an eccentric weekend running club or maybe an idiosyncratic tour group. It's only when you get closer that you catch sight of the posters some of them are holding, and see this is a rally opposing Covid-19 restrictions and the prospect of vaccines.

As we mill around, I am drawn towards the familiar outline of Microsoft founder Bill Gates, who adorns a poster just to my right, alongside a sinister-looking image of a vaccine. Gates's eyes are wild and blood spurts from the syringe he's holding. In the past few months, Gates has become the bogeyman for the Covid-19 conspiracy movement, and at rallies like this he's a prominent feature on several posters.

Folklore professor Timothy Tangherlini, who has looked into the link between witchcraft folk tales and these conspiratorial ideologies, describes Gates as a 'great villain' for the anti-vaccine movement.[5] After all, Gates has huge influence across the world in both technology and health. He's not just the founder of one of the biggest technology corporations in the world – although he's no longer Microsoft's owner – he is also the founder of the Bill & Melinda Gates Foundation, a multinational charitable organization that focuses predominantly on healthcare and poverty. Power and money – especially when an individual is not elected or easily held accountable – often leads to valid questions. But this goes far beyond questions about, for example, Gates's approach to some of the pharmaceutical companies and their decisions around vaccine patents. The extreme claims at the heart of Conspiracyland undermine reasonable discussion.

In Brighton it isn't just Gates's face on display. There are banners reading 'Covid is a HOAX' and referring to the 'Scamdemic'. They appear alongside more measured criticism of politicians and vaccine passports, but it's all very much muddled together.

Starting just weeks into the first lockdown, rallies like this became a regular weekend activity. They were initially organized on Facebook by grass-roots groups that sprang up to oppose Covid-19 restrictions. There are a whole mix of them, with different leaders that organize rallies all around the country – from Brighton to Newcastle.

Ostensibly, these groups are about opposing restrictions, but this has quickly snowballed into conspiracy theories about sinister global plots to harm people involving the pandemic. When the major social media sites cracked down on the disinformation – including attempts to organize large events contrary to the health guidance at the time – many of these groups' members went what you might call 'underground'. They joined large channels on Telegram, where there just isn't much moderation (though when I spoke to Telegram they said calls to violence are expressly forbidden on the platform, that moderators proactively patrol public-facing parts of the app and accept user reports in order to remove calls to violence, and that users are encouraged to report calls to violence using the in-app reporting feature). Still, Telegram was where a lot of the logistical planning for this rally happened.

I strike up a conversation with the man holding that Bill Gates poster. I'm here with BBC *Panorama*, I explain, gesturing towards the team weaving between protesters with a camera. Only minutes ago, they shouted at us to leave. Threats and hostility have been a pretty common response to any mention of the BBC at rallies like this one. It's for that reason that the politeness some show comes as a surprise.

My chatter with this man – who I'll call Denis – and his friend is initially relatively mundane. He's unsure about revealing too much about who he is to me. After all, I work for what he would call the mainstream media, which he doesn't trust very much. We talk a bit about how he likes to walk with friends in the sunshine, our mutual frustration that life isn't going to be back to normal for Christmas – and then I start to question the sign. His allegation is that Bill Gates was somehow involved in creating this pandemic, because he plans to depopulate the planet by injecting them with a killer vaccine. Pretty extreme, as the conspiracies go.

I quiz Denis on this. Why would Bill Gates want to do that? How would that benefit him? What would it achieve? Instead of launching into a complex conversation about sinister global cabals and efforts to make obscene amounts of money through genocide, Denis opts for something simpler.

'You believe all people are good,' he explains. 'I believe almost everyone is bad.'

This simple loss of faith in systems, humanity and the people in power comes up over and over again. In my experience, it often underpins belief in these conspiracy theories.

With that, our conversation dwindles to a close and he tells me that I'm far too nice and normal to be working for the BBC.

Although we didn't chat for long it seems that Denis's lack of faith in humanity is so deeply held that it's apparent it didn't start with Covid-19. The pandemic has just ignited and brought to the fore his deepest fears. But, rather than quelling those worries, these conspiracy theories are exacerbating them.

More than two years later, in April 2023, I find myself at an almost identical rally against the conspiracies these people believe are unfolding. Only, by this time, there are no lockdowns or Covid-19 restrictions in place. I'm also not by the coast in Brighton. Instead, I'm in Devon, in a town called Totnes. I've swapped the beach for a pretty square, in this town known for the way it embraces alternative cultures. Its unashamed sense of self was apparent the minute I set foot in it – I'm here for a new podcast, investigating what has happened to the UK's conspiracy theory movement.

In Totnes I meet a protester who reminds me a lot of Denis. She's what I imagine the Denis of the future will be like – someone whose views have now taken over their life and reached new extremes. Her name is Natalie, and she's laying out posters when I spot her. One features a large pair of red eyes – symbolic of how we're being 'monitored forever', as she later tells me. She's wearing a black cap embroidered with bright white writing that reads 'WAKE UP DEVON'. It's the kind of slogan favoured by conspiracy theory movements that believe we are all sheep blindly following those in power, and we have to open our eyes to what's really going on. It's also the name of the group she's part of. There are several that make up the conspiracy theory landscape in this area of the UK. Like two years ago, they organize online – usually on websites and Telegram.

We get chatting. Most of Natalie's concerns centre around the idea that governments and global organizations are looking to control us. Her greatest worry is measures to limit pollution. She tells me how human-caused climate change is 'pseudoscience and fraud' and that the planet is actually cooling down. This isn't true. When I push back with references to the overwhelming body of scientific evidence that contradicts this, she points to a minority she deems experts who disagree.

I begin to question her sources. That's often a lot more effective than getting into a debate, because she just doesn't believe what the evidence points to. She talks about a conspiracy theory newspaper I'm investigating called *The Light*. Set up in the first year of the pandemic, it has continued to share disinformation about a range of topics, both in its pages and on social media channels – from vaccines to climate change and wars and terror attacks. In its pages and on its Telegram channels, it also shares hate – for example, calls for doctors, politicians and anyone they believe to be complicit in these 'plots' to be executed. When I challenge Natalie on that, she begins to tear up. Her voice wobbles.

'I and others here have spent so much of our time trying to save humanity, trying to wake them up, trying to help them. We've lost our families, lost our friends, and we still stand in our truth because we know it is the truth and so… I'm sorry, it's upsetting me.'

I find myself comforting her. Her emotion has caught me off guard. It's raw and fearful, I'm struck by just how deeply Natalie believes all of this. She tells me 'they' – the allusive powers that be – want not just to 'control us' but also to 'kill us'. While Denis was mainly frustrated at the pandemic, Natalie has been wholly indoctrinated into this world. To believe you and those you love are being targeted in this way is really scary. I ask her about those feelings of fear.

I have heard so many times about the fracturing of relationships and families, but Natalie signals a new extreme. No one has ever burst into tears in front of me at any of these protests before, and Natalie seems so genuinely convinced of everything she's told me about that she's genuinely frightened. She can't seem to see the misinformation and hate she's being fed.

Moments later, Natalie is embedded in the procession that's heading off from the square. She clutches a megaphone and chants. Her warnings about these sinister plots hang heavy in the spring air.

* * * *

Both Denis and Natalie got to the heart of two important questions for me.

The first – why don't I believe in online conspiracies? There are multiple reasons for my lack of belief, but at the heart of it is a simple answer: trust. I have faith in a system and institutions that have not on the whole let me down, plus a doctor for a dad and a mum who was once a nurse. Both of them would certainly refuse to follow orders from a sinister overlord – contrary to what a lot of these protesters frequently suggested around the pandemic.

That leaves me far less vulnerable to online disinformation. Research tells us that those drawn to pseudoscience and conspiracy theories tend to lean away from rational fact and into spirituality.[6] That's to say, they are much less likely to rely on the evidence available and the experts who are sharing it. I've tended to find that's because their personal experience has led them to doubt those who the rest of us are more likely to believe – including doctors, scientists and professors. Maybe they had a bad experience and were let down or misled in some way, or maybe that happened to someone they know. Once you no longer trust the people with the expertise to explain what's going on, even when the weight of the evidence is in their favour, it becomes very difficult to make sense of what's happening.

The second question – who really believes this stuff? There's a realm of misconceptions we have about who becomes drawn into these online conspiracy movements. Stupid, bonkers, lonely – those are just a few of the words I was greeted with when, in the name of research, I asked passers-by on a central London street how they would describe a conspiracy theorist.

Denis, with his Bill Gates poster down by Brighton beach, and Natalie, with her megaphone in the centre of Totnes, are a starting point for countering some of the misguided stereotypes that exist about people like them. They were both engaging and interesting. At the same time they felt let down and exploited, and genuinely thought everyone was bad. The only difference was how deeply they'd become immersed in the world of conspiracy theories. Denis had just begun his descent into Conspiracyland, while Natalie was already engulfed – to the point where she seemed to have severed her connections to some of her family and friends. I don't think either of them were stupid or nasty. I think they both cared a lot about people, and they were hyper-curious. They both seemed to be looking for a sense of control in a chaotic world.

My impression of the true believers is backed up by studies too, which suggest people are sucked in by conspiracy theories when 'important psychological needs are not being met'.[7] Dr Karen Douglas talks about three different types of needs. There's the epistemic, which include 'the desire to satisfy curiosity and avoid uncertainty' – looking for patterns even when they don't exist. There's also a sense of existential threat. This involves attempting to restore a 'threatened sense of scrutiny and control' and regain power. For the true believers, it can be about a feeling of agency when they feel that is otherwise lacking. The third need is social[8] – again, relevant to both of these protesters. Even during our brief conversations, it was apparent to me that they both felt like they belonged, and to a group of which they were proud to be a member.

Heightened worry pushes people to seek out certain answers. Now, with social media at your fingertips, it's possible to do that and find yourself connected to a community like this – and the ideas they promote – quicker than ever before. The land of social media is not an easy one to navigate, and huge volumes of information – and misinformation – come from all sides.

* * * *

Though meeting them was instructive in some ways, both Denis and Natalie remained somewhat two-dimensional to me. These were fleeting conversations at chaotic rallies. But there are other people whose stories I've investigated in recent years, and they can help to deepen our understanding of who the true believers really are.

The first is a man named Gary Matthews, who died from Covid-19 in January 2021 at the age of forty-six, despite believing the pandemic wasn't real.

I first saw Gary in a photograph displayed at the top of a news site. I remember links to the article appearing all over my social media feeds, accompanied by stark warnings. Posts exclaimed how this was a reminder of the dangers of pseudoscience. Chatting to my editor at the time, though, we realized that the coverage raised more questions than it answered.

I started to read about who this man was. The image painted of him by different people seemed at odds – in the press, on Facebook pages, in the form of tributes from friends. At times he was painted as crazy, an idiot who should have known better. In other pieces, he was depicted as a sad and troubled man who had blindly followed the bad guys – or as a martyr for the Covid-19 conspiracy movement. Occasionally, people spoke about his sensitivity and artistic talent, but empathy seemed to be scarce. I wanted to understand who Gary really was, how he'd come to believe what he did, and how it had affected his actions.

Gary lived in Shrewsbury, a pretty market town in the UK. As I would discover from speaking to friends and family members, he loved art. He opposed war. He was a gentle man. He was loved deeply by those close to him. Gary did not fit the 'mad and stupid' stereotype often associated with conspiracy theorists.

Yet he did seem to believe much of the disinformation around the pandemic, according to those who knew him best. I turned to two of Gary's friends, Peter and Geoff, to understand why and how he came to believe what he did.

Peter and Geoff's beautiful old townhouse was located near the river in Shrewsbury. In the December sunshine in 2020, the river glistened. It almost felt like the house was floating. Inside, their ornate living room was decorated with trinkets from a life well lived. There was a certain peace that had settled over this home. Peter and Geoff told me how this was where Gary had sought solace as a young man trying to make sense of his place in the world. I could immediately see why Gary had spent so much time here.

Ardent protesters and champions of LGBTQ rights, Peter and Geoff had created a space where you could be whoever you wanted to be. That had attracted Gary, and he had been a fierce advocate for political causes. It was the *Socialist Worker* that had initially bonded the three of them. Gary would pop round to deliver the paper and come in for a cup of tea.

When Peter and Geoff first met Gary, he was fresh-faced – and a little bit broken. They gathered that life as a teenager had been hard for him, with bullying and taunting, accusations that he was gay, and repeated reminders that he didn't fit in. He relished the opportunity to become closer to the couple and the other people they took under their wing. There was a freedom to be who you wanted in their circle. The constraints and expectations Gary had grown up with dissolved to some extent.

'The thing about Gary is he knew who he wasn't. But he wasn't quite sure what he was or who he was,' Geoff told me. His shoulders sagged as he recalled the young man who had walked through their door what felt like many moons ago.

Soon, it was more than just weekly cups of tea. Gary spent time living with the couple when he fell ill with cancer in his twenties. Together, they got Gary back on his feet. But once he was better, regular catch-ups and conversations about politics started to change. Gary's advocacy and campaigning started to venture beyond advocating for LGBTQ rights and equality.

The Syrian civil war – which broke out in 2011 between the Syrian Arab Republic, led by President Bashar al-Assad, and opposition forces and groups – became a real worry for Gary. Peter and Geoff described to me how Gary hated war and feared for the people caught up in it. But, as Gary sought out more information about the conflict, he soon found himself exposed to disinformation online, often propagated by those who supported the Syrian regime. I've seen some of this propaganda, and it's easy to understand how emotive posts could draw in someone like Gary, who was advocating for peace. It was then that his conspiratorial worldview started to take shape.

'My view was that Assad was just doing the most appalling things to the population,' Peter told me, laying out some of the evidence he'd seen of what was actually happening. But the social media lens through which Gary was beginning to experience world events told him otherwise. Conspiracy theories had started to spread like wildfire, with the help of the Russian state propaganda machine after they entered the war in support of Assad.

'Gary was saying, "Well, no, actually, this is not true. Assad is not so bad." He was just so… He had changed a bit, he was very convinced and almost slightly insulting: "You're being brainwashed. Can't you see?"' Peter explained.

Both Peter and Geoff said attempts to challenge those beliefs and confront Gary with other evidence became futile. Geoff described conversations where there was no room for debate. It seemed to me that it had become a lot less about the ins and outs of what Gary thought was really happening in Syria, and a lot more about his belief that the mainstream media and politicians were lying about it. That led him to believe whatever was in opposition to what they were saying, even when the evidence suggested otherwise. This was the latest part of Gary's search to make sense of the world and everything that happened in it.

Gary was always drawn towards 'cultish groups', Geoff recalled. He wanted to feel a part of something that also helped him better understand the world; and becoming involved with the disinformation around Syria was a means of doing that. He thought life was unfair and laid the blame simply and squarely at what he saw as the mainstream media and the untrue narratives they peddled.

What had once been about challenging the people in power in the way that Geoff and Peter had done throughout their lives just became too simplified, until everything was actually part of a plot to harm the average person in Syria or the UK. Gary stopped challenging the powerful people involved in those wars, even when there was evidence of their wrongdoing. It seemed he stopped being able to see the nuance and complexities.

At the time – and this is still the case now – I struggled to square the circle. Gary was loved and accepted by his family and the friends around him. He was clever, creative, loving – and yet felt like he just didn't fit. Head in the clouds, seeking a purpose first through painting, photography and art, and then through something more – these conspiracy theory circles. They were like a drug that immediately offered the agency, connection and fulfilment he had been craving.

Geoff explained to me that 'the scar was so deep' when it came to Gary. This craving for meaning was one he'd had his whole life. He was enraged by injustice and wanted to stick up for others who were maligned or suffering.

As the pandemic approached, Gary was vulnerable to the slew of conspiracy theories claiming that this terrifying event was part of a plot to limit our freedoms. Lockdown pushed him closer towards his social media feeds and further away from real people. He became glued to the online world as he sat for hours on end at home on his own. One relative recalled that he seemed 'possessed' by the idea that the pandemic was a conspiracy and that it didn't exist.

I never had the chance to meet Gary, but I turned to his social media profiles for clues. On 15 December 2020, just weeks before he died, he'd liked a tweet proclaiming 'fresh air' and the 'immune system' as all that was needed to combat the virus. In the end, Gary showed that this wasn't the case. He contracted Covid-19 and died at home, seemingly without seeking medical assistance.

Gary's social media footprint, along with testimony from friends and family, became a way to understand how he had become immersed in Covid-19 conspiracy theories in particular.

For him, the bad information had started in a Facebook group called the Shropshire Corona Resilience Network. I got a sense of their beliefs by looking at a new version of the group set up after Gary died.

One post showed a wanted poster with a picture of then UK health minister Matt Hancock – accusing him of committing 'genocide by vaccine'. Another long post described how the virus was '100 percent a dark magic ritual'. These weren't exactly legitimate political debates about, say, the impact of lockdown measures, or the viability of vaccine passports.

Links on that group led Gary to various conspiracy influencers with growing followings – and mainstream commentators flirting with the conspiratorial. They populated Twitter (now renamed X), Facebook and Instagram – and of course Telegram, the social media app whose membership was growing rapidly as the pandemic dragged on.

Geoff and Peter remembered watching Gary's Facebook feed shift before their eyes. When he began sharing specific posts denying the pandemic, while they sat bored and scared at home, they just found it too difficult to communicate with him anymore. They stopped talking to him or looking at his feeds.

But while they might have stopped encountering his posts online, they did bump into him on occasion during the Covid-19 lockdowns. One of the last times was out and about in Shrewsbury. Gary was with his mum, who Geoff and Peter said diligently wore a face mask, while Gary's face was bare.

When they found out Gary had died from Covid-19 not long after that last encounter, they were both so upset and angry. 'It didn't have to happen. And yet it [did],' said Geoff.

When I interview people who believe these conspiracy theories, I often think about how stressful it must be to think that almost everyone is part of an elite cabal. But I didn't ever get the chance to ask Gary how it made him feel.

Peter and Geoff gave me the impression that, while Gary derived purpose and community from this world, he did find it terrifying – a bit like Natalie from the protest in Totnes. But they saw him far less in the period when he truly became immersed in the Covid-19 conspiracy theory movement. To figure out what he was thinking and feeling then, I turned to a different friend – who saw him fairly often during the lockdowns.

His name was Adam. He used to meet Gary for walks during the pandemic at the Quarry, an extensive parkland in Shrewsbury. As they wandered around, Gary would talk about his deep fears for the future of humanity. He seemed anxious, frustrated and tortured.

I met Adam on a freezing cold day in that same Quarry. We sat on a bench close to where he had last seen Gary, and Adam told me how they used to paint together and discuss ideas. Kindred spirits in some ways, but different in other respects.

'This wasn't somebody with tinfoil on [his] head. This was a very intelligent chap,' Adam explained, casting his eyes over the river and the frosty pastures of the park. 'He's a beautiful man. I mean, he was very gentle, and very delicate. You know, he was kind of pure. There's very few pure people.' Adam was still struggling to talk about his friend in the past tense, having only lost him a year earlier.

That conversation with Adam was a reminder of the profound impact this all has. On the lives of those drawn into online conspiracy claims – and on the lives of those left behind. Adam's grief hung between us.

Adam gave me the impression that he shared with Gary a certain suspicion of authority and the systems that had somewhat let him down. I could tell he'd carefully considered whether to speak to me. He also shared Gary's dream-like view of the world. Together, they would talk about a world free of conflict, evil and war. They cared deeply about injustice and poverty. But Adam saw the difference between political criticism, concern and suspicion and the outlandish conspiracies that Gary had struggled with.

In Adam's view, it was the lockdown restrictions that truly pushed Gary into conspiracy theories. Gary was stuck at home in a small flat with too much time on his hands. The places he'd found fulfilment before – like his artwork – disappeared. He started to spend hours and hours online, where he sought out meaning and community.

Adam noted that there were social factors at play here too. In the big houses just down the road from where Gary lived, people often had home offices or gardens. Lockdown wasn't so hard for them, and so they were less likely to turn to social media to make sense of how uniquely awful their own lives had become.

Those who believe conspiracy theories can also be wealthy, however; many I've interviewed are. It's also important to state that some of the fiercest opponents to conspiracy theorists are people who are not wealthy at all. But Adam said that for Gary, this inequality was important. Gary believed he was being wronged, and that others without the means to make lockdowns comfortable were too. It wasn't just about the unfair circumstances; it further fuelled his belief that this was somehow part of a plot by the powerful to control or harm the powerless. There are others I've interviewed since who struggled to make ends meet during the cost-of-living crisis, and who were spurred deeper into the world of conspiracy theories by the inequality they experienced. It fuels distrust in authority.

'You have this disparity,' Adam explained to me, 'and I suppose in a place like Shrewsbury it's more evident. It's quite small, but the affluence is evident, and the lack of it is obviously very demonstrably obvious.'

No attempts to challenge Gary worked. As much as Adam would indulge legitimate questions about lockdown measures and their proportionality, he couldn't seem to get Gary to see that it didn't mean the conspiracies about the government creating the pandemic to control our lives were true.

Adam described the 'off' feeling he'd sensed when he and Gary last chatted. It wasn't long before Gary died. He put it down to the toll of restrictions, or Gary starting to feel ill. He'd never see Gary again. When I spoke to him, he was unsurprisingly still finding it very hard to process that he couldn't speak to his friend anymore. 'You just assume that this will pass, and he'll be around the corner in a minute and this will just go away.'

Adam couldn't fill in the gaps for me about those last few weeks of Gary's life, but there were others who could. His immediate family weren't able to talk to me directly, but were happy for his cousins to share more information about what happened. Gary's cousin Tristan talked me through what the family knew about his last moments, and shared conversations he'd had with Gary's close family.

Gary's sister Emma and mum, Kate, told Tristan how, on 7 January 2021, they received a call from Gary. He told them he felt ill – but he thought it was the flu. At that time, he was working at a local hardware store where he still came face-to-face with customers, and friends and family recalled he refused to wear a mask or take other precautions. Some suspected that was where he caught Covid-19. Ultimately, though, it's impossible to know for sure. From the 7th to the 10th of January, according to his family, Gary became increasingly sick. On the 10th he called his mum again. That's when he'd finally decided to go and get a test.

Having thought for months that the virus was a hoax, Gary's illness started to erode these beliefs. He recognized he needed to check if he had Covid-19 – and he was suddenly cautious about meeting people and potentially infecting his loved ones. His sister later found that he'd been googling the symptoms of Covid-19.

Gary walked to the Shirehall testing centre. That's a round-trip distance of around two miles, even though he was struggling to breathe. His family said he didn't ask anyone to drive him for fear of spreading the virus.

On 12 January – the day before he died – Gary phoned his mum again. The test was positive; he had Covid-19. His family advised him to take some painkillers and rest. After all, they'd known people who'd had the virus and recovered – lots of us had. They thought it would be the same for Gary. But it wasn't. Gary's dad went around to the flat the next morning and found him collapsed. He'd died.

Although he did get tested, I've never found any evidence that Gary went to hospital or sought professional medical attention. Tristan was sure that Gary didn't seek help, and Gary's sister and mother didn't mention Gary calling a doctor or an ambulance, or visiting the hospital or a GP surgery.

Gary, rather than being an outlier, matches up with a lot of what studies and analysis tell us about people who believe conspiracy theories. Some believers turn to these theories in an attempt to find 'an accurate and consistent understanding of the world'.[9] That seemed to be one of Gary's main goals, and it came from a place of worrying about humanity, rather than any kind of malice.

Being bullied in his past and a difficult lockdown had left Gary feeling powerless. From conversations with those who knew him, it seems as though he felt like he'd been dealt a bad hand and was consistently wronged. In his eyes, the causes he fought for were consistently ignored by those in power, whether they were to do with the war in Syria or the pandemic lockdowns in the UK. Various experts point to how those who really believe conspiracy theories often see themselves on the 'losing side of political processes', which Gary seemed to.[10]

After talking to his friends and a couple of family members, I finally had a sense of who Gary really was: a well-meaning and intelligent man who seemed able to make up his own mind, but nonetheless was misguided. It was the combination of who he was and the circumstances he found himself in that seemed to cause him to lose his own life in the name of disinformation.

* * * *

By the time the pandemic eased, it was already too late for Gary Matthews to escape the conspiracy world. But even if he had survived those months of lockdowns, would he have been able to get out? For many of the believers I've met, the pandemic totally altered their worldview and left them vulnerable to a whole range of conspiracy theories.

In the summer of 2022, I spotted Alicia commenting on one of the social media posts of a prominent UK conspiracy theorist, Richard D. Hall. He dabbles in pandemic disinformation, but his area of expertise is fabricated terror. He also tracked down the Manchester Arena survivors to see if their injuries were real – and he casts doubt on the reality of other terror attacks, including the 7/7 Tube bombings. (There will be more about his conspiracy theories, tactics and those he has targeted later in the book.)

In the post Alicia commented on, he was advertising a market stall he ran, selling books and DVDs promoting lots of these ideas. Alicia said she was looking forward to visiting it. I messaged her, and she agreed to speak to me. When I arrived at her home in Wales I was greeted with a warm welcome. I found her to be a lovely woman, very chatty and likeable. We got on well.

Alicia had long black hair and a black cat that guarded the window. Her cosy flat, located just outside of a busy Welsh city, was decorated with home-made ornaments. As we entered, she gestured to an empty fish tank in the hallway. She was no longer able to run it, she told me. She just couldn't afford to. It just stood there, a relic from a more prosperous time. She carefully switched off all the lights and said she was worried about paying for the heating as winter approached. Struggles with money were at the forefront of her mind.

When we sat down on the sofa, she talked me through other difficulties she'd experienced in her life. She'd struggled to have children, and had had some bad experiences with doctors. She also lost her mum during the pandemic, which she'd found really difficult. She talked to me about her family and friends with such pride, and it was obvious immediately that – like Gary – she cared deeply about people.

Alicia told me she was often unsure of who to believe and trust, and that sense of confusion was apparent from the beginning. She said she found the news depressing, but was also overwhelmed by the conflicting narratives presented to her on social media. She was also very disillusioned by politicians. She'd lost faith in the government over the past couple of years, especially the way they handled the pandemic. Revelations that ministers and politicians had broken rules they'd set made her question why they weren't taking it seriously. Alicia had been stuck at home all on her own. It really stung. 'There's no trust. People don't feel safe anymore because they've got nobody to look to who tells us the truth. That's quite scary, actually,' she said.

During the pandemic, she'd found herself contemplating alternative explanations for what was really happening, and soon enough she was exposed to disinformation online suggesting the pandemic was staged in some way or that vaccines were part of a sinister plot. She just wasn't sure who or what to believe anymore.

She'd been hopeful that life would improve when pandemic restrictions were lifted, but instead she faced a new struggle with money. She could hardly pay her bills. Pandemic disinformation led her to the pages of conspiracy theorists like the one in question here.

'I like Richard D. Hall. He's quite interesting,' she explained. 'He's down to earth.'

She'd considered a range of views he'd promoted, including his suggestion that terror attacks like the Manchester Arena bombing were staged in some way. You might think the very act of contemplating these views makes Alicia cold or cruel.

But, face-to-face, I could see this loving and kind woman was struggling with the huge amount of content she was sifting through online. True to that, she told me that she didn't want it to be true that the Manchester Arena bombing was a hoax, but it really frightened her that it could have been. It felt as though she was using these conspiracy theories to try to make sense of something terrible that had happened – which did nothing to lessen the blow for the survivors of the attack who'd lost loved ones or had to live with life-changing injuries. When I revealed to Alicia that I'd spoken to some of them directly and they'd contradicted Hall's narrative, she was shocked and dismayed.

'It's really upsetting if that is the truth. Like you said about the victims. That is appalling.'

I was struck by how quickly Alicia backtracked when confronted with the evidence. She was a living, breathing, compassionate human being, but it was as though – until then – she hadn't let herself think about what these kinds of conspiracy theories meant for the very real people who became their targets.

Alicia's experience and views aren't as uncommon as people might think. Research by King's College London, which the BBC fed into, has sought to understand the relationship between wider social issues like the pandemic and the cost-of-living crisis, and belief in these sinister conspiracy theories. They surveyed 4,000 people on the issue, representative of the UK population.

The research suggests the pandemic was a gateway to more sinister conspiracies, with a third of respondents saying it had made them more suspicious of official explanations of terror attacks. Professor Bobby Duffy, who led the research, expects that poor economic climates pose the same problems. 'If everything is spinning out of control, like a big economic crisis is making my life very uncertain and anxious – that is one of the conditions that we know is related to belief in these types of theories, which give more sense of certainty or give them someone to blame.'

And while it's worth noting that according to this research four in five people do recognize that serious terror attacks have occurred in the UK, a significant minority have doubts about the truth of these attacks. 'This not only disengages people from society generally. For that small minority who get really caught up in conspiracies it can actually affect their behaviour, which then affects other people,' says Duffy.

The research distinguishes between those who can't work out the truth of attacks and those who believe attacks like the bombing at Manchester Arena are a hoax. According to Duffy, anxiety, uncertainty and social media habits can push someone from understandable questions to extreme beliefs. Of the 14 per cent of those surveyed who stated they believed crisis actors (people hired to portray disaster victims) were involved in the Manchester Arena attacks, 44 per cent used Telegram as a key source of information on news and events. They were also more likely not to have voted at the last election – and to be younger, which fits with high exposure to social media.

* * * *

For those who truly believe in one particular conspiracy theory, others 'seem more plausible' as a consequence.[11] That's because the same idea underpins them: important things are covered up or hidden, in a way that goes beyond genuine examples of political corruption and institutional wrongdoing. And this doesn't just apply terror attacks; there's climate denial, too.

I first came across Matthew in a channel on Telegram, which connects conspiracy believers all over the world. Founded in Russia but popular globally now, you can join large groups with thousands of members on the app. People share links, videos and ideas in these groups. Users can also chat to each other individually. Each user has a profile picture and description, but that's about it. The appeal compared to other social media platforms is the hands-off moderation. It also claims to be more secure than other sites. All of that can be positive, especially in places where authoritarian regimes are in charge. But it's also helped Telegram to become a hub for disinformation – one that Matthew likes using.

In one of the pandemic conspiracy channels, he shared a message that read: 'I'd love to date someone who wasn't duped by alarmist climate change and covid propaganda.' I wanted to speak to him to understand how he not only believed the pandemic was part of a sinister global plot, but that climate change was too.

A few days later, very early in the morning to account for the time difference – Matthew lives in New Zealand – I found myself on the phone to him. Matthew, left frustrated by the repeated harsh lockdowns in New Zealand, truly believed the conspiracies about Covid-19.

New Zealand was one of several countries that aimed to stamp out Covid-19 through strict lockdowns. Troubled by the government's approach, Matthew turned to social media for news and community. The online groups he joined – all opposed to vaccines and masks – exposed him to conspiracy theories about sinister global plots.

He sent me pictures of stickers from a group called White Rose, which he'd attached to lamp posts near his suburban home. These stickers featured QR codes that linked back to the conspiracy-theory-ridden Telegram channels he was a part of, and condemned sinister plots to kill off the world's population with the Covid vaccine. One of them was decorated with a scary-looking Bill Gates, with crazed eyes and pointy teeth – a lot like the image on that placard from the Brighton rally at the start of this chapter.

Matthew was convinced that those same shadowy forces at play during the pandemic also lay behind climate change. He believed we're not being told the truth. 'This whole campaign of fear and propaganda is an attempt to try and drive some agenda,' he explained. 'It doesn't matter whether it's climate change or a virus or something else.'

Matthew had looked me up before we spoke, and you might

have expected a certain degree of hostility. Why had he agreed to speak to me when I was likely to say the conspiracy theories he promoted were contrary to evidence? I think some believers, like Matthew, think they can convince me of their world view, and I'd guess that me being a young woman plays a part in that.

Matthew saw 'Covid and climate propaganda' as part of the same so-called plot being waged by the rich and powerful across the world. In his view, the world leaders and billionaires were all in on it. But like with others I've interviewed, when I tried to drill down to the specifics he shied away from giving too much detail about this alleged cabal.

I wanted to know whether his belief in such a plot was actually just a way of coping with the reality that the planet is in a bad way and life as we know it could change forever. I'd find it quite comforting to believe that everything was going to be fine.

But Matthew told me it was the opposite. It was a huge stress rather than a relief, and he found it easier to go along with the so-called narrative rather than oppose it.

'I have woken up every day the last three or four months feeling very anxious about the world and what's happening. And I often wish I hadn't [woken up feeling that way]. I wish I felt differently.' When he said this, his voice was tinged with something like despair.

Holding these beliefs was having a real impact on his life, and his views set him apart from the people he was closest to. He was having to hide in the garden to speak with me, as he didn't want his partner overhearing our conversation. She became too upset and angry, he explained, as she was someone who campaigned to better protect the planet – which is why he'd posted on Telegram saying how much easier he'd find it to live with someone who believed the same things he did. He even felt uncomfortable because his daughter, who was only nine years old, was doing a presentation about climate change at school.

* * * *

Matthew, Alicia and Gary were all cut from the same cloth. They were all fearful of crises outside of their control – which pulled them into that social media rabbit hole and left them all the more obsessed with what they found there.

Gary feared war and the harm it caused. Those anti-war beliefs drew him towards disinformation about the conflict in Syria, and it led to him believing that Covid-19 was part of an evil global plot. Alicia was overwhelmed and confused, struggling with money and isolation. She no longer felt like the institutions she'd relied on were protecting her anymore, and her legitimate concerns left her vulnerable to more sinister disinformation that told her this wasn't just incompetence, it was deliberate and part of a plot. Matthew was fearful of the way the government had strangled the joy from his life while he struggled through the harsh New Zealand lockdowns, and this then caused him to explain away other stressful global phenomena with false ideas.

Evidence suggests 'the aversive feelings that people experience when in crisis – fear, uncertainty, and the feeling of being out of control' – feelings Gary, Alicia and Matthew all had – increase 'the likelihood of perceiving conspiracies in social situations'.[12] They turn to these theories to try to quell those fears and get a grip on what's out of their control.

It's less about what you believe than why you believe it. That might explain why no amount of evidence will persuade the likes of Matthew and Gary. It's about a deep distrust and worry, not really about facts – or the lack of them.

In a time gone by, these three people may have found community elsewhere. Perhaps they would have been more involved in organized religion (and that's not to compare the two). They could have gone to chat to others in a real town square. Now, they found themselves frequenting a virtual one, where polarization, conflict and disinformation seem to be more pronounced. Instead of encountering a range of people and beliefs, social media algorithms drove them towards others who looked at the world in the same way. But the conspiracy theories they were drawn to weren't a remedy; instead, they added salt to the wound. Gary, Alicia and Matthew found their personal relationships fraying, along with their connection to the wider world.

The families and friends of people who fell down the conspiracy rabbit hole during the pandemic message me all the time to tell me how, as the pandemic eased and restrictions were lifted, their loved ones started to wrap new events into the sinister world plot. They couldn't seem to stop, even when it was having a great personal cost to them at home. It left them vulnerable to extreme political ideologies on both the far right and far left. Their relationships with those closest to them fractured, and so they turned to these online communities even more for support.

Sasha Havlicek heads up the Institute for Strategic Dialogue (ISD), a think tank which focuses on exposing extremism and disinformation. She describes conspiracy theories found on social media as 'an entry point to detaching you from mainstream society and leading you into more and more extreme environments'.

Rather than helping believers gain agency, these conspiracy theories do the opposite. The true believers become even more powerless, because ultimately they can't resolve the fabricated plot they think they've uncovered. They also find themselves exploited by new powerful people – the leaders of this conspiracy world. All this is likely to 'further fuel mistrust and cynicism and increase people's feelings of isolation and marginalisation'.[13]

When people fall deeper down rabbit holes, they – and we – lose what Havlicek describes as the 'shared concept of reality'. This is something that is fundamental to functioning societies and democracies. We don't have to agree, but we do broadly have to accept the same truths and facts. Ultimately, Conspiracyland threatens the social fabric that binds us all together.

* * * *

But let's get back to the million-dollar question – who really believes this stuff? Dismissing these people as stupid and mad is not just wrong, it's damaging. The easy stereotypes mask real problems – and suggest this is fundamentally about the responsibility of the individuals caught up in this. It's more complicated than that.

Conspiracy theories and falsehoods help believers feel powerful in a world where lots of people feel powerless. Individuals are responsible for their participation in these acts, but they can also be victims of the lies they believe in, and they are often powerless to deal with the injustice – or perceived injustice – that led them there in the first place.

You might think I'd feel pessimistic about these people. But really, I think they often have good intentions, even when what they believe causes harm. They are misguided and misled, vulnerable to the worst liars and lies. They are let down by systems and social media sites – and pushed to a point where their beliefs become so tied up with their identity that escape looks impossible. They feel as though the alternative to not believing is just so much worse.

What is terrifying is how powerful these conspiracy theories can be.

Believers can't just climb out of the rabbit hole. Leaving is complex. Everything it affords them – whether that's a sense of power or community – draws them further in, and all the while they're exposed to more and more of the same, or more extreme.

Research has found that people who are more sympathetic to conspiracy theories are more likely than others to agree that 'violence is sometimes an acceptable way to express disagreement'.[14] It's not hard to see how, if you genuinely believe people are out to harm you and your family in a way that totally surpasses the evidence, you might be inclined to take more extreme action.

In 2022, twenty-five people were arrested in Germany on suspicion of plotting to overthrow the government. The Reichsbürger – the movement linked to this alleged coup attempt – predates the pandemic, and believes that the current German state is illegitimate. Its followers want to return to the Second Reich – the German Empire from 1871 to 1918.

However, the support for this movement – and the commitment from those drawn towards its ideas – seemed to increase during the pandemic. Once you falsely believe in these sinister conspiracies under the guise of Covid-19, you want to overhaul the entire system.

During the months leading up to the arrest, Telegram groups related to the Reichsbürger (meaning 'citizens of the Reich') had become populated with conspiracy theories not just about murder by vaccine, but also suggesting the war in Ukraine was a hoax and that satanic cabals of paedophiles were out to get former US president Donald Trump. You could see the real-time fusion of all of these different ideologies, all ultimately underpinned by the same guiding thought: there are secret groups of very powerful people doing unimaginable harm, far beyond the known examples of powerful people doing bad things.

Several months before the alleged coup attempt, German authorities uncovered how several members connected to the group were plotting to kidnap the German health minister. Why the health minister, you ask? Well, because they genuinely believed he was somehow committing murder or treason by introducing a Covid-19 vaccine that saved millions of lives. As of 2023, according to the Office for National Statistics, there had been a small number of deaths reportedly linked to the jab in the UK – out of over 50 million people who've had at least one dose.

This coup attempt might seem extreme, but when I think back to Natalie crying at the rally in Totnes, genuinely convinced of the conspiracy theories she believed, it doesn't come as much of a surprise. If I believed the same thing, I can imagine wanting to do anything and everything to put a stop to it. And that's terrifying.

When I'm targeted with death threats and harassment online and offline, it's this idea that worries me the most. These comments aren't meaningless, but are coming in some cases from people who are so terrified or so angry they'd really be willing to do something extreme.

What all of these true believers have taught me is how much these conspiracy theories are about apportioning blame. They're about finding someone you can direct your fears and frustration at. If you're looking for a sense of control, you want to know very clearly who the bad guy is and then focus all your efforts on them – when in reality there are lots of bad guys and sort-of-bad guys and maybe-not-so-bad guys. Issues like inequality and lack of opportunity or community can be the fault of the politicians in charge combined with the circumstances we find ourselves in, also combined with big events like pandemics that to some extent are beyond our control. Those issues are hard to remedy, whereas conspiracy theories give you a quick fix. Here's who to blame, here's why – let's go for them.

My fear is that, while I think all of the true believers in this chapter are genuinely kind people who wouldn't behave violently, it only takes one person engulfed in this world and spurred on to take matters into their own hands. By understanding the true believers, and *why* rather than *what* they believe, we can expose and identify some of the root causes. And then it's up to policymakers – whether local leaders or MPs – and social media sites to come up with the solutions to tackle them before it's too late.

2

THE NON-BELIEVERS?

What if someone told you that the worst day of your life had never happened? That's what internet trolls told Martin Hibbert, who survived the terror attack at Manchester Arena on 22 May 2017. Twenty-two people were killed and more than 1,000 injured when a suicide bomber exploded his device in the foyer at the end of an Ariana Grande concert. Despite the facts, several conspiracy theorists have suggested that the bombing didn't actually happen.

It was sitting in Martin's living room on a sticky day in August 2022 that I realized how low conspiracy theorists and trolls had sunk not just in the UK, but all over the world. In this chapter I want to tell you about the conspiracy theorists who aren't just devoted followers of these theories.

The term 'non-believers' in some respects can be applied to everyone who believes these conspiracy theories – because they are so often about disbelieving that events occurred in the way the evidence suggests. What I'm looking at in this chapter, though, is whether the people who are the main propagators of these ideas really believe the conspiracy theories they're pushing, or whether they're motivated primarily by the power and money they can gain through sharing them with an online following. And the story of the Manchester Arena survivors is the best place to start.

Conspiracy theories claiming that Martin and his daughter Eve are acting and the bombing was really a hoax have plagued both of their remarkable recoveries from their life-changing injuries. The conspiracy theorist Richard D. Hall even went so far as to track down Eve at home, attempting to film her to check if her injuries were real. He shared a video showing off his tactics to his thousands of committed followers online. In the footage, he holds up a very poorly camouflaged camera, which is propped up on a stick adorned with leaves. He explains how he's going to attempt to gather evidence with it. The whole scene verges on the absurd, almost like it's a joke. But it's not, and absurdity would have done nothing to lessen the shock felt by Martin and his family when the police made them aware of Hall's attempts to spy on Eve.

As you might imagine, Eve's injuries are very real. Just fourteen at the time of the attack, she experienced a serious brain injury and has since lost the use of her left arm and leg. A lot of people didn't expect Eve to survive, and she relies on round-the-clock care. Martin recounted all of this to me as we sat in his living room. His own injuries, too, are very real. His wheelchair was propped up neatly beside the sofa; Martin is paralysed from the waist down. The light that had filled his face as he spoke about his daughter quickly drained when we began discussing the conspiracy theories and hate.

'I'm all for freedom of speech,' Martin explained. 'But it crosses the line when you're saying I'm an actor or I've not got a spinal cord injury or Eve's not disabled, she's not in a wheelchair.' Martin's courage and resilience were very apparent, but even I could tell he was fearful of how the tactics Richard D. Hall was using to target his family could escalate. Martin told me he just didn't know how far this man was willing to go for answers.

And Martin and Eve are far from the only targets. I first realized the Manchester Arena victims and their families were being targeted by trolls and conspiracy theorists when I saw an anonymous account replying to the posts of a grieving mum who'd lost her son in the bombing. (I'm protecting her identity here because she doesn't want to experience any more of this hate.) The troll was tweeting out pages of a book written by Richard D. Hall – the same conspiracy theorist targeting Eve Hibbert – that claimed the victims who had lost their lives in the bombing, including this woman's son, were really in hiding in places all over the world. This troll account was denying that this mum had lost her child. In a message, she told me how she would 'give her last breath' to have him back.

Weeks after I first met Martin, I went to the office of a boatyard on the beautiful west coast of Wales to see Lisa, who had also been injured in the Manchester Arena bombing. Richard D. Hall had documented online and in his book his attempts to use a hidden camera to spy on her while she worked. He'd wanted to check whether Lisa was really injured too.

I saw with my own eyes Lisa's missing finger – the one Hall alleged was still there. I saw the scar left on her face. She described the years it had taken for her to come to terms with those injuries and to be comfortable enough to let others see them. She wasn't wearing make-up on the day she met with me. We were filming an interview, and she hoped Hall would watch it when it aired and realize just how real her injuries were.

Lisa's quiet courage sat between us as she relived the worst day of her life. She described being in the lobby of Manchester Arena to collect her daughter when the explosion happened, and how guilty her daughter felt about what had happened. She recalled sitting on the curb, injured and bleeding, as a little girl and her mum tried to help her. Lisa became very upset at various moments in our conversation. She'd found it hard to deal with her injuries. She'd had to wear a glove for months because of losing her finger, and she described how hard it was to take off. And then to be told that none of it had happened, that her injuries weren't real and that a traumatic moment that had shaped her life was fake . . . well, it was devastating.

This wasn't just online either. Hall had come to this remote location to film her while she was unwittingly going about her work – an invasion of privacy that had left her fearful for her safety. 'You just don't know who's out there and who might be lurking in a garden or standing round a corner with a hidden camera,' she said.

Why would someone do this? That's a question I've asked of almost every conspiracy theorist I've investigated.

It turns out that promoting conspiracy theories can be a profitable business. It's possible to build a profile online in a way you may never have been able to before – and cultivate a following of committed social media followers who make you feel important, almost like a celebrity. They hang on your every word, and you don't need a huge number of them to be greeted with regular praise and donations. It can be hard to untangle intention, though, because these people also seem to convince themselves of the ideas they're peddling.

After talking to the Manchester Arena victims, I wanted to figure out whether Richard D. Hall – the most prolific proponent of the conspiracy theory claiming that the attack didn't happen – was a non-believer. Working with the teams at BBC *Panorama* and Radio 4, we pieced together the clues we could find about him online.

Hall is a former engineer and failed comedian who has been sharing conspiracy theory videos online since around 2011. First it was UFOs, but then it turned into more sinister conspiracy theories about fabricated terror. In recent years he's made money through selling DVDs of his online shows, as well as books and tickets to live speaking tours. Videos of his tours show packed pubs, and his book alleging the Manchester Arena bombing was staged sells for about £20.

In that book – as well as various videos on his website – he researches the lives of every single person who lost their life in the attack or was injured, and includes intrusive photographs and details. He falsely suggests their injuries were faked, and that those who died are somehow living elsewhere in hiding. Towards the back of the book there's a table showing every victim of the bombing and their alleged new location.

Hall used to have a YouTube channel with more than 80,000 subscribers. But the platform took it down after I approached them for comment about the theories he was pushing. From analysing his various streams of income, it seems to me that he makes his living from conspiracy theories. He doesn't have another job. Although Hall's operation isn't exactly a multimillion-pound empire, that doesn't diminish the distress he's caused to the real people caught up in the Manchester bombing.

To understand what was driving him, I turned to those who had encountered Hall up close, hoping I might find out if he really believed the theories he was pushing.

I first met with Neil Sanders in a pub in Nottingham. A lot of people Neil knows would see me as the enemy, and his loyalty to the conspiracy world was apparent to me during that meeting. Nonetheless, he was willing to share how someone he had once associated with seemed to have gone off the deep end.

From 2010 onwards, Neil was invited to appear in several of Hall's videos talking about one of his specialist subjects – mind control. This is the idea that the media, politicians and the global elite are doing something far more sinister than just lying to us. Those who are interested in mind control often talk about secret signals and signs these powerful people employ – and the way they covertly control what we think and do.

Although the two still shared an interest in supernatural phenomena, Neil outright rejected Hall's more recent claims about terror attacks being faked, and seemed to recognize the harm that such theories could do. But he thought that Hall, though misguided, was acting with sincere motives. 'A lot of people will look at this and say: Richard must be monstrous and appalling. And he isn't, which is the incongruity between the two things.'

According to Neil, Hall had once expressed scepticism about the conspiracy theories suggesting school shootings were in fact staged, and he recalled a conversation in which he was sure Hall had dismissed them as untrue. This was back when Hall preferred UFOs to terrorism. But as time went on – and he became more embroiled in this world, both online and off – Hall seemed to convince himself of the truth of these theories. 'He's coming at it from the perspective that he's unearthed a massive fraud that has been perpetuated on the world, essentially,' Neil explained. 'And so he's wanting to uncover that for the greater good.'

I challenged Neil on this notion several times. I found it very hard to understand how anyone could promote theories this extreme because they saw it as being for the 'greater good', as Neil put it. Neil's view was that opposition to the conspiracy theories Hall promoted just made Hall think that the 'mainstream' was trying to silence him and cover up the real truth.

He then talked me through the money aspect. Rather than relying on hundreds of thousands of adoring fans, all Hall really needed was a few hundred committed ones who'd be willing to buy his books, attend his talks and watch his videos. And Neil said he had them. 'They would try and involve themselves with him as much as they possibly could, in the same way that somebody who is a fan of a band or a football team would.'

Ultimately, the conspiracy theories Hall was choosing to pursue and promote – including those concerning fabricated terror – were the ones that seemed to spark the greatest interest from his audience. Neil mentioned how 'the more outrageous and the more bizarre and the more wacky theories' are the ones that 'actually get the most traction'.

Neil had given me a lot of insight into how this particular conspiracy theorist operated, but I still wanted to speak to the man himself. I emailed with Hall for weeks, with no luck. He rejected my approaches for an interview and wouldn't answer the questions I asked him directly.

So, as a last resort, I went with producer Alys Cummings and camera operator Tom Traies to Wales where Hall was based, to get answers for the survivors – and made an unannounced visit to the market where he had that stall selling his DVDs, books and other merchandise.

It was a dreary October day, and we splashed through puddles as we approached the escalator leading to his stall. When I first saw him, Hall was sat behind a desk wearing a black T-shirt emblazoned with his website's logo. There was a very brief second where his expression was open, almost welcoming – before he saw the camera behind me, and his face dropped.

My approach was not hostile. This wasn't a world leader or a CEO accused of corruption. I genuinely just wanted to find out more. But when I asked if he'd be up for answering my questions, he politely declined. Within minutes, he'd pulled out his own camera and started filming me back. It threw me off-guard. I thought he was about to get up and leave his stall unattended, and I took a step backwards.

We went round in circles, with Hall dodging my questions about why he was promoting these theories and why he wouldn't do an interview with me. Journalists think very carefully about these encounters known as doorsteps. I had wanted to ask him enough questions to hold him to account on behalf of the Manchester Arena survivors – but once he'd decided he didn't want to cooperate, that was my cue to back off. I opted for one final question about money.

'You're selling books here, you've got your DVD. You're profiting from the worst day of these people's lives. Do you realize that? How does that make you feel?'

'If you read my book, all the answers are in there,' he replied.

'I have looked at your book, and in it there are claims that are contrary to the evidence.'

Hall told me I was wrong and that he didn't believe I would represent him 'correctly'.

It was only after that visit that he finally answered some of the questions I'd asked. Not directly, but in a video he posted on his website.

In it, he said he hadn't put a camera outside the home of Eve Hibbert, but he did admit to leaving 'a camera rolling' in his van which was 'parked in a public place'. He claimed he had made 'polite door-to-door inquiries in order to gather evidence, which is a perfectly legitimate activity when doing research', and that his appeal for information from the public did not make him 'responsible for hateful messages sent by people'. But he also held firm to his 'opinion [that] there has been no satisfactory evidence presented to the public, which proves that the Manchester Arena incident was not staged'.

While Hall hadn't directly responded to my questions during our encounter at the market, meeting him had revealed a lot to me about who he was and what could be driving him.

To me, it felt like this was perhaps the first time he'd been confronted about the harm he had caused to terror attack survivors. Until then, he'd been able to inhabit a bubble disconnected from reality. I got the sense that he'd convinced himself of the truth of these conspiracy theories because they made him feel important.

I don't think this is about whether Hall actually believes these conspiracy theories at all – which is almost impossible to ever know. What really matters is that he's created a conspiracy world that causes real-world harm, and he's willing to keep it up because he seems to like being at its centre. That, to me, is what separates him from the 'true' believers. These devoted followers tend to sit at home, watching, commenting and sharing. They want to be a part of something, rather than its beating heart. They want guidance and answers, rather than influence and followers.

In the reality Hall has constructed, his actions don't have consequences. Only he knows whether being asked questions about it – face-to-face – did anything to puncture that fantasy. Although his behaviour since suggests he's only doubled down.

Tired of the lack of accountability from someone who had caused serious distress to his family and the family of other survivors, in 2023 Martin Hibbert brought a case for defamation and harassment against Hall, on behalf of himself and Eve. I chatted extensively to the lawyers representing Martin in this case. I also saw how – in his defence case – Hall remained adamant that his book and videos are in the public interest – and that he's right to question whether the terror attack was staged.

It seems to me that, for Hall, retaining his followers is more important than the financial risk of not owning up to the mistruth he's promoted and the tactics he's deployed. After all, if he admitted he'd got it wrong – whether accidentally or very deliberately – his followers would leave. His 'career' and purpose would disappear.

* * * *

Trying to figure out what the leaders of these conspiracy theory movements are driven by is no easy task. Conspiracy theories are essentially an industry. Those in charge can gain profit and fame, power and agency – but as Richard D. Hall demonstrates, it's a risky game to play with very serious consequences, especially when legal action is on the cards. It's also a difficult position to climb down from, especially when it's brought you attention and power.

Hall's tactics are imported from overseas, and before him came the alt-right radio show host Alex Jones. After setting up his own channel, Infowars, in 1999, Jones made his name by suggesting the Sandy Hook school shooting in 2012, which killed twenty-six people, was staged. It was a particularly shocking shooting because the victims were mainly children.

The average person tends to be shocked by such conspiracy theories. Nonetheless, they helped Jones rack up more than 2.4 million YouTube subscribers on his Infowars channel before it was booted off the platform in 2018. Jones's career, though, predates the social media age. Since his start on local cable TV in Texas more than two decades ago, he has projected a larger-than-life image of himself as a fearless truth-teller exposing evil. The conspiracy theories he's pushed have, to varying degrees, always focused on evil and elite cabals plotting sinister wrongdoing.

But his claims about Sandy Hook were the ones that really caught people's attention – and meant more clicks. And it wasn't just the clicks themselves that made Jones money. It was the health supplements, the survival gear for living 'off grid' to escape the cabal, and the other merchandise he could sell to all of those viewers that made him rich. Marketing is inextricably entwined with Jones and his mission.

I reached out to Alex Jones, but he didn't get back to me. I did, however, hear back from someone who used to work with him.

His name is Rob Jacobson and he was a video editor at Infowars. He worked at the company between 2004 and 2017 – and watched how the dawn of social media propelled Jones from a local celebrity in Texas to one of the biggest conspiracy theorists on the planet. The more people Jones could reach, the more fans he could recruit and the more money he could make.

Rob watched in real-time as Jones began claiming that the Sandy Hook school shooting was part of a bid to ban guns in the US. From there it evolved into allegations about crisis actors and claims that 'no one died'. It was a topic Jones covered again and again and again. It proved to be a hit with the audience – with a knock-on effect in the Infowars store.

'Whenever Alex brought it up, his ratings were going up – and he definitely caught notice of that,' Rob recalled. 'It was such a horrible tragedy that perhaps people just didn't want to believe that it was true. And Alex was giving them the way out to sort of escape from this horrible tragedy.'

Rob told me he didn't work directly on the Sandy Hook coverage, and he didn't pay much attention to it until he realized the harm it was causing to the families affected by the attack. He raised the alarm internally, but his concerns were met with laughter and jokes.

For Rob, the question of whether Jones really believed the conspiracy theories he spread about Sandy Hook wasn't all that relevant. 'Did Alex really believe it? I mean, I would personally say he doesn't care whether they are crisis actors or not. What he cares about is being extremely rich, and he cares about being the king of this world he created.'

That became apparent when in 2022 Jones was ordered to pay over a billion dollars to the families of the victims of the Sandy Hook shooting, because of the conspiracy theories he'd spread and the hate they triggered. In court, Jones acknowledged that the Sandy Hook shooting was '100 per cent real'. But when broadcasting to his fans as the verdict came in, he doubled down. He was calling for donations on the right side of the screen. On the other side you could see the parents of the Sandy Hook victims. One was in tears.

'The money you donate does not go to these people. It goes to fight this fraud,' Jones declared. He was already attempting to claim the verdict as further proof that the state was trying to stop him from telling the truth. Never had his words sounded colder than when contrasted with the emotions of the grieving families.

Rob Jacobson told me that Jones would struggle to continue if he did have to pay these damages – and true to that, Jones declared bankruptcy after the verdict. But keeping the attention – and the money – of his committed fans seemed to remain a priority no matter how callous it appeared. In Rob's eyes, Jones was driven by that rather than an unflinching ideological belief.

* * * *

While I have never met Alex Jones face-to-face, I have met the editor of a different outlet here in the UK – a newspaper called *The Light* which was set up during the pandemic. With its anti-vaccine, anti-lockdown stance, it grew to be a focal point of the UK conspiracy theory movement.

When I questioned Richard D. Hall at his market stall in Wales, I had been surprised to see *The Light* proudly displayed on his counter – months after lockdown restrictions had been lifted. But then I received messages from followers about how *The Light* was still being given out in their town, often at regular rallies or weekly market stalls. I set out to investigate.

The paper is handed out free by volunteers in around thirty self-appointed hubs across the country, from Brighton to Leicester and Manchester to Totnes, and local leaders have accused it of inflaming division and harassment with false and misleading claims about vaccines, the financial system and climate change, among more mundane articles on local politics, health and wellness. It seems to print over 100,000 copies a month and it had, at the time of writing, more than 19,000 members on its Telegram channels.

In its pages and on Telegram, *The Light* has shared hateful and violent rhetoric towards journalists, medics and MPs. Articles and content shared by the paper have called for them to be punished for 'crimes against humanity' in war-crime-style trials they sometimes call 'Nuremberg 2.0' – referring to the trials and execution of Nazi Party members after World War Two. The paper and its supporters have suggested the government, doctors, nurses and journalists are complicit in sinister plots to harm people with vaccines and the pandemic.

Recent articles in *The Light* have declared 'it's just a matter of time before these worst perpetrators of war crimes are facing trial' like in 'November 1945' – and 'MPs, doctors and nurses can be hanged'. Posts shared by the paper on Telegram have featured cartoons of gallows and included the work addresses of 'liable people to be held to account' for taking part in plots to harm people with vaccines – plots for which there is no evidence.

The paper has defended far-right figures accused of antisemitism, and there is evidence of its links with far-right groups like Patriotic Alternative, endorsing their content promoting rallies and posts talking about the 'replacement' of white people and asking people to '#GetInvolved'. It has also shared posts from the extreme group Alpha Men Assemble, which offers military-style training to anti-vaccine activists and says 'it's time we show them who rules this country'.

I wanted to know more about Darren Nesbit, the editor of this paper. As I looked into *The Light*, his name came up again and again. On social media there were pictures of him performing with his band. He'd written articles and shared posts online with ambiguous references to 'coming for those at the top' and how the time 'is coming' for some kind of punishment. Some posts on *The Light*'s Telegram channel were signed off with his name and a row of kisses or smiley-face emojis, which felt at odds with the content *The Light* was putting out.

When I emailed him initially he refused to speak to me, and then hung up when I called. But after a back-and-forth where I said that, as long as I could interview him, he could ask me questions in return, he agreed. This is becoming more of a trend, with high-profile people like Twitter boss Elon Musk and self-proclaimed misogynistic influencer Andrew Tate insisting on the same set-up in interviews with the BBC in 2023. Then they tend to share the recording of the whole interview with their followers.

I'm more than happy to answer questions about my journalism. So I practised with my team, coming up with questions and predicting what he might quiz me on. I travelled with my producer Emma Close on the train to Manchester in the evening, running on about one hour's sleep and almost forcibly holding my eyes open as I squeezed in the last bits of preparation.

The next day, I found myself sitting opposite Darren Nesbit in a pub in the town of Leek, not far from his home turf. The upstairs function room felt like it was more accustomed to birthday drinks than an interview between a BBC journalist and conspiracy theory newspaper editor.

Both of our teams set up their kit, and the room became a tangle of cameras and microphones. Darren was frustrated that he couldn't seem to load videos on his laptop. Then he told me I looked like I was going to a disco. Interesting initial comment, I thought. Bald with a beard, he was wearing a white T-shirt with the name of his guitar company on the front – but I didn't comment that he looked like he might be dressed for a gig. It felt like we were two boxers ahead of a fight, and he referred to it as a 'horse race'.

Copies of *The Light* and his extensive notes surrounded us on the table. I clutched my questions in my lap. His views quickly became apparent when we began, as he talked about many of the conspiracy theories populating the pages of *The Light* and its Telegram channel. It felt a bit like conspiracy bingo.

While the pandemic seemed to have energized Darren's views, that wasn't where it started for him. He told me he'd been awake 'for ten years' and referred to himself as a 'complete believer'. He said he'd always been sceptical of the government and corporations – but for him this past decade was more than that. He referred to it as a 're-education'.

'It was great to be able to go back and revisit all the things that we've been told, whether it's science, history, geography, cosmology, health,' he said. 'We don't have to accept to what the BBC tells us. We don't have to accept what the official narrative is.' There's a big difference, though, between holding institutions to account and some of the conspiracy theories about evidence-free plots *The Light* shares.

He had insisted that we alternate questions one at a time, and I noted down my follow-up. When it was Darren's turn to quiz me, he asked why opposition to the government was always conflated with online abuse and the extreme views held by a tiny minority. I told him that I always endeavour to separate very legitimate and reasonable concerns and questions that people have from the more extreme views and ideas that are contrary to the evidence.

According to Darren, the paper cost about £20,000 to print, which means annually the paper could be costing him around £240,000 per year to make. That's a fair bit of money, which he said came from subscribers and advertisers. I wondered whether he had any major donors – but there's currently no evidence to support that idea.

The financial commitment from a portion of the paper's readers also suggested there's a commitment on their part to some of the world view *The Light* pushes. While some of the content is mundane, I voiced my concern that some of it could be a gateway to something more extreme. I quizzed Darren on the paper's links with far-right and antisemitic figures, which he denied. When I asked why he allowed them in his paper, he told me: 'Because if they write good articles on topics that are, you know, useful topics that are interesting to people, then we should have them.'

Darren made it clear that he believes free speech to be hearing from people you don't necessarily agree with, and even 'some whose ideas abhor you'. This gets to the heart of one part of the conspiracy theory movement. Freedom of expression with zero limits – even when it can affect the right of others to speak freely. Targeting journalists with hate and suggesting they should be executed doesn't sound very much like a democracy that honours free speech to me.

'As an editor, do you feel responsible for what you put out there?' I asked. By this point we'd stopped with the one question each, although Darren's team and mine were keeping a close eye on who had more time to ask questions.

He replied that he wasn't promoting hateful ideas and I confronted him with some of the books recommended in the paper, including ones written by a white supremacist, Eustace Mullins, who the paper had described as a 'renowned author'.

'Eustace Mullins is not a white supremacist, he's a historian,' Darren said.

'But he's specifically written books including ones like *The Biological Jew* and *Adolf Hitler: An Appreciation*,' I responded.

'Okay, I've not read that,' he replied. When I pushed harder on whether he was exposing his readers to the hateful ideas someone like Mullins was promoting in their books, he denied that, too.

I quizzed Darren on an article in which *The Light* defended Cornwall radio host Graham Hart, who was sentenced to thirty-two months in prison for making antisemitic remarks on his show. He'd said Jews were filth, like rats, and deserved to be wiped out. Darren agreed it was 'pretty harsh stuff' but the paper defended Hart's 'right to say it'.

The interview was a constant back-and-forth. He'd deny what I said to him, I'd present him with evidence to the contrary, and then he'd just brush it off. He was adamant that if he said it wasn't true, even when the evidence says otherwise, it wasn't true. That's how Conspiracyland works. You can build a whole world where objective truth is irrelevant. At one point I even told Darren that he was a very tricky interview. He and I might decide we had different views about the table in front of us – I might love it, he might hate it – but if he didn't believe the table was even there, then we were talking at totally crossed wires.

When I questioned him about *The Light*'s Telegram channel, he told me that he didn't directly control it, even though some posts featured his sign-off. I asked him about posts from far-right groups that had been shared and endorsed.

He just shrugged. 'People can make up their own minds, they're all adults.'

I asked him about articles condoning 'the use of force only to defend against aggressors' and referring to some of the conspiracy theorists who are a part of this movement as 'extremists'. He immediately condemned any violence, but said it would be in self-defence if there were forced lockdowns or evacuations – and then he offered some more cryptic answers about how people could make their 'own decisions'. It was like he was playing a game.

I wondered why he didn't just disown the violent rhetoric if he didn't agree with it.

'I might be wrong,' he declared.

'So you think violence is justified?'

'No, I don't. But I might be wrong.'

Weeks later, Darren would publish my email address on Telegram, in a post he had again signed off himself. It triggered a wave of hateful messages, including an email at midnight saying

'Tick, Tock'. This confirmed my impression of him as clever, and also quick to wash his hands of any responsibility for others' actions on the basis of content *The Light* shares.

Ultimately, I can't know whether Darren actually agrees with the rhetoric and people he publishes. What I can conclude is that he is willing to publish this kind of content regardless of the harm it can cause. After three hours of talking to him in that pub, I felt a bit like I'd been in a tumble dryer spin cycle all day. I was dizzy with the whiplash from the various contradictory denials.

Given it's no easy task conveying the entirety of our hours-long chat, there are a few things I can deduce about Darren from the evidence and situation that unfolded in front of me. Darren struck me as akin to a political leader – one that wants to position themselves outside of the framework of traditional politics and appeal to the disillusioned. At one point he asked me gleefully if I'd like to get rid of the government and political institutions, to which I pointed out that getting rid of all of those established structures might be a bit chaotic. Darren is emblematic of a new divide. Not between left and right – though his paper's social media channels have shared openly far-right posts and ideas – but rather between those who trust democracy and institutions and those who don't.

He's also a perfect example of how most clues about these conspiracy theorists don't come from the endless documents and videos they cite, or the details of their beliefs. They come from the way they interact with you before, during and after you meet them. At the end of our chat I asked him whether our conversation had changed his impression of me, and to my surprise he was very complimentary. He said I was 'smart, bright, full of energy'.

But, days later, a poem appeared on Darren's Facebook, featuring a photo of me from our interview. It read: 'Her name is Marianna Spring, Shilling for cash is her thing, In disinformation she finds inspiration, her eyes light up and go ker-ching.' In the rest of the post, he claimed I planned to discredit him and the paper by associating them with people promoting hate, disinformation and antisemitism.

I realized I was watching him distort the reality of what had happened in real time. There was a disconnect between the way we'd left the interview and what happened next. And I think that's perhaps the most revealing part of this. My experience of interviewing Darren suggested that he wanted to present a certain image to his followers of him being powerful and in charge. He seemed to want to up the trash talk and draw in eyeballs. That's his identity – and his community looks up to him and expects a performance. I think he has convinced himself of some of the world view his paper presents, but I also think that he's a very clever man who knows how to fan the flames without getting burned.

* * * *

That disconnect between social-media and real-world personas reminds me a lot of another conspiracy theorist I have spent time with. But instead of meeting me at the pub, she welcomed me into her home. Which is how, in December 2020, I found myself trying to fit a Christmas jumper over the leg of a chihuahua.

Before the pandemic, Kate Shemirani was a fan of alternative medicine and saw herself in opposition to the mainstream. At that time, though, she didn't have much reach on social media. I had certainly never come across her back then, although those who have known her for years tell me unscientific cures were high on her agenda.

A nurse by trade, Kate became especially interested in alternative health when she developed – and recovered – from breast cancer. She even started a business and brand called 'Natural Nurse'. That was how she sold treatments and advice to her followers.

Then Covid-19 gave her a voice like never before. Shemirani insisted that the virus causing Covid-19 did not exist. She called the global pandemic a 'scamdemic' and a 'plandemic'. She stated the symptoms of Covid-19 were caused by 5G radio waves and that Covid-19 vaccines would be used to implant microchips in order to track and control people. She was reaching thousands with these claims on social media, racking up followers on Twitter and YouTube in between being suspended at various times for sharing disinformation.

Her regular speeches at anti-lockdown rallies were plastered all over social media. I remember seeing her speak at one in London in 2020. Gaggles of people in shorts and T-shirts sporting backpacks and carrying picnic food were gathered around the fountain in the centre of Trafalgar Square. There was a stage set up where the Christmas tree stands every December. Music was blaring out. There were posters and flags and T-shirts with slogans.

But, as you moved a little closer, you realized those flags were declaring that Covid was a hoax, and the posters featured cartoons of politicians next to nooses. There was opposition to vaccine passports – and a lot of anger at anyone who passed by wearing a mask. There were big banners supporting Donald Trump's re-election campaign in the States and mentioning the QAnon conspiracy theory.

Those in the crowd had their mobile phones at the ready, eyes and ears eager to see who would grace the stage. Then, she arrived. Glamorous, with long blonde hair. Wearing a dress and heels, Kate Shemirani looked like she might be speaking at a business conference. But the words that blared out from the loudspeakers weren't the kind you'd usually hear at a conference. There was talk of mass genocide by vaccine – how it was all part of an elaborate plan, a hoax. Political criticisms became muddled together with extreme views.

For Kate, speeches like this one were the beginning of her celebrity within the conspiracy world. But she truly broke out of the conspiracy echo chamber and into the mainstream when, at one of these rallies, she suggested doctors should be hanged like Nazi war criminals for their role in the pandemic 'hoax'. Her comments sparked outrage from government ministers and the general public. She was even struck off the nursing register by the Nursing and Midwifery Council in the UK. A leading tabloid newspaper questioned whether she was the 'most dangerous woman' in Britain for peddling life-threatening health disinformation. Was she? Well, that's what I wanted to find out when I arrived at Shemirani's house.

By lunchtime, we'd already been filming for several hours. We'd drunk several glasses of Kate's famed juices and eaten a platter of fruit and vegetables. Once populated by her several children, the house was now inhabited by Kate and her chihuahuas and a gaggle of cats, one of whom was blind and kept bumping into things. Beaming with pride, Kate informed me that these cats were not vaccinated.

The house felt like a relic to a time gone by – a time when there were children at home and family life was busy. At least one of those children, smiling from the photos on the walls, said he was no longer speaking to his mum because of the conspiracies she promotes.

I was already a villain to the conspiracy movement, so you might be surprised Kate had agreed to do an interview for BBC *Panorama* with me – let alone welcome me into her home to dress up her chihuahuas and drink juice. But I found that, once we'd chatted on the phone, the barriers began to lower. She wanted to convince me of her point of view, and she wanted to draw attention to her own conspiracy theory mission.

Kate's charm offensive had begun almost as soon as I'd entered the house. She was very easy to chat to, and she heaped praise on me. I enjoyed her conversation, although given her opposition to me and the BBC, my guard was still up. She was in her mid-fifties – although she looked a lot younger.

Kate had recently featured in a video promoting some anti-vax conspiracies, along with various people based in the UK, US, Spain and Sweden with impressive medical and scientific titles. Several alleged that the Covid-19 vaccines were unsafe, that they could alter a person's DNA – and that the pandemic was somehow not real. The video was produced by a media company called Oracle that had turned its attention to promoting conspiracy theories about the pandemic. Social media, smartphones and editing software have enabled almost anyone to call themselves a journalist, and Conspiracyland is populated with these media outlets which create slickly produced and convincing content to recruit others into their way of thinking. Except, unlike journalists, they're not subject to any kind of regulation. They don't have to uphold certain standards. These videos are posted on alternative video-sharing sites before finding their way to WhatsApp groups. They're designed to play on very real fears, questions and concerns.

One of those featured in this particular video alongside Kate Shemirani was Dr Vernon Coleman, a veteran of the pseudoscience world here in the UK. A former medical doctor born in the West Midlands, he relinquished his medical licence in 2016. He has called the pandemic 'the greatest hoax in history', similar to a newspaper article he wrote in 1989 saying that AIDS was the 'hoax of the century, the crisis that never was'.

Anti-vaccine disinformation is Coleman's bread and butter, and while he may have been able to write for mainstream newspapers back in the late eighties and early nineties, his reach is now through YouTube videos and interviews shared on social media.

Also in the video was Dr Rashid Buttar, who was reprimanded by an American medical board in 2010 for using untested treatments on four cancer patients. Then there was surgeon Mohammad Adil, investigated by the UK's General Medical Council after sharing social media videos claiming that Covid-19 was a hoax. He was suspended for twelve months. *Panorama* invited Oracle Films, which produced the video, to comment. The filmmakers chose not to.

Both discredited former doctors, Buttar and Adil seemed keen to grow their online reach after finding themselves under fire for their decisions and opinions before the pandemic. Covid-19 was a new opportunity for them to employ tactics they were already well versed in, and to sell a new alternative to social media users. And they were just two of many.

When the BBC wrote to all thirty-three people in the video, eleven responded, four defended the video's contents and five said if we referred to them as 'anti-vaccine' they'd take legal action. One made no comment. Another acknowledged the virus was real and the cause of disease and deaths – but said the measures to manage the pandemic were disproportionate.

This video didn't just spread within a bubble. I heard about it after a woman in her eighties called Rosemary got in touch. It had scared her out of getting her first vaccine. And it wasn't just Rosemary either. Westminster City Council was compelled to issue a warning after it began circulating in Asian and black communities, which seemed to be contributing to a lower uptake of the vaccine. I wanted to understand why Kate Shemirani had taken part in a video with these people. What did she get out of doing this?

In our conversation, Kate listed conspiracy after conspiracy, bouncing around every time I tried to push on anything specific. She told me the government was incompetent – and then found herself tied in knots, unable to explain who was really behind a pandemic plot that would require lots and lots of competence.

It's again impossible to convey every minute of our conversations, but there are a few things I can deduce about Kate from them that I hope can offer some insights into what drives her. I remember thinking she liked the conversation and camera and performance. She even lent me a pair of wellies before we headed out to walk the chihuahuas, and I realized she wanted me to like her. She was trying to offer me an escape, I think, from the dark BBC overlords.

Narcissism is just one of the characteristics that can draw someone towards conspiracy theories,[15] and that's a term that's been used to describe Kate by those who know her well. What are the traits associated with it? A sense of self-importance, a preoccupation with power, beauty or success, a need to be admired, a lack of empathy – tick, tick, tick, tick. Kate Shemirani exhibited all of these in her behaviour towards me. It seemed to me that she wanted me to like her, but didn't appear to care about the people who could be harmed by the disinformation she shared. She wanted me to know all about her and – as is pretty evident in the clips of her at rallies – thrived being the centre of attention, surrounded by fans hanging off her every word. When we chatted in her kitchen, I was left with the impression that this was about power and attention. It was a chance to command the room. It's exciting and terrifying to be hated and loved in extreme ways.

At first I found I did actually quite like her, which came as a surprise and was definitely her intention. It wasn't the compliments, though, but rather her willingness to talk to me. But then, when she was delighted as I told her about Rosemary, scared off a vaccine because of bad information Kate had readily put out, my opinion changed. She told me she was happy Rosemary had decided not to take the vaccine. In fact, she seemed to relish the idea that someone had followed her advice.

Social media combined with the pandemic offered Kate the opportunity to build a following like never before. It was easier to reach those already susceptible to alternative health ideas, as well as the newly disgruntled. Their engagement was immediate. She was a celebrity in their eyes.

The effect of social feedback on conspiracy theorists is crucial – because they seem to feed off reactions more than non-conspiracy theorists do. A recent study in the *Journal of Experimental Social Psychology* found that a 'considerable proportion' of people explicitly acknowledge that 'when the social engagement reward was sufficiently large, they would be willing to share inaccurate information'. Trading the truth for likes, they know full well that the conspiracies will get you more clicks than the facts ever could.[16]

This is why one of the risks of talking to conspiracy theorists is that you might amplify them to more people – and motivate them to keep at it. But I believe that covering them in a responsible way – when their reach is sufficient and the harm they cause is too – is vital. Pretending these people don't exist does nothing to expose the harm they do. And in many cases, they already have hundreds of thousands of online followers, so it's hardly like we'll be providing them with a platform they can't already access.

* * * *

I was left asking the same million-dollar question about Kate Shemirani as with all the others. Did she really believe all of this – or did it just benefit her to promote these ideas? I got the impression that she'd push whatever was most likely to attract attention and rack up the clicks and likes.

The person who shed light on the years before her social media career was actually her son, Sebastian. He'd reached out to me by email in 2020. The last straw for him had been seeing his mum in video clips at these rallies, encouraging people not to take precautions against Covid-19, which at this point had strained hospitals and left tens of thousands dead, and not to take a vaccine that would save millions of lives. He'd written: 'Sebastian here – I am (unfortunately) the son of Kate Shemirani, the notorious 5G/Coronavirus conspiracy theorist. I'm reaching out to you because I am trying to limit her platform and prevent others from falling down the rabbit hole, because what she is doing is dangerous.'

I met Sebastian close to where he was attending university in London at the time. This was the first time he had ever spoken out about his mum, and he took me all the way back to the beginning.

Sebastian thought Kate had felt lonely – and at times unfulfilled – when she was at home while her kids were at school. But he said the interest in pseudoscience really started after she was diagnosed with cancer. She'd recovered, but the conspiracy theories hung around and became a lot more than just questionable ideas about alternative medicine.

Sebastian told me how at home he was shown videos on YouTube when he was little more than ten years old. Videos about how the very powerful Rothschild family were plotting to go to live on a space station. There was mention of mass genocide. 'It sounds like a bad Hollywood plot, but at the time you know I'm ten, eleven years old and I'm bricking it. I can't believe the genocide was coming.' Sebastian's brow creased as he remembered.

Then, one year, he was given a book by one of the UK's most prominent conspiracy theorists, David Icke. 'It was all about the lizard people that live under the surface of the earth, and they also impersonate the royal family and they also impersonate David Cameron and for some reason they're plotting.' Sebastian trailed off as I tried very hard not to smile. 'It's just so crazy talking about it. I can see you smiling. I'm smiling but it's just so bloody mad.'

It could be quite funny, if it weren't so sad. Sebastian, though, wasn't bitter or distressed about that childhood exposure to conspiracy theories. Rather, it seemed to have shaped his outlook on the world, and pushed him in the other direction.

It was when he attended boarding school as a teenager that he began to question why the genocide his mum had predicted hadn't happened. Being at home wasn't easy, especially after his parents split up. With some distance, he began to see flaws in the world his mum had constructed. The question he asked himself was one he encourages others to ask of their conspiratorial parents or friends or family members: who does this conspiracy actually benefit?

'This big genocide plot just doesn't seem like it would benefit anybody. I don't know why you would kill your entire workforce if you're the global elite.' Sebastian talked me through the thinking of his fourteen-year-old self.

I later spoke to psychologist Jovan Byford about how Sebastian had challenged his conspiracy upbringing, rather than allowing it to inform his view of the world. When he watched back the interview, he was shocked. Not by the lizard books or the YouTube videos. He was surprised by how Sebastian had managed to endure this upside-down way of looking at the world and go in the opposite direction.

Years of exposure to these conspiracy theories had not made Sebastian susceptible to believing them. They didn't change the way he looked at the world, and he didn't think they'd changed the way his siblings looked at the world either. That in itself, in Jovan's view, gives an important insight into how this works. Being hyper-exposed to conspiracy theories is not the only factor in believing them. You have to be vulnerable to them as well – whether that's linked to a sense of distrust or a desire for fulfilment.

By 2020, Sebastian had reached his wits' end. His relationship with his mum was distant, and they stuck to conversations over text. He was living his own life in London, and his mum was in Uckfield, East Sussex.

But then, in the early days of the first lockdown – one of his siblings called. 'Mum's got a load of YouTube followers, look!' Sebastian's heart sank. Up and down the country, people were trying to make sense of the pandemic. It was a time of restriction, upheaval and stress – and stuck at home and turning to social media for answers, they were finding Sebastian's mum telling them that nurses were part of a sinister plot to harm people and that the pandemic was a hoax.

At first, he wasn't sure what to do. He hoped it might just go away. He feared the public harm that his mum was causing, but this was also deeply personal. It was about salvaging some kind of relationship with her. He attempted to talk to her about it, but he had no luck.

Sebastian showed me some of their text conversations in which Kate implored him to listen to her, saying that if he didn't, he and his sister would die as the result of a CIA plot. She said half the UK population would be killed within the next five years. Then there was talk of cities being turned into fortresses, covert military operations that would mark the end of life as we know it. Sebastian said he'd tried to engage in a constructive way, and to suggest this might be worth rethinking. She'd just told him he was brainwashed. If this was an acquaintance or even a friend, he might have just disengaged – but this was his mum.

'My mum is completely unsalvageable – there's nothing I can do,' he explained to me from the get-go. His tone was matter-of-fact and defeated. We were talking because he had reached a point where he felt like he could no longer change his mum's mind. Now he wanted to warn other people – and condemn someone spreading what he termed dangerous disinformation. He believed that, if by speaking out he could limit her platform and deter some of her fans, he should.

While a lot of what Sebastian revealed to me was about the lasting and devastating impact online conspiracies can have on one family, he also gave me a lot of insight into how, in his view, his mum had arrived at this point. And that tells us something about who spreads disinformation and why.

Sebastian thought it was about the attention and the power it afforded her. For him, the applause and reaction she received at anti-lockdown rallies was miles away from the life his mum was leading back at home.

'She's got a big God complex and she loves playing that role,' he said. 'It gives her this confidence and it [fuels] her addiction.'

Many of the people in attendance at those rallies felt betrayed by the media. Signs describing the journalists as the 'enemy of the people' and the BBC as 'Satan's advocates' were a common occurrence, whereas they saw Kate as real, attainable, one of them. These rallies also attracted far-right political groups, seeking to co-opt the message. It was this part that really made Sebastian angry. It was the closest he came in our conversation to losing his temper.

'There are not enough expletives in the English language for me to go at it, but that really, really annoys me,' he said. But rather than shutting it out, Sebastian found himself drawn towards these rallies. He'd look up videos of his mum speaking at them, and attempt to cycle past them when he could, looking for the protest signs and listening to her speak. He described it as a macabre fascination. It seemed to me like it was part of his attempt to hold on to a connection with his mum. He said all he could think of when he saw the crowds of people was *my mum is causing this*.

In Sebastian's view, his mum derives some feeling of intellectual superiority from conspiracy theories. It gives her the keys to the castle, and her followers hang off her every word. It's as if she knows what's really going on, whereas people like Sebastian don't, won't and can't.

Sebastian said he doesn't think his mum will ever say sorry for any of what she's promoted – even when it's been linked to real harm and her predictions have been proven wrong. To an extent, he's right. His mum has been booted off social media sites, and she lost some of the public's interest as pandemic restrictions eased. But even when her prophecies about vaccine deaths and Covid-19 'genocides' failed to come true, she kept pushing the idea that the jabs were part of a sinister plot.

'This is her five minutes of fame, and when this is over in three or four years' time and everything she said is forgotten, she's going to feel lonely again. It will be the next thing, but you know the disaster that goes on within my family,' Sebastian said.

Kate's most recent texts to me suggest Sebastian's prediction is coming true. She's turned her attention to war and climate change – to any narrative that fits with the sinister global plot she's convinced of. 'I'm not sure how you could have missed it in your latest position of fairy on the Christmas tree and all that is nonsense,' she wrote, underlining her belief I was peddling myths.

'I'm never going to have a relationship with my mum again,' Sebastian admitted. He hoped that others might be encouraged to speak to their family members before the rabbit hole swallowed them up entirely. He said it takes a couple of years to totally lose them. But when you are collateral damage like this – and your relationship is suffering – can you ever open their eyes to the truth?

Sebastian offered some advice, born of years of experience. First of all, try to stop the descent as quickly as you can. You've got to keep trying until those initial seeds of conspiracy are killed. Sit the person down and keep talking for hours until they realize what they're saying is untrue. If you allow it to grow and flourish, it becomes all the more dangerous. Sebastian kept reminding me just how quickly you can lose a person.

He said it's also about discrediting where they're getting this information from: the sources. That's the exact reason he decided to speak out about his mum – so that those who follow her can at least see another side.

I wanted to match up Sebastian's advice, as someone who has watched this up close, with an expert in the field. Jovan Byford agreed in principle with what he suggested. But for Jovan, it also depends on who you're dealing with and when.

'I think annihilating a conspiracy theory can be done, but only with people already sceptical of a conspiracy theory,' he says. Often, the counter-arguments alone are not enough if someone is adamant that they're right. Establishing a basis of understanding is key. Approach them on their own terms and avoid sweeping dismissals or simply saying 'you're wrong'. Jovan advises trying to get to the bottom of the often-legitimate concern at the heart of the conspiracy theory. Present them with facts and research – and try to do this neutrally. You can't force anyone to change their mind, but you can make sure they have valid information.

Perhaps the most difficult thing to hear is that there is no silver bullet, no quick fix. Something Sebastian knows all too well. 'The point is to infuse their thinking with counter-arguments,' Jovan explains. In some way, by sewing those seeds of doubt, you create the ability within those people to encounter a conspiracy theory in a new way. You equip them with the right tools.

Since my conversation with Sebastian, his relationship with his mother has unsurprisingly not improved. He has been living on the other side of the world, in Hong Kong. Under new Twitter ownership, Kate Shemirani is back on Twitter – and still a key figure in the UK conspiracy movement.

* * * *

There are different types of non-believers and believers who join the wider conspiracy theory movement, and they sit in a hierarchy. At the very top you have the conspiracy theorists like Alex Jones, with a huge reach and international reputation. Below that there are other leading conspiracy theorists with varying reach – often with their own niche, whether that's health, climate, politics or another area. At their heart, though, they essentially propagate the same idea: an evil cabal of elites are plotting the unspeakable all over the world.

Beneath that are the wannabe conspiracy theorists. They're the people who begin as adoring fans of their leaders, and then attempt to copy them. They want to open up local conspiracy theory branches, encouraging protest and direct action. They are the minions – the local celebrities.

They have fallen under the spell of those in charge and so they are simultaneously victims and bad guys. The misled who go on to mislead. It doesn't take long to realize that, while they might want to paint themselves as all-powerful leaders, they are anything but.

In the original coverage of Gary Matthews's death from Covid-19 (from Chapter 1), a man called Charlie Parker was painted as the villain. He ran the local Facebook group pushing conspiracy theories about the pandemic and vaccine, and he'd been arrested during anti-lockdown rallies in Shrewsbury. He seemed to be the ringleader of the group that Gary had become a part of. It was suggested that Charlie and Gary were friends – and that ultimately it was Charlie who had pulled him into the murky world of online conspiracy theories, something which Charlie denied.

Charlie's name came up so many times. Everyone I interviewed or spoke to seemed to have heard of him. So I reached out to Charlie on Facebook, and after numerous exchanges he agreed to meet. I wanted to ask him about this group and movement. I also wanted to understand who he was, what he believed in, and why.

When I met Charlie, not too far from Shrewsbury where he grew up, he appeared to be in his thirties with scruffy brown hair. He was dressed in an extravagant fur-lined jacket. It looked more impressive from a distance. As he drew closer, it was clear that the coat was faded, frayed and grubby. I'd heard from various local people that he worked as a children's entertainer and rode a unicycle.

Charlie arrived for our interview armed with a stack of papers and some leaflets. We began by talking about Gary Matthews and how Charlie had known him. He described seeing him around Shrewsbury, how he was part of the furniture, someone he'd say hello to every now and then.

He said they'd really bonded on Facebook in those early weeks of the pandemic, when they both became suspicious about lockdowns. He explained how he and Gary would message back-and-forth, sharing their notes and research – he'd brought some with him today. He described the two of them as equals, contrary to the suggestion that he had somehow led Gary astray.

After that, the conversation very quickly veered from talking about Gary to talking about what Charlie believed. Mainly about the pandemic – the sinister global vaccine plots and how Covid-19 was all part of an elaborate hoax. We discussed his concerns around doing an interview with the BBC, which he was deeply critical of. Along with producer Ant Adeane and editor Mike Wendling, I challenged the conspiracies one by one, but made very little progress.

It became apparent to me that he really wanted to believe that the government was plotting to control and murder a whole population. He really wanted to believe in a battle between good and evil being waged on his doorstep; and he wanted to believe he was a crusader on the right side. He didn't trust me one bit, even asking me if I had webbed feet like a lizard. Dear reader: I do not.

Why would anyone want to believe anything so terrifying? Well, because for the first time, Charlie was not just the quirky character on the unicycle who people dismissed or chuckled at pitifully. He loved believing in this stuff; it made him feel important and valued. Various people had told me he'd struggled at school, and most of the locals I'd chatted to had painted him as the town jester – or nuisance.

Whenever I tried to talk to him about normal stuff – like his family, or what he liked to do – he shrank back into his shell. But when he was discussing conspiracy theories, he was talking at a mile a minute and brimming with confidence. He was powerful Charlie saving the world from an evil cabal. He could explain the world through this new belief system to which he'd subscribed.

His beliefs had also given him followers and friends who trusted what he said and praised him. Before the pandemic, Charlie had been somewhat of a lone wolf, according to everyone I'd spoken to. Footage I saw of him at anti-lockdown rallies revealed how popular he had become. People were excited to see him. He had a new community and purpose.

No amount of challenging Charlie on his beliefs was able to provoke any reflection on his part. He just ploughed through. What he believed in seemed fundamental to his sense of self. Why would he shatter the one thing that had made him feel a bit better about life – even if it was just a short-term fix?

When I really pressed Charlie about Gary, he didn't tell me a story or describe a cherished memory. Instead, he read off a handwritten set of notes. 'Gary was a unique and highly regarded individual to all those who met him. He was highly intelligent and had a variety of interests from fine art to photography,' he said, his head buried in the pages in front of him. 'Gary had a zest for truth and a passion for knowledge.'

When I asked when they'd first met, Charlie couldn't remember. It seemed to me that their friendship was purely about belief. He didn't see Gary as a son, a friend or a cousin who loved art and painting and spending time with family. His testimony starkly contrasted with my conversations with Gary's other friends. They were comrades in the trenches, and Charlie would continue to espouse the belief system he maintained they were both dedicated to – regardless of the harm and hurt that it had caused.

Regardless, too, of the fact that Gary had died of the very virus Charlie didn't believe existed. It seemed he would stop at nothing to come up with reasons why it couldn't have been Covid-19. He wouldn't let the facts disrupt the fantasy world he'd constructed. He believed that Gary had died in some other way, but struggled to define exactly how. He even let Gary's family know that he didn't think it was Covid-19 that had killed him.

'I knew there was such large grounds for foul play that I felt it out of moral obligation, I should approach his family to notify them in the most empathic way I could. And that was such a difficult thing to do,' Charlie told me.

I quizzed him on this – could he see how for those close to Gary it was really hard to be approached in that way, and to see Charlie's posts online casting doubt on Gary's death while they were grieving? But he didn't think he'd done anything wrong.

'I tried to contact certain members of his family and I was accused of harassing his family, which is complete nonsense,' he said. 'I simply messaged a couple of members of his family to notify them about my concerns [about] circumstances surrounding what had happened to Gary. That's all I did. And because I received no response, I saw a post in memory of Gary and I wrote a tribute to Gary.'

I pushed harder. 'But can you see it from their point of view? Gary's not coming back. Gary's dead. They don't get to ever speak to Gary again. Gary is their son, Gary is their brother. And they've got to see this kind of stuff on Facebook. Can you see why that might be really upsetting? Do you see how hard that must be when they've lost someone who means so much to them?'

'I appreciate that they were in their own mourning, as we all were. But I could also see how wrong and immoral the situation was. Anyone who cares about anyone would want the circumstances to be investigated promptly and effectively.' Charlie seemed rattled, frightened and confused. He was uncomfortable facing the consequences of his actions.

Charlie may have been painted as the fairy-tale villain in early media coverage of this story – as the all-powerful leader who'd somehow created this mess – but he was far from that in reality. Those like Charlie are followers of the major influencers. They are also to some extent leaders, inspired to grow their own small communities of believers in their home towns, like Shrewsbury. They impart wisdom through local Facebook groups, all the while evolving and growing their belief system – concentrating on the bits they like best.

Charlie has a lot in common with Kate Shemirani, Richard D. Hall, Alex Jones and Darren Nesbit. They all seem driven to some extent by the attention and the social acceptance. Gratification trumps fact – and the danger of pushing harmful conspiracy theories. But, unlike the others, I don't think Charlie is so aware of what he's doing. He's not calculating.

For Charlie, there isn't really any money or much power involved at all. He just wants to feel valued and important on a much smaller scale, and his influence is dwarfed in comparison to Conspiracyland's leaders. The way that he defended himself, especially when we discussed Gary, felt different to how several of the others responded to my challenges, too. He desperately wanted to justify himself, and he didn't want to have been the reason Gary lost his life. Charlie is a hybrid between true believer and non-believer, and teaches us about how to climb the conspiracy theory ladder – or not.

* * * *

Conspiracy theories aren't just shared by the leaders in Conspiracyland – powerful among their committed followers but lacking in any real authority. Elected politicians who inhabit the so-called mainstream can also fan the flames of unfounded theories that feed into this world.

When Candy video-called me from her car in Connecticut before she headed into work, I quickly realized that no amount of evidence would convince her that the 2020 United States presidential election hadn't been rigged. She'd propped her phone on her dashboard, her blonde hair was tied back from her face and she was wearing sparkly eyeshadow, which I complimented. That sparked a five-minute chat about her favourite eyeshadow palette – and where I might be able to buy it.

When we got on to the subject of the election, Candy cast her mind back a few days. It was the middle of a frosty November night, and the 49-year-old was curled up in bed after a long shift at work. She unlocked her phone and began scrolling through her social media feed. It was election night, and the result was still hanging in the balance. So she scrolled and scrolled, catching up on the night's news and waiting for her favourite presidential candidate to speak.

It was just after 1 a.m. when she first heard Trump allege 'fraud' had occurred, even while the votes were still being counted. The frustration rushed through Candy – and she was desperate to do something. She lived in a democracy after all – supposedly the most free and fair in the whole world. How could her vote be discarded like this? How could the election be rigged? She quickly joined a Facebook group, invited by one of her best friends. It was called Stop the Steal.

'The Democrats have said since the beginning of all this Covid stuff that they're going to do whatever it takes to get Trump out – and I think that they have succeeded,' she told me, pushing a strand of blonde hair away from her face. That wasn't a view that Candy had suddenly developed on election night.

It wasn't actually triggered by Trump's shocking early morning speech. This was something she'd been expecting. Candy had been primed.

For months, allegations of 'rigged elections' and 'voter fraud' had been punctuating her Facebook feed. And she wasn't the only one. The man at the very top – President Trump – had told her and his millions of followers, again and again, that the election could be rigged, that voter fraud would happen. According to BBC research, between April 2020 and the election Trump mentioned rigged elections or voter fraud more than seventy times. And it wouldn't stop there; in the months and years after the election he has continued to push the idea it was stolen.

Just to give you a flavour – on 22 June 2020, Trump tweeted, entirely in capitals: 'RIGGED 2020 ELECTION: MILLIONS OF MAIL-IN BALLOTS WILL BE PRINTED BY FOREIGN COUNTRIES, AND OTHERS. IT WILL BE THE SCANDAL OF OUR TIMES!'

Trump was no stranger to claiming elections were rigged. He'd even made claims of voter fraud back in 2016. But the evidence suggested that this time many more people had been seeing these unsubstantiated claims all over their social media feeds. Candy was just one of them. In 2020, Trump's audience was larger and more willing to hang on his every word. He was the president, after all. The lie travelled through the vessel of social media in a more turbocharged way than it had four years before. Mainly because, in 2016, Trump had won.

Hundreds of thousands joined big Facebook groups under the Stop the Steal banner, just as Candy had. Like her, they'd seen disinformation about voting online for months. The claims didn't just come from Trump, either. Influential right-wing accounts with sizeable followings had been instrumental in amplifying the idea that the election was 'rigged'.

The name 'Stop the Steal' itself went viral on Twitter on election night, accompanied by what would turn out to be one of many misleading videos claiming voter fraud. This particular video showed a poll watcher – people who observe the election process – being denied entry to a Philadelphia polling station. It reached almost 2 million views on Twitter, and was shared by multiple pro-Trump accounts.

The man featured in the video was asked to wait outside by officials – with a woman telling him that the certificate he had showing he was allowed to watch voters and ensure election integrity was not valid at that particular polling station. The BBC worked to verify this video was real, looking for clues from the scene and messaging the people sharing it. It was genuine – and the woman in the video was wrong. It was true that there was confusion over the rules. Poll watchers used to only be allowed into a particular station in Philadelphia, but they could now visit multiple sites across the city. The situation was later clarified and the man was allowed into the station and given an apology. None of that was reflected in the video of course – and the hashtag had already gone viral.

It was from that moment that 'Stop the Steal' became the rallying call for those who had bought into these cries of voter fraud. The large Facebook groups that sprung up cumulatively amassed more than a million members in the days following the November election.

I had scrolled through the comments in various groups. Threats of violence and calls for 'civil war' were not hard to find. It was this kind of rhetoric that would eventually lead social media sites to take down some of the groups, with Facebook underlining its commitment to protecting election integrity – but at this point, the movement had taken on a life of its own. Attempts to shut it down were like Stop the Steal whack-a-mole.

For Candy, violence wasn't the answer. She was outraged to hear that people in the movement were trying to start riots in different places in the country. The Facebook group she was a part of, though, was one of those shut down. Candy's big concern, one she reiterated to me in earnest, was finding out the truth. I genuinely do think she bought into these narratives. She wasn't sure who to trust anymore. The problem was that the truth she really wanted to believe was contrary to the evidence.

'Everybody was just putting out what fraud they were seeing going on with the election,' she explained, occasionally pausing our video call to take a look at some of the examples on her social media feed.

She mentioned the claim that certain types of pens were handed out that would invalidate ballots, or that ballots were being dumped or ripped up. One example: a man said that he had thrown away Trump ballots in Wisconsin in a video that went viral on Facebook. But it turned out that he lived in the suburbs of Detroit in Michigan – a totally different state. When I contacted him about it, the 32-year-old butcher insisted he'd had nothing to do with counting any ballots – in Wisconsin or anywhere else. The post, he said, was simply a joke. He couldn't quite believe how quickly it had caught on, and how much his joke had fanned the flames of those election fraud claims.

Misinformation, funnily enough, is often born from jokes gone wrong. I spoke to a prankster during the pandemic who'd joked about fines for leaving your home more than once during lockdown. People had believed the rumour he'd started. He insisted on wearing a balaclava when we spoke because he was fearful of the repercussions of what he'd done.

Candy readily told me how she thought she spent too much time on Facebook. Social media was her after-work companion, a place she connected with people – and it was also her main source of election information, even though she wasn't too sure who or what she could trust.

No surprise then that Candy had come across a popular conspiracy theory: QAnon.

It's the one everyone asks me about. The one that's caught the attention of the media and public alike. In essence, it suggests that Trump is waging a secret war against Satanic cabals and paedophiles in government, media and business. Really, it's a conspiracy octopus that wraps its tentacles around just about anything and everything, exploiting feelings of deep distrust and shape-shifting so that it can appeal to even more people.

QAnon started back in October 2017, following the election that saw Donald Trump become president, when an anonymous user posted several times on the message board 4chan. That user called themselves 'Q', suggesting they had a level of US security approval referred to as 'Q clearance'.

The 4chan posts shared by Q became known as 'Q drops'. These posts were cryptic and coded; you almost had to learn a new language to be able to understand them. They talked about Donald Trump a lot – as well as alleged secret plans and pledges. This wasn't limited to niche messaging boards, though. The QAnon conspiracy theory that these posts started and fed spread everywhere, from Reddit to Facebook, Twitter to YouTube. During the pandemic, it boomed, finding a more captive audience than ever before, all willing to believe that almost everything was part of a sinister plan. A September 2020 Pew Research Center study found that nearly half of all Americans had heard of QAnon. That was double the number of six months before.[17] It was only during the pandemic that the major social media sites really began to crack down on groups linked to this particular conspiracy theory, removing them and attempting to limit its spread.

QAnon's main goal has been to target the politicians, celebrities and powerful people who they believe are part of this cabal. There have been threatening messages online – and QAnon believers arrested offline too. But the riots at the Capitol in January 2021 are perhaps the starkest example of how QAnon and conspiracy theories in general can inspire offline violence.

QAnon's election rebrand in the months leading up to the riots was based around the phrase 'Save the Children' – in response to the idea that powerful cabals of people were stealing, abducting and even eating kids. It was a conspiracy theory unfolding at a time when worrying allegations of sexual abuse were being levelled at very powerful people who didn't appear to have been held to account for years. Understandably, parents were worried about this, and elements of this sprawling conspiracy theory played on their pre-existing concerns when it was shared in local Facebook groups.

Trump had never officially endorsed QAnon, but he'd flirted with it. He'd liked tweets from major QAnon influencers on Twitter, and shared memes they'd created. Plus the ideas he was promoting – especially the concept that everything was rigged against him – fed directly into their beliefs.

Around the 2020 US election, I interviewed Professor Whitney Phillips of Syracuse University, who studies online misinformation. It was her view that QAnon helped to explain just how the rumours of a rigged election had spread so viciously and quickly among people like Candy.

'Journalists and commentators have focused on the satanic child sex ring elements of the theory,' she told me over a video call. 'But buried within that narrative was a deeper "deep state" narrative' – and it was this which caused Trump supporters to question and doubt almost everything.

In Dr Phillips's view, even before the first vote was cast there were 'breadcrumbs and a whole narrative framework' that the Democrats were going to steal the election. She told me she was less worried about violence on the streets than she was about the erosion of faith in democracy. But it turned out that both of those things were very legitimate fears.

Less than two months after I spoke to Candy – in January 2021 – my phone buzzed with a flurry of messages.

'They're inside the Capitol!'

Soon videos spread online of crowds pushing their way into the most important government building in the US. These were mostly filmed by protesters who not long before had gathered at a Trump rally. There were some from the few journalists who had found themselves rammed in with the crowd. Terrified members of Congress also shared their own pictures and footage. There was shouting, crashing, screams.

From the start there were explicit links to the QAnon conspiracy and other far-right groups, including several individuals present who had known ties to QAnon. One was a man called the QAnon Shaman – real name Jake Angeli. He was memorably photographed in horns and a fur hat, with the American flag painted across his face – and his picture went viral. Others at the Capitol were associated with various far-right groups including the Proud Boys and the Oath Keepers. Evidence that emerged in the hours, weeks and months afterwards would further substantiate those links.

It was all at once impossible and predictable – proof that a significant number of people really seemed to believe that the election had been stolen. And it had very real, direct consequences. Five people died who were caught up in or connected to this.

The events of 6 January shook the foundations of democracy in the world's most powerful country. The heart of the US government had been overrun with protesters who effectively wanted to stage a coup. They were – in part – inspired by what they were seeing online. And some of those posts came from one of the most powerful men in the world.

Hearings to establish what happened at the Capitol that day have sought to confirm exactly what role Trump played in the riots. Unsent tweets and testimony have been used to suggest he was aware some individuals were armed. Questions have been asked of the social media companies, too – what role did they play? At the hearings, social media moderators whose job it was to monitor content on the sites talked of sleepless nights, fearful of the destruction and death that would come on 6 January.

A few days after the riots, I messaged Candy to see what she thought – and to check she hadn't been there. She still believed not only that the election had been stolen, but that Trump was, yet again, being set up. It wasn't pro-Trump supporters causing trouble, she said. In reality, they'd been infiltrated by anti-fascist activists and Black Lives Matter campaigners. Candy's faith in institutions was so shattered that she couldn't even begin to believe that maybe she'd been misled.

Trump has since been indicted several times – including on charges of plotting to overturn the 2020 election defeat. He has been accused of four felony counts, including conspiracy to defraud the US, tampering with a witness and conspiracy against the rights of citizens. This specific indictment capped the inquiry into what happened on 6 January. The case against him alleged that he did know his claims the election was stolen were not true.

I spent time lurking on the sites where Trump's most committed devotees gather, to gauge their reaction to events in the real world, and each time news of his indictments has broken, they were bubbling over with outrage and anxiety. Many of them said that the indictments were part of a plot by the Deep State. And there were two competing narratives unfolding simultaneously.

The first involved angry and sometimes violent rhetoric directed at the government, along with cryptic calls to action. Messages included 'Here We Go!!' and 'Their turn is coming soon'. Others referred to the false claims that the 2020 election was rigged and Trump was the rightful winner, explaining 'see if we'll stand against this fake government should Trump [be] arrested'. The more extreme messages called for followers to 'Kill the Deep State', but there was no visible evidence of plans to riot.

There was some talk of pro-Trump rallies, but the mood felt different to the lead-up to the US Capitol riots, which were preceded by a social media movement with hateful language and calls for violence. Several posting on Telegram feared there was a sinister plot enticing them to take to the streets like some did on

6 January, and that they would be arrested. They stated there was a bigger plan where Trump would emerge victorious – if they could stay out of trouble. The officials in charge of bringing and handling these indictments had made Trump the most 'prolific political martyr in history', one pro-Trump account wrote.

Now, for some of the followers of both QAnon and also Donald Trump, everything is part of the conspiracy. Their faith in the institutions and democracy at the heart of their nation is totally shattered. The genie is out of the bottle. When a conspiracy theory is fuelled by one of the most powerful people, that's very hard to undo.

There are quite a lot of differences between a committed disaster troll or conspiracy theory newspaper editor and the president of the United States. But, ultimately, this is all about the benefit incurred by pushing unfounded or evidence-free ideas. In the age of social media, such disinformation is not just permitted but essentially actively rewarded – with views, followers, money and power.

Before social media it was easier to ignore people sharing conspiracy theories – and there was not necessarily such a clear incentive for them to be shared. But now conspiracy theorists have their own platforms where they can build and shape their idea of the truth without being held accountable. Whether we ignore them or tackle them, they continue to cause harm. I hope that by exposing who is involved in Conspiracyland, I can shine a light on why and how this happens – and its consequences.

Ultimately, it is very difficult to figure out whether any of these people really believe the ideas they promote, because of the benefits they gain from sharing them. So, perhaps whether they believe in them or not is the wrong question to ask. Instead, we have to stick to interrogating what purpose spreading these conspiracy theories actually serves. Perhaps it is useful to convince themselves of these ideas – and only they really know how much of it they actually believe.

3

COLLATERAL DAMAGE

I was scrolling on my TikTok account in early 2023 when a photo of a woman appeared on my screen. She was in her forties, dressed in sportswear. I'd never seen her face before, but it was about to be plastered everywhere. Her name was Nicola Bulley, she was forty-five years old, and she was missing. She had been walking her dog along the river in the small Lancashire village of St Michael's on Wyre when she vanished.

Witch hunts began on the popular video-sharing platform not long after her disappearance, with people falsely accusing Nicola's friends and family of being involved in what had happened. They analysed social media posts and CCTV footage, statements and reactions, racking up millions of views in total.

When Nicola's body was found in the river several weeks after she disappeared, and her death was ruled as accidental drowning by the coroner, the heart-breaking truth could not undo all of the speculation and mistruths that had spread in the meanwhile. The damage was done – and the conspiracy theories had taken root in people's minds. Within the first three weeks of her disappearance, videos I found using the hashtag of her name had 270 million views on TikTok.

But what was astonishing was just how many TikTokers were actually going to Nicola's village. Amateur sleuths turning up at the scene of a crime is nothing new – but the number of them who were turning up combined with the level of conspiracy thinking, suggesting that what had happened was staged and, in addition to the wild accusations, surpassed what I'd seen before. The tactics were more extreme, too; there was a willingness to break into properties and trespass, to confront locals and post everything on TikTok.

Wall-to-wall coverage by the press was partly blamed for the chaos unfolding – but it was on TikTok where the lies and misinformation that couldn't be aired on traditional media spread like wildfire. It was out of control. It even triggered statements from the police, who issued a dispersal order. It also began to seriously affect the locals; they were the collateral damage.

Oliver Fletcher's family own the caravan park close to where Nicola went missing. His grandmother Penny, aged seventy-eight at the time, was the person who found Nicola's phone and dog after she disappeared. Some of the wild speculation flying around online accused the whole family of being involved in what had happened to her, even though that was contrary to all of the evidence. They were terrified. Penny was frightened to leave the house.

As Oliver walked me around the grounds of the caravan park a couple of months following Nicola's disappearance, he told me how – at the time – the theories just became 'wilder and wilder'. People had actually suggested that his grandmother was somehow hiding Nicola or had abducted her.

'Within days, if not hours, that quickly escalated to people finding out what my grandmother's name is, the address being posted online. People started to physically turn up in the village and take photos of the house,' Oliver told me as we watched his clearly very capable grandmother whizzing around on her lawnmower, preparing the grounds of the caravan park for holidaymakers.

He talked me through an incident involving one particular TikToker – footage of which I'd seen online. He'd achieved notoriety for his invasive videos about the case. Oliver described to me how this man had allegedly trespassed onto the caravan site and started speaking to customers, before approaching his grandmother and quizzing her. 'He stood in front of her asking her questions, trying to provoke or antagonize her.'

In the clip, I can see how Penny tried to escort him off the property as he kept asking questions. 'She said that she felt like someone may come and attack her, and try to kill her,' Oliver explained. 'It's been intrusive, intimidating, antagonistic, and also getting clicks and likes to earn money online.' At the time of writing this, the TikToker in question had been arrested on suspicion of malicious communications, perverting the course of justice and stalking.

In Oliver's mind, it wasn't just the TikTok creators them-selves he blamed for what unfolded, but the social media sites that he thinks incentivize this kind of behaviour. 'I do think that the sort of popularity of the TikTok videos almost gives legitimacy to these people's actions, and people now think that it's acceptable to invade people's privacy and make people feel unsafe in their own home. I think twenty years ago this simply wouldn't have happened. The concern is that the escalation of people coming to the house to film my grandmother will encourage others to do so, because they have assumed that that's perfectly acceptable – which is, of course, [it is] absolutely not.' Oliver became emotional as he reminded me that his grandmother and his family were real people, and how he couldn't believe people would accuse them of such awful things.

What happened during the Nicola Bulley case appears to be part of a wider phenomenon, where TikTok drives disproportionate amounts of engagement to some topics. Speaking to former staffers, users and analysing data for a BBC Three investigation, I found that these 'frenzies' then lead to disruption and disorder in everyday life.

Ultimately, it seems to come down to TikTok's algorithm and design. When you post a video on TikTok, it will appear on the feeds of other users who TikTok thinks might be interested in it, rather than just being promoted to your friends and followers. Depending on how users engage with that video, the algorithm might decide to push it to millions more at a speed and scale seemingly greater than on the other social media platforms. Former employees have also explained to me how – rather than remaining passive and just consuming content – TikTok users are much more likely to make and post their own videos.

If you do use TikTok, think of when a particular topic or trend takes off with unusual vigour or unexpectedly. At times, those 'frenzies' might be more mundane, with less serious consequences. Those that I've investigated, though, have been linked to harm in the real world. The combination of encountering content you've not seen anywhere else, high engagement and increased participation seems to distort perceptions of what's socially acceptable and validate antisocial behaviour, encouraging people to take part and copy in a way that they wouldn't normally.

When it comes to far more important topics – like the disappearance of Nicola Bulley – users can feel like they are participating in a sort of mystery game. But a lack of control over what's being posted means it all gets out of hand pretty quickly, and misinformation about blameless bystanders is enjoyed by millions.

I wanted to speak to one of the TikTokers caught up in this particular frenzy – were they just collateral damage in terms of the social media site's algorithm, or did they need to take some responsibility for their own actions? So, I met Heather, who had posted several very popular videos speculating about the Nicola Bulley case. Unlike the TikToker who turned up at the caravan site, she never went to the scene of the disappearance, but she did find herself caught up in this frenzy.

Heather, with her blonde hair tinged pink and wearing a bright smile, told me she'd never really posted on TikTok before. A busy mum, she hadn't really had the time. She said she'd wanted to get 'the real person's perspective' on what was happening after Nicola Bulley disappeared – and that TikTok had inspired her to get involved.

Heather described the first posts she'd encountered: pleas for information about Nicola, little descriptions of what she was wearing, retracing her footsteps from the day. But then she'd seen the darker side: the conspiracy theorists unpicking Nicola's life and focusing on her family and friends. On TikTok, Heather found she was being fed more and more of this kind of content.

'I think it's very easy to fall down like a conspiracy hole, isn't it?' she said. 'You start to scrutinize things, and any little thing can become suspicious when you're looking at it over and over and almost wanting to find discrepancies in people's stories.'

True to that, Heather posted a video scrutinizing doorbell footage of Nicola leaving the house on the morning of her disappearance, and falsely implying the footage was actually of Nicola's best friend, Emma, pretending to be Nicola. Emma had spoken to the media about Nicola's disappearance, which led to TikTokers analysing her behaviour and claiming she was involved. But Emma was totally innocent.

According to Heather, her video got 3.6 million views in seventy-two hours, which was totally unexpected. She said that TikTok sent her emails of encouragement for going viral, telling her how many views she'd received, calling it a hit and encouraging her to keep posting.

In her mind, TikTok changed how she thought it was OK to behave. 'Whereas before you might not have had that level of empowerment or entitlement, all of a sudden you feel that you've got this authority to keep posting,' she explained.

Misinformation has proved a particular problem for TikTok, with a study by the Integrity Institute finding that misleading and false claims can be amplified up to twenty-five times more on the video-sharing platform than the likes of Instagram and Facebook.

'I've had to remind myself these are other people's lives. And it's not just a video that's going to go nowhere. It's potentially going to blow up in your face. And then you are accountable,' Heather said.

I could tell that she regretted getting caught up in the frenzy – and she'd since deleted her videos. While she was capable of making her own decisions, I couldn't help but think that without social media – and TikTok in particular – Heather just wouldn't have become involved in the case. Without a doubt, people like Oliver and his granny Penny are collateral damage in these situations – but in a very different way, so are those like Heather who seem to be spurred on by the social media sites they use.

I met with an insider at TikTok for more answers about what was happening here. I'm calling him Lucas to protect his identity. He worked in data strategy and analysis – and his main focus was on revenue and the profit-driving side of the business. Before we met, he was really fearful about the repercussions of speaking to me, and cited allegations that TikTok monitors and tracks its former employees.

TikTok, which is owned by the Chinese company Byte-Dance, grew exponentially during the Covid-19 pandemic. It became known for fun dancing and lip-syncing videos when much of the world was stuck at home – and for its very powerful For You page (FYP) that constantly feeds you more videos that you likely wouldn't have encountered before.

But soon, TikTok was so much more than an innocent pandemic hobby; the home of viral dances and life hacks. Almost every major global news event – including ones I hadn't heard about in the media yet – seemed to unfold in real time on my feed. Different topics were up for grabs, and a younger user base became especially involved. Lucas thinks TikTok just wasn't equipped to deal with that evolution, which in his mind explains the frenzies like in the Nicola Bulley case.

'They didn't necessarily have all the systems to handle things properly. It grew so fast that they couldn't possibly keep up with or predict every single way the app was going to go,' Lucas said, adding that he'd never heard of TikTok 'trying to proactively prevent' dangerous content from getting big. 'In general, they don't want to. They don't want to stand in the way of entertainment growing quickly on their platform.'

I asked him if it came down to money. His answer – yes. After all, more users spending more time on the platform means they can sell ads at a higher price. 'It's probably the most addictive platform that we've encountered yet. And I think that's a real danger, especially because of how young the audience is and how impressionable they are.'

TikTok maintains that it tackles hate and disinformation on its platform and protects its users, but it is clear to me from speaking to Lucas and other insiders that the social media arms race to create the most popular site seems to be connected to some of this harmful behavior offline. A highly powerful algorithm and clever format draw you into worlds you would never have entered, and distort your perception of what's socially acceptable. After all, what we consider acceptable behaviour is based on our interpretation of how the majority perceive it. If harmful or antisocial behaviour is viewed by millions and even actively endorsed and rewarded, it can seriously disrupt the social code we rely on. The damage isn't just done to the people who find themselves the unexpected targets of conspiracy theories and trolling. It's also to users who are being affected by the social media sites profiting from them.

When I put these allegations to TikTok, a spokesperson told me that its 'algorithm brings together communities while prioritizing safety'. It said it recommends different types of content to interrupt repetitive patterns, removes 'harmful misinformation' and reduces the reach of videos with unverified information.

It also says it has more than 40,000 'safety professionals' using technology to moderate content, with the 'vast majority' of videos with harmful misinformation never receiving a single view. It told me that users 'naturally' take more of an interest in stories at 'moments of national conversation, which are intensified by 24-hour news reporting'.

'Prioritizing safety is not only the right thing to do, it makes business sense,' the spokesperson said.

* * * *

The small Devon town of Totnes is very different from St Michael's on Wyre, where Nicola Bulley went missing. I arrived there on a rainy Tuesday, and I was greeted by its high street, lined with independent shops and art galleries.

I'd come to Totnes because, like in other places across the UK, people living there had told me their town and its residents had become collateral damage in the ever-committed UK conspiracy theory movement (you might remember this protest from Chapter 1). But, rather than a swarm descending on the town like in the village of St Michael's on Wyre, this happened more gradually over the pandemic. And Totnes was one of the hubs where a motivated minority, who'd once protested lockdown measures and vaccines, were continuing to distribute the conspiracy theory paper *The Light* (you met its editor back in Chapter 2).

To find out more, I got in contact with the town's former mayor, Ben Piper. He grew up in Totnes, and knows it like the back of his hand. We arranged to meet on his home turf in the town's market square, though it was busy, so we sought solace in the nearby church. Ben was wearing a cap, an earring sparkling in one of his ears, and had brought along someone else – Georgina Allen, former deputy mayor of the town. Their friendship was immediately apparent, and they teased each other like siblings – interrupting one another as they spoke.

When the conspiracy theory newspaper *The Light* first appeared on the streets of Totnes, Ben was in the midst of trying to protect the town during the pandemic. He was tasked with enforcing restrictions, and that quickly made him a key target for the conspiracy theory movement that sprung up here. While the movement began as an opposition to lockdown measures, it soon spiralled into the repertoire of conspiracy theories about sinister plots you will now be well familiar with.

It was as the conspiracy theory movement in Totnes started to become more vocal and almost evangelical in its approach, attempting to recruit other residents of the town, that Ben and Georgina spotted *The Light* being handed out and put through doors. It appeared to be a publication brought into the town from outside, rather than something produced by the people who lived there.

Ben said that at that time the harassment he was facing from members of the conspiracy theory movement started to get worse. 'I've been shouted at in the street. I've been accosted and had cameras shoved up my nose and had people drive their cars at me.'

He recalled standing on the side of the road when a man swerved his car at him. He had to jump out the way. The hardest part was that it was someone he'd known for thirty years. He described this to me as the 'personal emotional cost' of 'divisive manipulative politics' packaged up as conspiracy theory movements. 'I've had peculiar phone calls in the middle of the night. And suddenly there's somebody on the phone going, "Yeah, it was really easy to get your number" and it's like, "Who are you?" "Oh well, you don't know me, but I know who you are" – you know?'

Ben was concerned that the level of abuse was being exacerbated by the conspiracy theory newspaper handed out on the high street. It's impossible to prove that people acted directly in response to content in *The Light* – but in Ben's view the publication and wider movement played some role in stoking the hate against him. He told me about an article where he was described as the 'cowardly mayor of Totnes'. Having met him, I really don't think 'cowardly' is the right adjective.

But this wasn't just about the targeting of individuals in the community by this movement. It was also the wider impact on local democracy. After all, it's a worry when an elected official is targeted offline like this anywhere, and by anyone. Tensions really escalated when an almighty row broke out with the council. Some local conspiracy theorists going by the name the New World Alliance – a group central to the movement in the town – attempted to book the Totnes Civic Hall as the venue for a 'conference of truth-speakers'.

Members of the group were also known to hand out *The Light*, and Georgina was well aware of the conspiracy theories and ideologies it shared. She told me she became 'really alarmed really quickly', and took a more detailed look at posts from the scheduled speakers and some of the other people involved with the conference. It didn't take long before she uncovered antisemitic ideas they'd posted online. 'You can't just say freedom of speech, let it happen, it'll be fine,' she said. 'Because, you know, the people involved were extremely nasty.'

Jewish groups in the area were also concerned about the implications and had started to write to some members of the council. To Georgina, this conference was the exact opposite of what the town should be all about.

It was around this time that Georgina and Ben started to realize there was something akin to what they'd describe as a recruitment process happening in their town. Some people in Totnes seemed to be very susceptible to the rhetoric being promoted. Georgina told me how the conspiracy theory movement began 'whipping up emotions and fears about the pandemic', pushing some residents towards the far right.

I wanted to find out a bit more about the conspiracy theorists that Georgina and Ben had mentioned, so I reached out to local artist Jason Liosatos. His name had come up several times in different conversations. I wondered how much individuals like him were responsible for the division in their communities.

Jason's videos online contrasted quite starkly with the peaceful art gallery he ran, located on the high street. 'The systems rotten at the core, it's a Frankenstein's monster system that's perpetuating slavery. It should be crushed to its knees. It should be deleted,' he declared in one angry rant. 'The system's horrible and the system is slavery, that's what it is. Don't get angry. You should get bloody angry!'

His other videos included 'JAB JUSTICE STOP THE JAB AND CLIMATE FEAR' and 'Saying no to the digital identification slavery'. They tended to be underpinned by the idea that we are being constantly tracked and trapped – in order to control us. But when I spoke to Jason on the phone before my visit, there was no anger. He was kind and open. He welcomed my visit and told me he was happy to be grilled.

When I first entered his gallery, Jason was deep in conversation with a fellow Totnesian. As they said goodbye I overheard him tell the man to take care of himself. It was clear that with a certain section of Totnes, Jason had cultivated a reputation as a peace-loving confidant.

At first glance, he looked very Totnes. His hair was tied up in a ponytail and he was wearing a light linen shirt. As we got talking, he told me he loved the town's quirkiness. He'd moved here from Wales eight years before, and championed sustainable living alongside his artwork.

The gallery was light, and airy. Every inch of the walls was covered with his paintings. Large abstract canvases bursting with colour, watercolours of rippling seascapes, and several portraits of cows. He described the gallery to me as a 'hub' for people to come to, to tell him their problems. This made him seem more like a pillar of the community than a wrecking ball taking aim at it. I thought that Jason had many of the hallmarks of a political activist, or even a political leader of some description – but he didn't seem to see it that way.

Like other people in the UK, the pandemic changed Jason's life and perspective. 'I just think it accelerated and magnified how people felt within themselves,' he said, describing the impact of being stuck at home for so long. At this point, Jason just sounded like someone who was politically frustrated and concerned about issues – like the cost-of-living crisis – that were affecting the lives of those around him. But then our conversation started to become stranger, even extreme – and shifted beyond the pandemic. I found myself hearing again about sinister plots and the government trying to control our way of life and cause us harm.

'To be honest with you, I think they're using it as a Trojan horse to bring in that great digital cashless reset,' he said in a very matter-of-fact way, as though I'd be used to talking about the cashless reset. And to some extent I am – but the average person likely hasn't heard of this before. The 'digital cashless reset' conspiracy theory is one that suggests that government and the banks are plotting to control access to all your money and therefore also you.

'I hate to talk about this like I'm a conspiracy theorist,' Jason said. 'I'm not. I'm a realist. I look at facts, yeah?'

I was reminded of how frequently these beliefs hide in the most unsuspecting corners of communities like this one. Conspiracy theorists can come in many forms; they can be a doctor, a nurse, a teacher or an artist. And according to Jason, people who had never been interested in this world before had started watching his videos since the pandemic. 'We've got literally queues of people saying I want something different. I think there is a hunger for questioning the usual narrative.'

But while what Jason was describing was a utopic ideal, where people rejected society and joined together in peace, some of his online rhetoric was very different in tone. There, he rallied about the battle between 'good and evil' on the planet, and encouraged his followers to take action. 'Let us not wonder how to do it, but do it then wonder how we did it!' he exclaimed in one video.

At the time I was speaking to Jason, despite him saying he was a 'political atheist' he was running for local office with the Heritage Party, who describe themselves as 'socially conservative' – opposing gay rights and abortion access and rejecting severe punishment for hate crimes. Jason said he didn't support all of the party's views.

He seemed to be somebody who embraced the wellness and alternative community more traditionally associated with the left, and yet his political affiliations suggested he was much further to the right. Dr Karen Douglas told me how 'people from more extreme political ideologies are more likely to believe conspiracy theories than people who aren't particularly committed to politics… you have people on the far left and the far right who are much more likely to engage with these sorts of narratives, and people in the middle who are less likely to engage in these sorts of narratives.'

Jason in many ways tallied with that description, and so did a lot of the content in *The Light* – which was another place he felt he'd found others who shared his values and ideas. 'I know most of the people round here that give *The Light* paper,' he said. 'They banned them from being put through doors I think… I'm not sure who decided that – it might have been the ex-mayor who called me evil incarnate.'

While Jason claimed he was an advocate for peaceful change, I've found that hate – and antisemitism in particular – often go hand in hand with the kinds of conspiracy theories he was talking about. Hateful tropes are woven into the fabric of these beliefs; they're looking for a bad guy, and more often than not it's the so-called powerful Jewish globalists who they believe play an instrumental role in what is happening.

'Before, when we first spoke, you said grill me grill me,' I said to Jason.

'Grill me,' he replied.

So I asked him about antisemitic comments he'd posted online. One, in December 2022, had said: 'The Jewish chosen ones, superior to all other races, especially blacks, let's send some of the boats with migrants from the shores, to the shores of Israel and make some nice mixed race to dilute their Israeli arrogance.'

Jason immediately denied this comment was antisemitic. He became visibly agitated by my question, fiddling with the coins in his pocket, and a tension hung in the air.

'[It's] the Israeli arrogance, like they're the untouchable chosen ones. If you look at religion, they'd say, well, they are the chosen ones. I used that as an example, a radical example, because I knew it'd make a point that I was trying to make.'

If that wasn't antisemitic in Jason's view, I challenged him, what was? The extremity – and violence – of his answer to this question really shocked me.

'Anti-Jewish [would be to] get a big knife and stab someone who's Jewish or Israeli [saying] I hate Jews and Israelis. That'll be anti-Jewish and anti-Israel.'

As he spoke, Jason made a stabbing motion with his hands.

'That would be murder,' I responded in a quiet voice.

'Right, it would be murder.'

Jason told me he'd had no involvement in the incidents of aggression former mayor Ben Piper had described. And there was no evidence he'd acted violently on the basis of his beliefs. But it wasn't hard to see how a town could become so divided when this kind of rhetoric became acceptable among a certain group. To some degree, while Jason was entirely accountable for the ideas he was pushing, he was also a victim of the conspiracy theory media he was consuming – which shared hateful ideas that normalized this way of approaching the world.

When I'd spoken to Georgina and Ben, they'd been clear that *The Light*, a paper from outside Totnes, was a key part of what had drawn people in the town towards a new way of thinking, even though its editor strongly denied his publication and its linked social media channels fuelled division in Totnes or elsewhere. They went a step further, too, and directly compared it to religious radicalization, as it's causing a committed minority to adopt radical positions on political or social issues – in this case, based on disinformation.

I asked Matt Jukes, the head of Counter Terrorism Policing in the UK, about this. Is it fair to liken conspiracy theory movements to other forms of extremism? His simple answer was 'yes' (though he wasn't commenting specifically on *The Light*).

'Our casework is no longer restricted to clear-cut terrorist ideologies, and we are seeing an increase in mixed, unclear and unstable mindsets in our investigations. Where we are seeing threads of misogyny, racism and homophobia, we are also seeing evidence of conspiracy theories being interwoven with extremism, particularly online. This connection is very much on our radar and in our sights as investigators.' He suggested that, while conspiracy theories are at the forefront of some of our minds following the pandemic – more so than before – many of these theories have 'deep and historic roots'. 'For example, we still see the echoes of nineteenth-century antisemitism revived and recast in today's terrorist ideologies.'

One of my main takeaways is that it isn't just individual people who are the collateral damage here – it's the fabric of the community and the tenets of local democracy. Conspiracy theories serve to undermine social cohesion. In Totnes they have disrupted the work of a committed local council, and elected representatives have been targeted in the process. This is much more sinister than just small-town vendettas. It becomes a whole lot scarier, too, when those caught up in it genuinely think hateful ideas are acceptable, and can't recognize the impact that their antisemitic or violent rhetoric can have.

* * * *

It's not just British communities who have found themselves affected in this way by conspiracy theories and the algorithms and conspiracy-theory media outlets that drive them. In Ukraine, communities and families have been fractured very acutely by state-sponsored disinformation.

That's what happened to Kristina, who spoke to me from a hotel room in Poland after fleeing her home in Kyiv after Ukraine was invaded by the Russians in early 2022. Let me start by telling you her harrowing account – the one that couldn't convince her family of what she was living through.

If I had to leave my house with no warning, the honest truth is that I'm not really sure what I'd take with me until the time came. I think that's what Kristina felt, too. In her moment of panic, she took with her a design book called *100 Interiors Around the World*. It was big and bulky – meant for a coffee table – and delicately decorated with Post-it notes on her favourite pages. She realized on her tricky journey out of Ukraine that it wasn't the wisest thing to take. But the Ukrainian graphic designer – who was thirty-one years old at the time – couldn't bear the thought of a Russian soldier storming her home and getting his hands on the book, tearing out pages or ripping out Post-it notes.

Kristina's story was such a poignant reminder of real people living through war – and the real harm done when someone you love doesn't believe you. I clung to her every word. She talked about her life back 'when it wasn't the war' – going to work and coffee shops, and designing animations. Then she told me about going to bed late one night in February, waking to loud explosions and having to hurry with her mum to a shelter with their passports and backpacks. She described desperately packing up the flat, and realizing that if they didn't leave soon they very well might die.

'I was just taking pieces of me,' she said, with the same poetics she used so effortlessly throughout the interview to capture the horror of what they'd been through. As she'd rushed to find her book, she'd found her mum trying to pack Kristina's clothes. She reminded her, 'Ma, you have to take your own things, not mine.' Her mum replied, 'You're my daughter. I want to take care of you.'

Kristina's story was so relatable and unimaginable all at once that you can picture my reaction when she told me her Russian cousin didn't believe any of it. She didn't believe Russia was attacking Ukraine. When she'd first awoken to those explosions, Kristina had frantically called her family and friends to wake them up, telling them to get to a shelter. She also called her cousin in Russia, whose response, at first, was exactly what you might expect.

'She was crying. She was really sad. She was like, "Oh my God, I don't want to lose you, I love you too much,"' Kristina recalled. But when Kristina explained how Kyiv was under attack from Russian forces, her cousin told her that she no longer believed her. She said she wanted proof – because she thought Ukraine was attacking itself. It was a war among Ukrainians. It didn't involve Russia at all.

Kristina began to protest, but she had enough to deal with at the time. That included comforting her two-year-old nephew who was hiding in the shelter with her, her mum and her sister. His only lullaby was a cacophony of dogs barking, babies crying and explosions that terrified him. 'We told him that it was just thunder. He [didn't] know the reality. I understood that we create the reality for our children.'

That idea of creating reality is at the heart of Kristina's story. While she was creating a reality where her nephew would feel safe and less frightened, Putin's Kremlin had created another reality in Russia where the war wasn't down to Russian forces. One where Ukrainians were fighting off the Nazis in their ranks – and Russians should be greeted with open arms.

Kristina was determined not to give up on her cousin, and after she'd emerged from the bomb shelter that first day she video-called her. Maybe seeing her face and her tears and her terror would help her cousin to understand. It became apparent, though, that her cousin had made her choice. Her husband worked for the Russian government and she made clear to Kristina that she couldn't even think about posting anything on social media about the situation in Ukraine, despite Kristina's pleas that it might help others in Russia to understand the reality of what was going on. She kept asking for evidence that it was really Russia attacking Ukraine, and Kristina became exasperated.

'We are being bombed. I don't know what proof I should give her. Should I wait until the rocket is close enough to me to take a photo of it?'

Kristina did everything she could to open her cousin's eyes. Why would Ukraine be bombing themselves, she reasoned. It was an overnight ambush. Her cousin then came up with a new excuse: it was only military targets being hit. Kristina's tear-stained face as she shuttled between her apartment and the shelter, fearful for her life, said otherwise. They were hitting civilians, she explained.

Her cousin's source of information wasn't – at that time at least – the disinformation hubs that thrive on social media. Rather, turning on her TV and tuning into state channels, she was seeing videos of Ukrainian soldiers allegedly holding civilians hostage.

War is complex and messy, but in those early days of the invasion it was immediately clear that Russian forces were attacking Ukrainian people in a way many of those in the centre and west of the country had not experienced before. The disinformation narrative that Russia spun to justify its invasion was that it was somehow 'liberating' Ukrainians from Nazi violence and nationalists in a 'special operation'. This was a narrative escalated for months by the state media in Russia – and pushed, hard, in the days after the invasion.

While it hurt her, it didn't take long for Kristina to make sense of the way that her cousin had started to view the world through this distorted lens of state-controlled media. Older viewers in particular still relied on the TV for their news, and the propaganda effort was seeping into other forms of media, including online. When there is an absence of a free and varied media landscape, the reliance on state media is greater – whether that's on TV, in the newspapers or on Telegram.

Back when Kristina was last in Russia, she'd seen the effect of state TV on her grandmother. Her granny would berate her for working too hard and tell her to come and find out 'what's going on in the world' – her eyes glued to pro-Kremlin channels. According to Kristina, they repeated again and again that Ukrainians didn't want their president – and that they want to be reunited with Russia.

'It took years for them to prepare Russian society for this war. They didn't do just in one day,' she explained. The same narratives were being repeated incessantly on state television and across the tightly controlled media in Russia. Unsubstantiated allegations that huge Nazi groups were running riot in Ukraine, with suggestions made repeatedly that the West wanted nothing but to harm and weaken Russia – stories occasionally woven together from grains of truth, and at other times entirely made-up. They were spun to make Russian people feel like they were constantly under threat.

Experts like Oleksandr Pankieiev – editor-in-chief of the *Forum for Ukrainian Studies*, the research publication of the Canadian Institute of Ukrainian Studies – have written about the onslaught of narratives vilifying Ukrainians ever since the invasion of Crimea in 2014. They talk about influence operations and attempts to exploit division in other countries. In Pankieiev's view, this was all building up to that moment of invasion.

Kristina was more forgiving of her grandmother than her cousin. It's easier to believe fairy tales when the reality isn't so frightening. Plus, the situation was complicated. Living through the breakdown of the Soviet Union had left her grandmother questioning what it meant to be Russian. It made much more sense that she would be vulnerable to this way of looking at the world – largely contrary to facts. But Kristina had hoped that her cousin, faced with all-out war and hearing directly about Kristina's experiences, would be different.

Once she'd reached safety, Kristina's conversations with her cousin did continue. But they followed a similar and unproductive pattern. Her cousin would express her fears for her and sympathy for her situation, and Kristina would respond with the cold, hard facts of what was happening. Then her cousin would get upset and tell her she'd got it all wrong.

It came to a head when Kristina started sharing posts about the war on her social media profiles. On Instagram she'd post photos and videos of the violence. In one video, you can see a fireball explosion over the top of blocks of flats in Kyiv. Another post is a photo showing black plumes coming from a residential building in Bucha. Kristina wanted her Russian followers to watch and react to the horror.

Her Russian cousin became increasingly distraught. She'd message her and ask how she could be so angry at Russia. She said Kristina was making everything worse. She never believed any of Kristina's evidence about shelters and bombs. It reached the point where Kristina felt like they were speaking entirely different languages, even as they both messaged in Russian. 'We spoke but we didn't understand each other. She was saying words I understand – but I didn't understand the sentences. The same for her.'

Their last conversation was about the homeware shop IKEA. Kristina had seen pictures of Russians desperately queueing to buy stuff from the shop before it closed its doors in the country. It came after many companies – including IKEA – decided to cease operations in Russia following widespread condemnation of the invasion. Kristina couldn't believe they were going to IKEA rather than protesting the war.

'I wrote on my Instagram story that when you have only ten minutes to leave your home you won't need anything from IKEA,' she told me, and even now I could hear the anger in her voice. Without a home, there was nowhere to put the cushions or cabinets you'd bought.

After that post, her cousin unfollowed her. IKEA was more important to her than her family, Kristina said. For Kristina, that was the end of their relationship. In her eyes, if her cousin didn't have the courage to hear what she was saying, and protest against the war, and do everything she could to reveal the truth, she didn't want to talk to her again. If the tables were turned, she told me, she would have fought for her cousin.

After our conversation, Kristina's book of interiors followed her from Poland to Berlin. She continued to post about the war on social media, even as her cousin's life carried on as usual in Russia and many started to avert their gaze from the horror of the violence.

* * * *

What have these encounters taught me? People like Oliver and Ben and Georgina and Kristina find themselves inadvertently affected by these mistruths – whether propagated by powerful states, fuelled by rich social media companies or fed by conspiracy theory media operations. They weren't necessarily the primary targets, but they suffered nonetheless.

What happened to them is the by-product of the primary goal of these kinds of disinformation and hate campaigns, which is to fracture and divide communities, and grow influence and profit. Conflict can drive people towards ideologies some of those leading these campaigns seek to promote, and negative sentiment can keep people addicted and engaged in a way that affords power and money to the operation driving what's happening. I think the most courageous thing we can do is resist the urge to be drawn into any of these kinds of narratives and turn on one another. Conspiracy theorists frequently claim they are the only ones standing up to power, when in fact they often cause harm to the average person and undermine cohesion in communities in a way that benefits the very people they claim to expose.

4

ESCAPING THE RABBIT HOLE

There's not much forgiveness in the world of conspiracy theories. Not from the conspiracy theorists towards the world around them, and not from the rest of society towards those who fall down the rabbit hole. But when I sat listening to former conspiracy theorist Brent Lee apologizing to a survivor of the 7/7 London bombings, there was forgiveness in spades.

Before we get to that, let me tell you how Brent arrived at this point. A softly-spoken man with long hair, he wasn't always so gentle. In September 2001, Brent was in his early twenties and living in Peterborough. He was playing in a reggae metal band called Optimus Prime, and describes himself as having been the 'scary screaming' guy in the group. When 9/11 happened, he came across some films on the internet that falsely claimed the terror attack had been orchestrated by a shadowy 'new world order'. It sparked an interest in conspiracy theories.

When I asked him about their appeal he said: 'I think the fact that the world wasn't fair. Corrupt people seem to get in higher positions. You're fed up with the lies of the world I guess. That's the only way I can think of it now.'

Watching these videos meant less time spent with his friends, and he'd write lyrics to the band's songs to reflect the conspiracy theories he was hearing about. Eventually he reached the point where he believed that everything was being run by an evil cult that even made human sacrifices.

What Brent was telling me was all beginning to sound a bit mythical – almost biblical. I have often asked myself whether the global decrease in religious faith has left a gap for belief in conspiracy theories. I'm not looking to directly compare the two, but rather to point out that perhaps the absence of that community and structure contributes to people like Brent – those who've never felt part of organized religion – turning to online conspiracy movements instead. Philosopher Karl Popper described conspiracy theories as 'the secularization of religious superstition', with abandoned gods replaced by 'the Learned Elders of Zion, or the monopolists, or the capitalists' – those key villains in the world of conspiracy. Such beliefs can make us feel like we have control over an unpredictable world.[18]

It's perhaps more acceptable than ever in some places not to conform; and at the same time, there are many who feel terribly isolated and sidelined because of who they are. Brent sought connection, answers and agency over what felt like a hard-to-change fate, and he thought he'd found that in conspiracy theories.

Just as Brent's beliefs were hardening, a major bombing took place on British soil. Brent's fascination with the events of 7/7 would eventually bring him into the life of someone who had actually survived the bombings.

On the morning of 7 July 2005, Paul Mitchell, a teaching assistant, was getting on the Piccadilly line at King's Cross. He was running late for work, after missing the first Tube on the platform. When he boarded the second train, he decided to head to the left and a little further down the carriage. At 8.50 a.m., as the Tube approached Russell Square, nineteen-year-old Germaine Lindsay detonated a bomb. If Paul had stayed where he was when he got on the train, he would have been about two feet away from the bomber.

When I spoke to Paul seventeen years later, he told me it still felt like yesterday. 'I remember just this massive pop sound, and a white light. I remember standing then I remember being on the floor. I don't remember any kind of point of falling, because it was that sudden, and that visceral.' He recalled that the train went from packed to just 'nothing around me'. It was only then that he realized he was injured. 'Sorry for saying this, but I reached down and my hand went inside my leg. And I went ohh, OK, then that's bad. And at that point – it's stupid [but] at that point I thought, "Yeah, I'm going to be late for work."'

Paul would later discover he'd been right at the heart of the most deadly of the four attacks that day. The bomb killed twenty-six people. Paul was taken to the hospital, and left fighting for his life.

Brent, meanwhile, was sitting at home. Once the news broke, he'd hopped on the conspiracy theory forums and chat rooms he frequented, and he and others started to make note of every detail that was emerging about the attack, in order to prove that the official version of events was suspicious. And so a conspiracy theory was born.

Brent falsely believed that the British government had carried out the attacks to get the public on side to support the war in Iraq. He thought the deaths were sacrifices. And for Brent, his involvement didn't stop with the forums or chat rooms. He'd rap about his theories, even doing so live at the locations where the attacks had just happened. His performances were filmed and shared online.

After the horror of the attack, the conspiracy theories were a further blow for survivors like Paul. He told me how they were all targeted like this to varying extents. 'I remember feeling very angry. I lay next to people who unfortunately didn't make it out of the carriage, you know, right next to people.'

It would be a while yet before Brent began to recognize the pain that his actions had caused survivors. Of all things, it was the false claims by Alex Jones that the Sandy Hook school shooting was a hoax that set him on a six-year journey out of the rabbit hole. 'I was like: "This doesn't make sense with my belief. My belief is that these deaths are rituals. And now you're saying the deaths aren't real. So where's the ritual?'

One day, in 2018, Brent disappeared from the conspiracy theory forums. He came to understand conspiratorial thinking differently, describing it like being 'indoctrinated into a cult'. He saw himself and others drawn into conspiracy theories as victims, but also took responsibility for how he behaved while immersed in that world.

Looking back on it, Brent maintained that during those years he was just trying to help. He genuinely thought that propagating those conspiracy theories was him exposing the truth to the average person. 'But the end result wasn't good. The end result was hurt. It hurt people.' He hung his head as he said this, and I could tell he felt ashamed.

Brent never took it as far as the conspiracy theorists who believe no one ever died at all. But in his view, it is beliefs like his that pave the way for the more sinister genre of conspiracy theory that denies attacks outright.

Paul and Brent lived too far away to meet in person, but they did agree to a video call. The two of them had never spoken to each before, but had already encountered each other on Twitter. It was this conversation I wanted to hear about – which had happened in 2022, on the anniversary of the attacks.

Every 7/7, Paul posts something to remember the other victims. Only this time, he saw a reply that surprised him. It was Brent, apologizing for being someone who had helped to promote the conspiracy theories about the attack. Paul could tell that Brent did mean what he was saying, so he decided to respond.

'I forgive you,' he wrote.

Brent was shocked. He hadn't expected to receive a reply like that. 'I ran into the bathroom and I cried. I'm six foot six, I'm forty-two years old. I'm a dude. But it stopped me in my tracks and just this humbling moment took over me,' he told Paul on their call. 'You know I was so moved, mate, I was so moved, thank you so much for saying that and for speaking me today.'

The two smiled at each other through the video call. Although Brent was of course no longer posting conspiracy theories about 7/7 online, Paul was still receiving them – almost twenty years after the event.

As for Brent, leaving behind his world view wasn't straightforward, and even now he sometimes finds himself drawn back towards it. But he had set up a YouTube channel and podcast where he talks about his experiences and tries to coax people away from conspiratorial thinking. He wants to use it to speak to other conspiracy theorists about the harm that they cause.

'How can I speak about it unless I confront my ex-community first? Here I am today and I want to let you know, we're wrong. We are completely, completely wrong. Conspiracy theories are dangerous and we're killing people. We need to turn around right now.'

Brent's tale is one of redemption. He's escaped Conspiracy-land – and he's willing to face the consequences of his actions. But Brent's story feels rare, and for him it's been a long journey to get to this point.

This chapter is about the few, like Brent, who make it out – and the light that can exist at the end of that tunnel.

* * * *

I found Catherine on a Facebook group that sought to counter pandemic disinformation, diligently posting evidence in the comments to conspiracy believers in a bid to win them around. In some ways, her experience was a blueprint for how to escape this way of thinking. Like Brent, her belief in conspiracy theories is somewhat historic.

A few months later, I sat opposite Catherine on her driveway at the end of a cul-de-sac on the Isle of Wight. It was freezing cold, and she headed inside to get a blanket to cover her knees. Her home looked cosy.

Catherine was thirty-seven years old, with blonde hair and sun-kissed skin from her time spent wandering the Isle of Wight's beaches, but the photos she showed me from a decade earlier painted a different picture. Back then, her hair was wild and her face was decorated with glitter, and many of the photos captured her dancing at festivals with a bunch of friends. These friends informed her world view right up into her early thirties. They believed anti-vaccine misinformation, and opposing vaccination based on dubious science became a gateway into a sprawling conspiracy theory world. Social media just amplified that network of beliefs.

At the time I was speaking with Catherine, Covid-19 vaccines had just become available. She told me a decade ago there was absolutely no chance she would have even considered getting the jab. She had been an ardent anti-vaxxer. Catherine's beliefs, though, hadn't started with her friends. The roots could be found in her childhood.

Catherine didn't grow up with much money – and described her mum to me as very anti-establishment. Her family had felt 'bottom rung'. Her mum's views went beyond just challenging capitalism and power, but in Catherine's view it was a legitimate distrust of a society that had let them down which left them vulnerable to conspiracy theories.

'We feel forgotten sometimes, there's a huge divide between the rich and the poor. I had some things running around in my head that, you know, the system was bad, the system was set up wrong, the system was set up for us to fail,' she told me. It was one of the first glimpses of her clear-sighted approach to her own identity and how it was formed.

That distrust meant that Catherine's mum was against a lot of science. She opposed medicine and vaccines, favouring alternative natural remedies. Hospitals and medicine were a strange faraway land, and vaccines were the enemy. Equipped with this mindset as a child, Catherine carried it through to her teenage years and then adult life. She surrounded herself with others who held the same views. Like Brent, she described it to me as cult-like – a whole community founded on conspiracy theories about vaccines and medicine. These beliefs became integral to her social identity and she liked being part of this world. She fitted in, in a way she hadn't with others when she was growing up.

'I hate to refer to anti-vaxxers as cult-like, because I know myself what it's like to be on that side and I would have hated to be referred to as that, you know. I was simply somebody trying to present the truth so I find it difficult to call it a cult. But in reality, yes, that's what it is,' she said.

Catherine's empathy set her apart from many people I'd spoken to about believing disinformation. Her view was that no believer would respond well otherwise, and I agree. If you don't afford people any respect, why would they respect what you have to say? It goes both ways.

Catherine's deeper descent into the anti-vax community did come from a legitimate starting point. She was suspicious of pharmaceutical companies and how they made money from people who were ill. But she started to believe that vaccines were part of plan – and that it wasn't just about increasing profits, but controlling people, too. She couldn't understand why you'd want to administer medicine to someone who was healthy. She started to weigh up the risk versus benefit and found it hard to see any good at all. Obsessively looking up the ingredients of vaccines, she became convinced they were packed with harmful and strange chemicals – formaldehyde, mercury, even aborted foetal cells.

There's a lot of legitimate debate about how for-profit pharmaceutical companies make their money off essential medicines and health care. And vaccines do contain some chemicals and additives in them, but in microscopic quantities. For example, aluminium in a vaccine could sound a bit worrying. But in reality there's less than a single milligram used per dose, and it's to help the body build stronger immunity against the germ that's included in the vaccine. Most adults will actually ingest several times that amount of aluminium via natural occurrences in food and drink – every single day.

The advent of social media only served to further Catherine's obsession. The videos she watched and the posts she read reinforced the idea vaccines were bad. People she didn't know, people all over the world, agreed with her – and the activists rallying around this issue were very convincing. They'd talk about their own qualifications and expertise, and she was won over. Little did she realize that many were discredited scientists.

'There were hundreds of YouTube videos, Facebook videos, memes, articles, clips that would catch your attention in the news feed and you'd think, oh yes, you know, this is finally going mainstream,' she explained. Catherine and her fellow anti-vaxxers were on the edge of their seats. This was it! The world was going to come round to their way of thinking. Everyone would finally realize this was a sinister plot and the jabs were part of it.

One thing that really struck me as we were talking was who Catherine had trusted and turned to for information. She'd been raised to doubt science, and yet she was prone to believing those who styled themselves as experts and doctors. What seemed to be crucial was that the 'experts' framed themselves as opposing the mainstream. They went against the grain and 'traditional' – factual – science, tapping into Catherine's belief that the truth was being suppressed and everyone was being silenced. She was convinced they were the only ones with the courage to tell the truth.

Catherine tried to give me a sense of her former mindset. 'The mainstream experts have clearly been bought off. They've clearly been paid by the governments, by corporations higher than the governments, by the global elites. The real science is hidden from us to maintain the façade that medical science is good.'

Conspiracy theorists often look at funding for answers. To some extent, that's what an investigative journalist does too – figuring out who may have an interest in a particular company and who could be driving what's happening. And following the money and asking questions about where it comes from is vital. There have, after all, been countless scandals and dodgy deals. But with conspiracy theorists, they'll see connections and sinister motives where they don't exist. Catherine believed that because some scientists and doctors were receiving funding at all, it must be dodgy – even when it was straightforward research grants.

For some, falling foul of conspiracy theories has little to do with gullibility and a lot to do with cynicism. It's very understandable to be critical of authority, government and institutions. But this same cynicism has left people like Catherine susceptible to demonstrably false beliefs. They become so trusting of anyone who challenges the mainstream that they forget to interrogate who is actually right – and who is wrong.

Years passed, and Catherine cocooned herself further in this world that is so often at odds with reality. By the mid-2010s, and her thirtieth birthday, Catherine had refined her conspiracy-style research tactics to an art. But this obsession with being critical that led her into the rabbit hole was what would, funnily enough, help her get out again.

Catherine's escape didn't happen overnight. Instead, it was little moments of questioning what she'd been told that chipped away at her whole-hearted belief in the conspiracy world around her. She began to notice that some of the alternative health influencers she followed promoted capsules and shakes that would somehow make you richer and healthier and happier. They'd change your whole lifestyle in days. Could that really be true, she wondered.

Others had warned her, but she was so convinced of her side's good intentions – and so angry at the world around her – that she'd been willing to accept they did without question. It wasn't just influencers, either. Some of the friends Catherine had made through the community started selling natural remedies on social media. When their businesses failed and they didn't make enough money, she started to see how these were pyramid schemes – and that, in some ways, the people she'd chosen to trust were using social media to exploit those she cared about. Until then, she explained, 'I thought it was for the people. I thought it was for us to share ideas and free speech and knowledge.' Her eyes opened a little wider.

But then she panicked and went into overdrive. Catherine had built her entire identity around this community she was beginning to realize was not what she'd thought. It was a mirage, an illusion. She still wanted to keep fighting for the cause, and so she'd find herself in heated debates with absolutely anyone who would listen. Not just about anti-vax beliefs, but that the earth was flat and 5G technology was without a doubt poisonous and that everything somehow linked back to the global elites. When she was confronted with evidence, she didn't even bother to look at it.

One day she got into an argument with someone online about the ingredients of vaccines. She told him it was impossible to deny there were bad things in jabs. He came back to her – did she realize that these chemicals she was talking about were used in lots of different stuff? Processed food, for example, or even naturally in other substances we digest. Did she understand how they were used and how these things really worked?

Catherine had become so stubborn and convinced of her world view; she was used to trotting out the answers she'd learned over several years, undermining the credibility of whoever she was arguing against. After all, they were from the other side – they were hiding the truth. Until now, she'd never really considered that they might be right. But this particular conversation caught her at the right time. His questions were so targeted that this time she realized she didn't actually have the answers.

She looked up formaldehyde, and read about how it's used to make vaccines safer. It inactivates the virus and detoxifies bacterial toxins. She found out that a baby already has a milligram of formaldehyde in its body. Vaccines contain far less than that. Maybe there were limits to her knowledge, she realized, and she'd been so swept up in everything else this world of disinformation had offered her – agency, power, community – that she hadn't really checked what she'd thought she knew.

Catherine herself acknowledged that it now sounded ridiculous that she hadn't done her own research. But, as she explained to me, when you're engrossed in this world, you become convinced that you're right. You don't properly interrogate the details. You hang off the words of these unreliable sources you trust, rather than really looking into it yourself.

Undermined and deflated, having realized she couldn't answer this man's questions, for the first time Catherine felt a bit silly. That feeling of silliness and inadequacy can often cause a person to double down, but for Catherine it was different. It was the moment things finally started to unravel. She saw that maybe the content she was consuming online was playing on her emotions and tapping into something beyond the rational. She started looking into the mainstream view on vaccines, and saw that it wasn't just one or two videos or a few hundred scientists. It was a huge body of researchers and experts who had spent years and years investing their knowledge.

From a young age, Catherine had been told by her mum and then the friends she'd made that this wasn't the case. This scepticism had surrounded her from when she was very little, and she'd been so convinced that they – and therefore she – was right that she'd never taken a step back and really looked at what it all meant. 'After a while I was able to recognize that actually conspiracy theories for me were approval-seeking behaviour. I wanted to feel part of the demise of governments, exposing the truth, fighting the good fight.'

It was realizing that the information she had been fed was misleading – and that the intentions of those promoting it might not be so pure as she'd once believed – that finally woke her up to the truth.

Catherine saw how social media algorithms had only further cemented her anti-vax beliefs, and knew she couldn't just sit back and watch. She could see the immediate threat bad information posed during a global health crisis, and she felt terrible. This could be a matter of life and death. So, she sought out a new community that battled the mistruths spread by people she used to be like. She found several in a Facebook group dedicated to debunking online myths, which she decided to join.

Catherine's experience has given her a series of questions to challenge those still embedded in the world she left. Her first is about whistle-blowers – the insiders who decide to reveal what's really going on. If there were all of these sinister plots playing out across hospitals and government departments, where so many people are employed, why has no one come forward? Why would doctors and nurses and the media and politicians across the spectrum all readily lie and harm people – and surely it couldn't be kept secret from everybody? 'If there was some grand conspiracy at play here, how many people would need to be involved in that theory all the way from the top down? You are talking hundreds of thousands of people... What are the odds of nobody saying anything?'

A conspiracy theorist might come back and argue that there are whistle-blowers. During the pandemic and the Ukraine war, for instance, there were people who built an online following by styling themselves as truth-telling doctors or bloggers opposing the establishment. Only, when you dig a little deeper, they appeared to have links to the Russian state, or they were struck off and discredited from the medical profession, and this was their way of promoting state propaganda or making a comeback.

Catherine also advises questioning how these plots would even work. Conspiracy theories rely on the belief that many, many people are almost superhuman, capable of plans that would be incredibly difficult or even impossible to pull off. When backed into a corner, conspiracy theorists afford magical powers to the cabal of powerful, corrupt people they believe are pulling all the strings. One Canadian anti-vaxxer I asked about this – after he'd made a whole YouTube music video dressed up as Bill Gates – told me ultimately the person pulling the strings at the centre of the evil plots was Satan. It's pretty hard to challenge that. But you'd hope you could provoke some reflection.

Finally – for Catherine – it's about showing patience and empathy. Labelling someone a 'conspiracy theorist' doesn't usually help. Rather, it pushes them deeper into their belief system. 'You need to be able to talk to people, understand their fears, their concerns. If they're willing then you can perhaps go into some discussions about why things might not be as they believe or why things might not be true, and it needs to be a much gentler approach.'

Staying calm is crucial, because the person you're talking to will be just as passionate as you are and willing to defend what they believe at all costs. Catherine's approach is one backed up by experts, including the science writer Mick West, author of the book *Escaping the Rabbit Hole*. He's dedicated many years to debunking pervasive myths – and looking into wider ways to deal with them. 'An angry, heated conversation will leave everyone feeling rubbish and further cement conspiracy beliefs,' he explains.

That's because this is about so much more than right and wrong. Psychologist Jovan Byford told me how all of these belief systems are underpinned by feelings of resentment, anger and indignation at how the world works. If you inflame those feelings and try to dismiss them, you won't get anywhere. Establishing common ground instead is essential. Show them where your world views may match, and that you understand the criticism and fears they have, before then addressing the ways they could have been misled or misinformed.

Claire Wardle from First Draft, a not-for-profit that fights misinformation, says that empathy rather than ridicule is key. If someone feels ashamed, your attempts to change their mind are much more likely to backfire. Shaming the person who is attempting to profit or to leverage power will be much more effective.

One of the main catchphrases in the conspiracy theory world is 'Do your own research'. It usually means watching endless YouTube videos and scrolling on social media, uncritically consuming misinformation promoted by those who often exploit distrust and play on emotions. It's a game of reaffirming what you already believe.

Catherine urges people to truly do their own research, which means consulting different sources, seeking out counternarratives, and questioning why people share what they do. Take a look at their workings, and engage in depth with the science. Has this source made predictions that were entirely wrong – or did they get it right? Find the right people to give you the answers to your questions.

Psychologists like Jovan Byford agree this is a useful approach. Explain how you value and respect the cynicism and scepticism they exercise, and encourage them to apply it universally – not just to those that they are much more likely to doubt. It's not about making them less curious or sceptical. It's about asking them to reflect on where they are directing that energy.

'I think part of me will always be attracted to the idea of things that make sense, understanding the world completely,' Catherine told me. 'We all like to feel in control of our lives and we all like to feel we've got some understanding of the way the world works, when in reality it's a lot more chaotic and almost too much for one person to understand in a lifetime even.'

* * * *

The journey out of the rabbit hole doesn't just happen all of a sudden. It can take a long time. For both Brent and Catherine, their escape came after realizing the people they believed were taking them for a ride. Those people gave themselves away when how they were benefitting from all this became apparent – and when the conspiracy theories they spread reached new extremes that felt uncomfortable for some believers.

I receive hundreds of messages from people on a regular basis who are hoping that their loved one or friend might be able to escape the world of conspiracy theories. Maybe you're reading this book because you're struggling with this too. I've become a bit of a conspiracy theory agony aunt, so I want to try to share some solutions.

Both Catherine and Brent managed to escape Conspiracy-land well before the pandemic. But it seems there's something different about the movement that boomed when people were locked down that makes it more difficult to escape. Some people were pushed towards ideologies they just wouldn't have entertained before, and they stayed there. As life moved on after Covid-19 restrictions disappeared, I thought the messages I was receiving would peter out. But they didn't.

In the spring of 2023, I received a message from someone I'm going to call Anna. She'd known her friend Millie for over a decade. Millie's descent down the rabbit hole began like so many others. She was interested in alternative medicine before, but during Covid-19 she was pushed to new extremes.

'It was during the pandemic that her views on vaccines really started to merge with other, less mainstream conspiracy theories,' Anna wrote. 'We met up for a coffee and I was shocked to hear that she believed that the vapour trails left by aeroplanes were chemtrails. She thought that maybe it could be the case that there's somebody controlling the global temperature to make it seem like global warming is worse than it is.'

In Anna's view, Millie's reason for turning to conspiracy theories comes down to a 'lack of trust in institutions and governments' rather than a confidence in 'facts and reality'.

Dr Karen Douglas explains how worrying about what's unfolding in the world, especially during turbulent times, can cause someone to 'look to these conspiracy explanations to feel a little bit more in control over the things that are happening to them'. The problem is that you then develop a certain dependence on them, and the ideas constantly reinforce one another.

What they think is a solution, she says, can just make the anxiety a whole lot worse. They become more isolated and are being fed even more terrifying ideas, and can end up in a vicious cycle. Her advice is to try to tackle the source. 'Talk to them about who is telling them this and how trustworthy and how reliable these sources are, to try to get them to think a little bit about what they're saying and what they're sharing and whether or not they should share it.'

Another person who messaged me, who'll I'll call Toby, spent a lot of time trying to break that vicious circle. Years before Toby reached out to me in 2023, his brother dipped his toe into the world of conspiracy theories. It started with a sudden interest in religion and talking about the Flat Earth theory, but his family just laughed it off as a passing phase. It seemed so harmless to begin with.

But then it got worse. Toby's brother became closed off to the usual things he enjoyed doing, like watching and playing football, and going to the gym. He stopped consuming any kind of mainstream media, saying there was too much subliminal and evil messaging. They couldn't even watch a film together.

Toby's relationship with his brother was getting tense. He was always so angry. 'Every single topic that we tried to talk about was brought back to being conspiracy, or worse yet, evil.' It felt like they were living on different planets. And Toby's brother – like Brent and Catherine – had this whole new social circle now.

'You don't necessarily want to chat with someone who believes in conspiracy theories, so they do have a negative effect on their interpersonal relationships and close relationships within a family. It can be really, really terrible,' Dr Karen Douglas explains.

And the deeper someone falls into the rabbit hole, the nastier disagreements and arguments can become. It can be hard to have a constructive conversation – but that doesn't mean a row is the solution. 'Hostility and ridicule is something that's just not going to work, because these people feel very, very strongly about what they believe in,' says Dr Douglas. 'And so going with these sorts of tactics is probably going to be unsuccessful.' But she acknowledges that this doesn't change how difficult it can be for family members, especially when they're struggling to talk to the person at all.

Toby's message to me, though, did end with some hope. He thought his brother was returning little by little to the person he'd been before conspiracy theories – mainly because his family had never allowed him to become totally isolated or estranged. 'I like to think it's because we as a family listened, we argued as rationally as we could, but we never ignored him. We always reminded him he was loved.'

In Dr Douglas's view, it's about offering this person some comfort, not more anxiety. 'How do you make people feel less uncertain about the political climate that they're living in? How do you make them feel safer and more in control? And how do you make them feel more secure and happy in the groups that they belong to and feel like they're appreciated?' Those questions, however, don't always have easy answers.

This is a long process, and multiple psychologists warn that it's not realistic to change someone's mind overnight. The superiority – and to some degree certainty and stimulation – that conspiracy theories can afford someone makes them especially resistant to change. This is about their self-esteem, and no one likes to be wrong.

Something I heard from both Brent and Catherine was how the work they do now on social media – whether on YouTube or in Facebook groups – to speak to true believers does seem to be proving effective. It's a tactic that's been used in other forms of de-radicalization, whether from far-right ideologies or religious extremism: if believers hear from someone who was once a part of their world, they're more likely to take them seriously. Crucially, they're more likely to feel as though they themselves are being taken seriously.

Ultimately, no one wants to be mocked or laughed at or ridiculed. There is of course more specific and tangible action that can help, from offering psychological support to putting them in contact with former believers. But, perhaps we also need to take a step back, and change our attitudes as a society towards those who are drawn into this world. Treating some of them more like victims than villains might prove helpful. Seriousness is essential here too, I think. We have to take seriously their underlying fears and concerns. We also have to take seriously the radicalization that's happening in some cases – and hold those responsible for this, whether the social media sites or conspiracy theory influencers, accountable.

The shame and stigma reserved for those who believe in conspiracy theories is very unhelpful. It's only by taking a new, less judgemental and more inquisitive approach that the likelihood of at least a few people clambering out of the rabbit hole becomes possible. The implication that conspiracy thinking only happens to the gullible has led to a dismissive and 'othering' attitude, rather than one focusing on the very real concerns and fears that can cause someone to tumble into Conspiracyland in the first place. The combative interview approach reserved for government ministers and corrupt CEOs doesn't work for the people who are also victims of this world themselves. We all need to practise the forgiveness Paul exercised towards Brent – with a dose of curiosity too.

5

THE LIFE OF A LIE

Conspiracyland is a place the vast majority of us don't venture into. After all, it's a sprawling belief system defined by an absence of evidence, which can become pretty hard to follow. It requires a lot of commitment.

We're all much more likely to incidentally stumble across disinformation on our social media feeds – a false or misleading claim, perhaps repeated or perhaps a one-off. Maybe you've received a WhatsApp spreading a baseless rumour about something unfolding that never really happened, or you've been recommended a video with misleading advice.

When it comes to misinformation and disinformation – the accidental or deliberate dissemination of falsehoods – we can all quite easily become a vector in its spread. We might forward on a message simply asking 'Is this true?' We might spread a rumour because it's a lot more exciting than what's really happening. Disinformation is designed that way. It tends to play on our emotions and draw us in. Shocking allegations catch our attention, when the truth is more complex.

History tells us that during times of difficulty or disaster, tales have often been used as a way of making sense of what's happening. In the past, 'access to trusted, consistent information was scarce', and so rumours would catch on in small communities with no counter-narrative to them at all. Now, in the age of social media, the 'overload of information online can produce the same effect'. [19] We're finding it hard to get the right answers.

While, once, those whispers might have been limited to one village or town, social media can now be weaponized to turbocharge a lie and spread it globally. And because these online lies have the ability to draw in – and use – a bigger crowd, they are all the more impactful. They can distort reality before our eyes.

While conspiracy theories tend to be quite unwieldy, a web of untruths and half-truths taking aim at a cabal of powerful people up to no good, disinformation can also be quite simple outright lies. But these can serve to some extent as a gateway drug into the more hardcore conspiracy theories. When you're bombarded with mistruths that start to form a particular narrative, you can find yourself on the path to Conspiracyland.

In this chapter, I'm going to track the lives of various online lies deployed by different activists and governments. It's only by unpicking them that you can understand exactly how this works, and just how hard it can be to stop a mistruth that's spreading like wildfire.

* * * *

I'll start with the most shocking lie I looked at – one which ended up being very difficult to unpick. It was about Marianna. Not me, but a woman in Ukraine. Hers is a tale of state propaganda machines and terrifying denial.

On 9 March 2022, Marianna was caught up in an attack by Russian forces on Mariupol, Ukraine. She was in the maternity hospital there, waiting to have her baby. Within hours of this attack, three photos emerged taken by Associated Press. They haunt me. Two are of Marianna – one where she is descending a flight of stairs in her pyjamas, a duvet around her shoulders and blood splatters across her forehead, and another of her outside the hospital, wrapped in that same duvet. In that second photo Marianna stares directly at the camera. Her eyes are glazed over. The third photo is of a different pregnant woman on a stretcher, severely injured.

For the Western media, these photographs were a shocking example – and proof – of the Russian state attacking and harming Ukrainian civilians. The images tapped into the vein of outrage already pumping across the world.

Only a few years older than me, Marianna's life could not feel more different to my own. Given our shared name, I couldn't help but compare her situation to mine. The contrast served as very stark reminder of the safety of my home, battling trolls from behind the protective jacket of the BBC, miles and miles from a war zone. I was haunted not just by Marianna's photos, but also by the wave of brazen lies that they triggered.

On what was supposed to be one of the most special days

of her life – the birth of her first child – the other Marianna had found herself at the centre of one of the most vicious disinformation campaigns and trolling storms I've ever encountered. She was accused of being an 'actress', and playing a part in all three of these 'staged' photos.

The allegations appeared to originate from Telegram channels, which supported the Kremlin in Russia. They were renowned for pushing out dubious claims about the fighting in Ukraine.

Soon, the actress accusations were picked up by Russian State media, and the Twitter accounts of Russian officials – including the foreign ministry. Not long after, it became a line parroted by Russian diplomats at the UN Security Council, accusing Ukraine of trying to frame Russia for violent acts it claimed it didn't commit.

It was clear that this was a lie endorsed by the very top. What was hard to figure out was whether this was a brazen fabrication that had been created on Telegram and the Kremlin had decided to use it to its benefit – or whether they'd sown the initial seeds. Faceless channels can be connected to state-backed journalists, and so it remains murky. Russia's government is known for its 'shameless willingness to disseminate' totally untrue claims.[20]

It didn't take long to figure out that the woman in the photo was likely not an actress. A cursory search on social media made it clear that she really was called Marianna, she lived in Mariupol, she was a beauty blogger and she was expecting a baby. Testimony from the Associated Press journalists on the ground who had taken those pictures, and clear evidence of a very real attack unfolding, backed all of that up too.

I put this all to Russian officials, who never responded to my request for answers. It was then that I went to look for answers myself.

I started by tracking down Marianna's family and friends in a bid to find her. In the days after the attack, news broke that she had given birth to her little baby. But she was still trapped in the besieged city of Mariupol. I reached out to one of Marianna's aunts in Turkey. As we sent messages back in forth in Russian, she was desperately scrambling to help her niece leave the city. She asked if I could help her find a car or any kind of vehicle.

I contacted friends of Marianna and her husband Yuri, messaging hundreds of accounts. One called Natalya, and her husband Petro, got back to me around a week after the initial attack. (I've changed their names out of concerns for their safety. If Russia took the town in Ukraine where they were living – and they actively spoke out against the disinformation campaign their friend had been subjected to – they could be at serious risk.) They were the first people I managed to record an interview with who could confirm that Marianna was definitely not acting and that those photos weren't staged. Relatives were fearful of the backlash that accompanied speaking out, and for several of them their relationship with Russia was more complex, as they were living in eastern parts of Ukraine already under Russian control. Their first priority at that time was ensuring Marianna, Yuri and their new baby were safe.

I then looked for clues about the couple who had agreed to speak to me. Their Instagram page was decorated with lovely family photos of birthdays and Christmas celebrations. There was a photo with Marianna and Yuri too, taken at a local café. These were relics from a time that, to them, felt like the distant past. Natalya and Petro had escaped Mariupol and found relative safety, but their lives had been turned upside down.

Petro had known Mariana's husband Yuri for years; they grew up together. And he and his wife had watched Yuri's very modern love story with Marianna play out during the pandemic. Marianna and Yuri had met online. She was from Donetsk, while he was from Mariupol. She'd found herself stuck there when the borders were closed because of coronavirus. Not long after that, they'd decided to get married.

I travelled back in time with Petro as he described the time the couples had spent together: Christmas, holidays as a group and celebrating their children's birthdays. For Petro and Natalya, it was difficult to reconcile the Yuri and Marianna who had sat excitedly in their home in January, talking about how happy they were to be expecting a baby and discussing buying baby clothes and decorating a nursery, with the couple fleeing a brutal attack.

As I watched some of the pictures coming out of Mariupol, it was hard to imagine there was ever such a time of happiness and hope, and that it had ended just weeks ago. At that time, Mariupol was the most heavily bombed city in Ukraine.

It was after Natalya and Petro had left that Marianna was admitted to one of the hospitals still functioning in Mariupol to have her little girl, close to her due date in March. She brought with her as much as she could to look after her new baby. Then, the attack happened.

The photographs of Marianna were how Natalya and Petro found out that she and Yuri had survived the attack. 'I felt joy that I knew [Marianna] was alive.' Natalya spoke to me in Russian, while her husband translated for the sake of those listening to BBC Radio 4's *War on Truth* podcast who don't speak Russian. It meant we were chopping and changing between languages, but Natalya's emotions were clear. She was shaken by the expression she'd seen etched across her friend's face. She described it not as fear or confusion, but just an emptiness.

Natalya was determined to show the world what Marianna and those in her home town were living through. So she posted the iconic images of Marianna on her Instagram story. But she got an unexpected response. She found herself inundated with hate meant for Marianna. She went to check on Marianna's own Instagram page and noticed how her and Yuri's holiday pictures and pregnancy announcement were littered with the same kinds of comments. Special moments spoiled by the nastiest of words from people they'd never met, all focused around this idea that Marianna had posed for photos.

The photo that seemed to pique their interest in particular was an image of Marianna on holiday in Turkey. In it, her blonde hair was tied up in a ponytail and her petite figure was dressed in some shorts and a black, sleeveless shirt. She was smiling at the camera, a million miles from the war zone. It was an image she'd shared while she was pregnant – a throwback picture. Only, the trolls were convinced that this was from now. That she'd never really been pregnant. That just added more fuel to the fire. Petro, Natalya's husband, kept reminding me how Marianna and Yuri were real people. How could people forget, he asked.

This was just over a week after the attack – and Petro and Natalya had not heard from Marianna and Yuri in days. My hunt for her continued. WhatsApp conversations with relatives and chats with her friends were the only places I could gather clues so far. Family members spoke cryptically – fearful of putting her at risk.

Not long after my conversation with Petro and Natalya, I got in contact with Yaroslava, another of Marianna's friends, this time based in the Russian city of Tver.

I'd found her excitedly commenting on Marianna's Instagram posts, talking about the gender of her baby, and clicked on her profile. It was dominated by selfies of a woman in her twenties with sleek blonde hair and wide eyes. Photos of shopping trips, new make-up products, dinners with friends. Her feed contrasted starkly with the Instagram feeds of beauty influencers from Ukraine, whose profiles had switched overnight from product promotion and glamorous portraits to shots of terrified huddles in shelters and posts about bombs.

Yaroslava's profile gave no sense of the war her home country, Russia, was waging against its neighbour Ukraine.

Yaroslava had become friends with Marianna as they were both in a circle of young Russian-speaking beauty bloggers, even though they technically were divided by a border. I messaged her, and she agreed to talk to me. The next day, we were chatting over the phone in Russian. This was for a podcast, and so I'd try to get people to speak in English when they could, but would often fall back on my Russian.

Just weeks before, she'd been commenting on Marianna's social media posts as any close friend would, and yet she'd entirely bought into the lies told by the Russian state about her friend. It became apparent straight away during our conversation that Yaroslava believed Marianna was pretending to be caught up in the attack on the hospital.

Yaroslava had come across these narratives on Telegram and state TV. 'We think the Ukrainian military paid to have Marianna in these photos,' she said, her voice rising in anger. In her eyes, this was all part of a plan by the Ukrainian military to make Russia look bad.

I explained to her how the photographs showed Marianna and another severely injured woman, who we had been told by that point had lost both her life and her baby. I tried to talk her through the evidence that this attack was real, including footage taken by journalists on the ground who had no interest in lying about what happened.

'Where is the guarantee that [the other woman] is dead? We can't tell from a picture whether a person is dead or not,' Yaroslava replied, and I could almost picture the shrug of her shoulders on the other side of the call.

I remember struggling to verbalize what I wanted to say next. I'd watched the footage Associated Press had released from the attack, and seen the horrific injuries sustained by the woman on the stretcher. They weren't visible in the photos that were released.

Yaroslava wasn't fussed as I probed harder. A part of me thinks she found this fairy tale she'd been told a lot easier to believe than the devastating truth. Having to accept your country is committing atrocities against civilians, some of whom you know and were friends with, is not so easy. It's made even harder when you've been bombarded with propaganda from a young age. Besides, it seemed challenging the state narrative was hardly a viable option. Yaroslava was adamant the Russian army wouldn't kill civilians.

But how was it that even knowing the person at the centre of this web of lies – in this instance Marianna – wasn't enough to make her see how she was being misled?

Day in day out, Yaroslava was glued to propaganda broadcasts on state TV and her Telegram feed. As Putin clamped down on access to certain social media sites, her ability to look for information beyond Russia was increasingly restricted. The world she experienced through her phone was totally different to the one a British person of a similar age would be seeing.

Living in Russia means you have fewer news sources, and nearly all of them are state-controlled – including the two channels that Yaroslava told me she watched daily. I asked her if she ever doubted what they were telling her.

'I do not question it. They show us a lot. Well, they show us what's needed. Maybe they don't show absolutely everything, but they show most of it. How everything actually happens.' Even with these caveats, her faith was unshakeable. 'We have a programme on Channel One called *Anti-Fake*. It says all this will be done on purpose against us, so that everyone thinks that Russia is the aggressor.'

Marianna's story shows how effective the Russian government's disinformation machine can be. It succeeds in presenting the most brazen mistruths to citizens like Yaroslava, who are ready to believe them. Which is not to say that other nations and governments don't spin. Of course they do – and they have for centuries. But in Russia, efforts to do this seem to be turbocharged, and with a high level of success.

The Russian propaganda machine has been referred to by academics as the 'the firehose of falsehood' because it's so 'rapid, continuous, repetitive' and full of 'partial truths or outright fictions'.[21] It can convince a nation to support a war and invasion that is harming people that they love, and make them think that it is Russia that is under threat. It plays on their complex relationship with their national identity, and exploits their distrust in the rest of the world. State propaganda leaves people like Yaroslava feeling proud of who they are and where they come from, even when the government is really rendering them powerless.

The final question I put to her was why we were seeing the war – and the world – through totally different lenses. I felt like we were living in separate realities. Her answers followed along the lines of 'well, they feed you what they want you to hear and me the same'. The truth, in her eyes, likely sat somewhere in between.

The problem with truth, though, is that it's cold and categorical. It doesn't conveniently position itself between differences of opinion, even though it can be nuanced and complex. Yaroslava's answer did, however, make me reflect on the presuppositions I'd carried around my entire life. To an extent, we all live in worlds created by the views of those around us, but for Yaroslava and others like her this is taken to the extreme. I'd like to think categorical evidence would change my mind.

* * * *

Finally, there was some good news. Marianna's aunt in Turkey shared an image she'd received of Marianna holding her new little baby, Veronika. Marianna looked exhausted. Her skin was tinged grey and her fluffy pyjamas were grubby. But the baby was there, and so was Yuri.

Just weeks later, I was finally on a video call with Marianna. I couldn't quite believe my eyes. Weeks of messaging and calls had led to this moment. She looked just like the photos, with her huge blue eyes and her blonde hair tied up. She was wearing a pastel jumper. She looked small and cold, but sure and ready to answer my questions.

Marianna was speaking to me from Russian-occupied Donbas, where she'd grown up – and where she'd evacuated to after giving birth to Veronika in Mariupol. Yuri and the baby were with her. Her family and friends had reassured me she was safe, although there was still the risk she'd be caught up in the fighting.

To speak to me, she'd travelled to the home of independent journalist Denis Seleznev, fearful of disclosing her exact location. He appeared to be organizing her interviews with the media and setting up her video calls. Before the interview, I'd tried to figure out more about who this man was and the role he was playing. I started with his social media profiles on VKontakte, the Russian equivalent of Facebook. He had a history of sharing pro-Kremlin views online in support of the Russian military in Ukraine. He was based in Donetsk, and the two seemed to have known each other for a while. They were friends, from what I could tell, and he appeared to be someone that she trusted.

He'd also been the first blogger to interview Marianna after her escape. By that point, his interview with her had already been twisted by Russian media to spin a narrative about the attack in which Russia was once again blameless, so I was wary of his intentions. But when I spoke to Denis over WhatsApp, he never gave any opinions or attempted to control the interview in any way. He was easy to deal with and didn't really ask many questions. He felt more like Marianna's assistant than a sinister minder.

He was present throughout the course of my interview with her, although Marianna had agreed to the interview without prior conditions. I concluded she was safe enough to speak; but ultimately it's very difficult to ever know the exact circumstances she found herself in.

My sense, as I spoke to her, was that Marianna was a single-minded person who wanted to speak out. She wasn't reading from a script and there were no interruptions – from Denis or anyone else. No one had vetted my questions, and she spoke quickly in Russian in what seemed to be her own words. Her reactions and answers felt fluent and genuine.

There were all kinds of complex reasons she might not be able to speak freely. The most obvious that sprang to mind – she had to protect herself and her family. Criticizing Russia directly could put them all at risk. She had already been targeted by a vicious disinformation campaign waged by a state with a track record of nasty tactics. Although she contradicted the misinformation spread about her, she never did take aim at the actual sources of the lies – powerful Russian officials and ministries – that she was somehow an actress. But there was something more complex at play here, too. Marianna had grown up in Eastern Ukraine, and so her own relationship with Russia was likely to be complex.

Covering stories like this is notoriously difficult. The information available can be scarce, and there are various different motives at play from governments and people with their own biases and goals. War is messy, and a fog can descend over things making it hard to figure out what is happening. Lack of phone signal and the ability to communicate, or a deluge of videos and photos online, plus fear and panic obscure the truth. Add to that states like Russia, with a track record of powerful propaganda campaigns – not just aimed at specific targets, but which have been used to distort reality for an entire population for years, through media and social media. The life of a lie is not straightforward, and part of unpicking it is acknowledging all of the factors at play that have facilitated its spread.

The concern at the heart of this: could Russia be using Marianna as a vector to disseminate disinformation to me? There was of course that possibility. But conversations with her friends and family – as well as her willingness to contradict Russian officials and say she definitely wasn't acting in those photos – suggested she wasn't doing that.

'I had to defend myself, because there was no one else to help, and I had to describe the whole situation as I saw it with my own eyes,' Marianna said. It's something she would repeat again and again, throughout our interview. The words of one of my editors echoed around my head. Marianna could not be expected to be an omnipotent witness. She was a human being. All she could do was be honest about her personal experience, which is what she seemed to be doing here. Her testimony to me focused on what it was like to be a first-time mum who'd suddenly found herself at the centre of this storm.

Caught between the weight of political forces, she refrained from political opinions. I took her back to the moment this all began to unfold – and she recounted the day of the attack for me blow by blow.

The hospital in Mariupol she'd been sheltering at wasn't the one where she'd planned to have her baby, but the war had changed that. She recalled how, moments before the bomb, the doctors and nurses had handed around little packages, with lots of bits and pieces you might need for a newborn. Then the windows smashed and the walls collapsed, and shrapnel flew around the room. She pulled a blanket over her head. The air was thick with the smell of dust; it was suffocating, musty. The sound of the explosion rang in her ears. It kept ringing and ringing as she and the other women headed down to the basement.

Then they were evacuated. She was one of the last to leave. Ahead of her were the severely injured. Then the mothers who had already given birth, tiny babies in their arms. Then the pregnant women, and last of all, the other people from the neighbourhood who had been sheltering in the basement. Marianna had some glass fragments embedded in her skin and a cut on her forehead – but a doctor told her she didn't need stitches. What she did need was everything she'd left inside, on the ward. Everything she'd planned to use to look after her baby when she finally arrived. She was terrified that she would have nothing.

It was once she'd collected that bag of belongings that Associated Press snapped one of those two world-renowned photographs. After that, Marianna was transferred to another hospital, where she finally gave birth to Veronika. As she lay with her new baby, survival on the brain, she had no idea of how the photographs had captured hearts and minds all over the world. She also had no idea of the social media chaos awaiting her. It was only once she had finally made the arduous journey to safety in her home town that she saw the photos – and the accusations that she was acting – with her own eyes.

'Of course, it was really offensive to hear that, because I actually lived through it all,' she said. She described it as a pity that people believed she was capable of something she'd never do.

One thing Marianna did wish was that it wasn't just her story and photos that had become central to understanding what happened on the ground that day. She thought photos and interviews with other pregnant women should have gone just as viral as her own. She feared that the focus on her alone was why people got the impression that it was all staged. But by Marianna's own account she was one of the last patients to be evacuated, and that was when the journalists arrived.

In our conversation, she never mentioned that it was Kremlin-linked media and Russian officials who'd actually put out the idea that this was an act. Instead, she criticized the AP photographers who had been praised globally for their courageous work in hard-to-reach war zones. But those journalists did interview other people at the scene – and they had nothing to do with the subsequent false story spread by Russian officials.

The lies about Marianna hadn't stopped there. They continued to spin out of control, and I navigated each twist with Marianna to hear her take. Strap in tight, because you're in for a bumpy ride of (at times, contradictory) falsehoods.

The false claims about Marianna acting formed part of a wider narrative that the Azov regiment – a controversial nationalist Ukrainian armed group linked with neo-Nazis – had occupied the hospital, which wasn't really functioning, and had staged the photos with pregnant Marianna to make it look like it was. The Russians wanted to make it look like they had hit a legitimate military target.

For starters, the Kremlin wrongly and repeatedly suggested the hospital that was involved in this attack was Mariupol's Hospital No. 1. Satellite imagery showed the hospital Marianna was at was No. 3, fully functioning according to its social media pages and Marianna herself.

She also contradicted the accusations that the Azov regiment had totally taken over the hospital – and the even more extreme claims that they were forcing women to act as human shields. The Ukrainian military weren't based inside her building, she told me. Rather, they were based in the oncology unit in the building across from the maternity ward – and some of them had family sheltering there too. That's not the same as the Ukrainian army closing down the hospital, occupying it – and then forcing women to pretend that they were real patients.

Her comments in her interview for Denis's blog, however, were also used to create new narratives that further undermined whether the attack had happened in the way it was reported on at the time. Marianna told Denis that she thought an air strike hadn't happened. Russian state media picked up on these comments to spin a narrative in which they were again blameless. Marianna was painted as a reliable witness, even though they'd attacked her credibility initially. Lies don't travel in straight lines in Russia. They are often contradictory and confusing. That's the whole point.

Marianna also told me that she never heard an air strike. She said she'd chatted to other women there and they'd also only heard explosions – not planes flying overhead. I challenged her on this – because the journalists on the ground had released evidence this was an air strike. There was footage where planes could be heard, and a crater that munition experts argued could only have been caused by a bomb dropped from above.

Her reply to me? She hadn't seen the evidence. Ultimately, Marianna was just one person caught up in this attack – and what she was telling me was what she'd seen and heard. And I did believe her – mainly because she admitted the limits of her own knowledge. 'In reality I can't blame anyone – because I didn't see with my own eyes where for certain [the explosions] came from.'

What's important to understand about the life of the lie is that it's not just the false claims that snowball and spread and evolve. It's the behaviour they inspire, too. In Marianna's case, it was the waves of online trolling and abuse her friend Natalya had described to me, accusing her of acting. When Marianna was able to log back in to Instagram, she saw swathes of abusive comments – and messages from all over the world. Some were supportive, but lots were incredibly angry.

The debate about air strikes and what really happened – a fire yet again stoked by Russian state media – sparked another round of hate, this time accusing her of lying about not hearing an air raid. This wasn't just disagreement, either – and she was frightened. What she found especially difficult was that her newborn daughter also became a target for the trolls. There were threats suggesting they would hunt her and her baby down – and that Veronika would be 'cut into pieces'. 'When they write threats and cruelty directed at my child, I do not understand it, because she has not done anything,' she told me. 'She has only just been born, and she has not even had time to live.'

Finding herself at the centre of this disinformation battle – as the war continued in Ukraine – had changed Marianna's life completely. She was finding it hard to think ahead. She wasn't making plans. Life felt uncertain – especially living in a war zone. But the glimmer of hope in her life was Veronika. I could see her eyes light up when she talked about her. She was so happy she'd arrived safely, but wished it had happened in a different way. That baby had found herself at the heart of this disinformation campaign along with her mum.

Marianna eventually returned to posting. Scrolling through her Instagram profile, I was struck by her photos of baby-grows and tiny hands. Life continued, even as the war raged on between Russia and Ukraine. The trolls turned their attention elsewhere. It may not have unfolded in quite so stark and brazen a way, but other individuals caught up in the war found the reality of what they experienced undermined by Russian propaganda. Ukrainian authorities on occasion also jumped to conclusions that contradicted the evidence. Trolls activated on both sides will always find a new target for their outrage. War moves quickly, and so do social media users.

More recently, Marianna was photographed at the start of the school year in Mariupol. In what appears to be a pro-Russian propaganda campaign, she gave little children ribbons. In other posts she can be seen handing out food and blankets in Eastern Ukraine with Russian groups. She even went to Moscow, and featured at glitzy events and high-profile talks. I received several messages from viewers and listeners. *Oh no!* they exclaimed – were they forcing Marianna to promote pro-Russian content? I think it is fair to point out that it may well be in Marianna's interests to support Russian causes, given that she is based in Russian-occupied Donetsk with her family.

But, having spoken to her, I think it boils down to something more fundamental. I had a strong sense during our conversation that Marianna just wanted peace and harmony. She wanted the fighting to stop. She wanted children to be able to go to school. She wanted life to return to some sort of normality.

There's also little doubt that her relationship with Russia was complex. In addition to the trip to Moscow and the various photo ops, after our conversation she began sharing explicitly pro-Russian posts on Instagram. I tried to reach out to her again, but she never responded.

I was also sanctioned by the Russian state for my investigations and reporting, along with other colleagues. In a similar way to my trolls, they likened my work to George Orwell's novel *1984*. That might explain why Marianna likely won't ever want to talk to me again.

I have spoken to some of her friends, who say they haven't really been in touch with her since she left Mariupol. I imagine it's very difficult for them to see her social media posts and the connections she seems to have to the Kremlin's propaganda efforts since the attack.

However misguided or not you might see her efforts, I still do think peace is likely the aim – for herself and her family first and foremost. The average person under the watchful eye of some very powerful people might find themselves in a similar situation, and that tells us just how extraordinary the life of this lie has been.

* * * *

Patricia was straightening her hair, face painted with tears. 'I'm so upset this happened,' she exclaimed. She was in snowy Houston. Meanwhile, I was squished in the corner of a booth at the BBC, trying to comfort her.

It had taken me days to track down Patricia, because it was her feet that became internet-famous, rather than her face. She was suffering from an unexplained skin condition, but a misunderstanding about what might have caused it had set off a chain of events that turned her feet into ammunition for anti-vaccine activists. They claimed that it was the Covid-19 vaccine that had caused her painful, swollen condition.

This hadn't required any help from powerful state actors or international disinformation campaigns. It was just a very committed bunch of online activists driven by false information, and some remarkably fast-acting conspiracy theory influencers.

Some of the accounts sharing Patricia's story seemed to have a long history of opposing vaccines. They had shared false claims linking autism and the MMR vaccine, something that had spread like wildfire in the late 1990s and early 2000s. These untrue allegations came to the attention of the wider public in a 1998 study written by Andrew Wakefield, who is still very much a hero of the anti-vaccine movement online. That paper was retracted in 2010 – but its claims are still cited by anti-vaxxers.

It wasn't just the established anti-vaxxers sharing these rumours about Patricia. There were also evangelical US Christian groups, who described vaccines as the 'mark of the beast'. Then there were the new anti-vax foot soldiers who had sprung up since the start of the pandemic. These people often started as anti-lockdown activists, but later found themselves immersed in more general conspiracy theories. The story they were telling about Patricia's condition matched up with what they believed about the vaccine, and it spread through their Facebook groups, Twitter feeds and Telegram channels at breakneck speed.

Patricia's story reveals to us just how effectively lies can be turbocharged with very simple tactics. A post picked up on information on a GoFundMe page, and used it to fuel an existing belief that the new Covid-19 vaccine was seriously harming large numbers of people and was very dangerous (contrary to the scientific evidence available at the time). The members of that group then jumped on this, and they spread it to other anti-vax Facebook groups. Then, they set out to spread their gospel further. The claims hopped over to Twitter, where other British conspiracy theorists started sharing them. The false claims also infected international anti-vaccine groups, who quickly translated the posts from English, and found their way to the most committed followers of anti-vaccine Telegram channels with thousands of members. They, in turn, shared this anti-vax version of Patricia's story on Instagram.

The way a network like this one connects, shares many similarities with the Russian one disseminating the false claims about Marianna. They push a convenient mistruth that hops between social media platforms. The difference is the power of the state propaganda machine, which can propel falsehoods from the online world to mainstream news, and get them parroted by key diplomats. That didn't happen to Patricia's feet.

Following the life of this lie, though, was still no mean feat. And tracking Patricia down was the first, very large, hurdle. I'll take you back to the beginning, so I can explain how I found her.

I came across her story when a picture of feet covered in purple and red sores, swollen and oozing with pus, appeared on my social media feed. 'Supposedly this is a [vaccine] trial participant,' read the text alongside it. 'Ready to roll up your sleeve?'

I tracked those feet back to the original GoFundMe page by using reverse image search, which is a way of tracking where a photo was first shared publicly online. That page made a direct link between the blisters and a Covid-19 vaccine trial, suggesting they were part of an adverse reaction. According to the GoFundMe page, they belonged to this woman called Patricia living in Texas. Armed with only her first name and a handful of pictures, I set about trying to find her on Facebook.

Hours and hours, no luck. I almost gave up until I found her commenting on a post – arguing with someone and defending herself. She'd changed her name because of the abuse she'd been subjected to since the pictures went viral, but a quick look through her pictures showed she was the woman on GoFundMe. This didn't seem to be a copycat account either, as there were lots of photos dating back years. After a quick message exchange, Patricia told me she was keen to reveal the truth of what happened. So, we hopped on a video call.

In between bouts of tears, Patricia explained to me how her illness had begun several weeks before we chatted. She'd felt pain in her left foot while she was on a walk. Her husband had suggested it might be her shoes rubbing. But when she got home, she realized the sole of her foot had become painfully swollen. A big blister had appeared, much too large to be caused by footwear. It was so big, in fact, that she had to use one of her daughter's nappies to dress it. She visited a number of doctors to show them, and they listed several potential causes.

One of several possibilities they mentioned was fixed drug eruption – a bad skin reaction to a medicine. Their minds then went to the Pfizer vaccine trial she was participating in at the time. She had received her second injection five days before the first blister developed on her foot. After seeing these doctors, Patricia talked to a relative who was so concerned that she set up a GoFundMe page to raise money for medical bills.

Under America's mostly private healthcare system, Patricia was already struggling with medical costs due to a back condition. She had to take time off from her job as an archival assistant due to the sores on her feet. Patricia originally agreed with the wording on the GoFundMe page, which mistakenly claimed the injury was linked to the vaccine trial. She had no idea how that misunderstanding would be used online.

It was then that her feet wandered all the way across the internet. As word began to spread, Pfizer and Patricia's doctors started looking into her participation in the vaccine trial. Normally, it's impossible for participants to find out whether they receive a vaccine or a placebo – that information is only revealed to researchers once the study is complete, so as not to influence the results. But Patricia says that because of the unusual circumstances, the drug company revealed to her that she had received the saltwater placebo, not the trial vaccine.

I spent hours attempting to contact those involved in the vaccine trial – from several doctors to the person who administered her shot. I was able to independently confirm she had received the placebo, after Patricia authorized me to speak about her case with the medical staff she'd dealt with. Plus, I double-checked with several independent dermatologists that saline solution injected in someone's arm would not cause sores like this to flare up on their feet.

Patricia admitted to me that she had played a part in how this mistruth evolved and spread. 'My injury had nothing to do with the vaccine. My bad. People make mistakes.' She regretted putting her story out there – and now realised just how nasty social media could get. She told me again and again how she didn't mean to deliberately deceive – and she was still desperately looking for answers from her doctors about what had actually happened to her feet.

The GoFundMe page was eventually updated – after it was briefly removed over fears it was promoting disinformation. This time it made clear that 'the cause had become unclear'. Patricia's relative also offered to refund anyone who had donated because they thought it was an injury caused by the vaccine trial.

By this point, it was too late. Her story had hit the sweet spot. At a time when anxiety about the new Covid-19 vaccines was high – as was worry about the pandemic – the misunderstanding tapped into the growing fears of a very loud minority on social media who became very quick at mobilizing online. She became somewhat of a celebrity among the denialism movement. So many people had seen Patricia's feet.

And it wasn't just activists sharing this either, but the average person who might stumble on the post and think, understandably, 'Wait a second – did the vaccine really do this?' They'd be left frightened and confused. They might share that post because they wanted to ask others whether it was real. The complex story of what had really happened wasn't yet out there at the time, and so there were only the conspiracy groups to turn to for yet more rumours.

Almost every single person I've interviewed who has found themselves the target of disinformation on social media has also been targeted with hate. The mistruths inspire a wave of vitriol.

In Patricia's case there was hate from all sides – just like with Marianna in Mariupol. Anti-vaccine activists berated her for taking part in the trial. Others sent her hate for what they saw as a deliberate fuelling of disinformation. She was called every name under the sun – from idiot and a drug addict to convicted felon, con artist – and much worse. Patricia had to go almost entirely offline. She hated that she'd caused all this harm, too. She'd taken part in the vaccine trial because she wanted to help scientific efforts, not hinder them.

Patricia's story is just one example of a recurring pattern. Fringe activists find a story that seems to support their entrenched views, and work to spread it rapidly online, regardless of the underlying truth. It's a blueprint that was used repeatedly by anti-vax activists long after restrictions had been lifted. There are real examples of vaccine injuries and deaths linked to the Covid-19 vaccine, although it is a very small number – and many of those used to push these ideas online aren't real examples.

Her story also serves as a reminder of how the average person can find themselves caught up in a disinformation storm, with no warning. There's no room for mistakes when it comes to the committed conspiracy theory community online. They're unforgiving – and they'll use anything and everything to further their cause, at whatever cost.

* * * *

Sometimes, the life of an online lie is unwittingly lengthened by people who aren't really conspiracy activists at all. They're what you might refer to as the accidentals, who find themselves vectors for something that's untrue, but not because they seek to gain from it in some way. They're not on a clear mission. They are friends or grandparents or neighbours, who sometimes really want to help and just don't realize how dangerous it can be to get tangled in the disinformation web.

On the brink of that first lockdown during the Covid-19 pandemic, there was almost endless speculation about the government's plans, with rumours flying around about tanks and soldiers being deployed to keep people at home, and countless dodgy health tips doing the rounds. This misinformation had a distinctly different feel to the conspiracy theories that would come later.

One of the most viral posts was a list of tips and advice – some true, some benign, and some possibly harmful – which circulated on Facebook, WhatsApp, Twitter and elsewhere. It was dubbed the 'Uncle with a Master's Degree' post because of the alleged source of the information. Along with my colleague, disinformation expert Olga Robinson, and editor Mike Wendling, I set out to find out where it had originally come from.

The lifecycle of this particular lie was by all accounts quite absurd – and, as I was to discover, totally fitting with how disinformation goes viral. At first glance it seemed legitimate because the information was attributed to a trusted source: a doctor, an institution or that well-educated 'uncle'. That's technique number one: persuade people that your source is someone who knows what they're talking about.

We used a program called CrowdTangle to find the earliest version of the post, which was shared on 7 February 2020 by a user based in Singapore in a group called Happy People, which had nearly 2,000 members. Not so happy if they followed this advice, mind. It read: 'My classmate's uncle and nephew, graduated with a master's degree, and work in Shenzhen Hospital. He is being transferred to study Wuhan pneumonia virus. He just called me and told me to tell my friends.'

Some of the tips that follow are misleading or wrong. One says that you don't have the virus 'if you have a runny nose'. At that time, it's true that this wasn't one of the most common symptoms. However, the US Centers for Disease Control and Prevention (CDC) and the medical journal *The Lancet* said it wasn't unheard of in Covid-19 patients. And as the months went on, we'd come to realize a whole range of symptoms could be associated with contracting coronavirus – and ruling out any one was pretty counterproductive. The post also encouraged people to 'drink more hot water' and 'try not to drink ice'.

The list picked up momentum several days later, when it was shared by an account called Glen DCruz in India. He posted it in several different Facebook groups, including ones focused on sharing memes and readings for Catholics. By this time the post contained new details – including accurate advice about washing your hands. It was also very specific about how the disease would progress. But doctors were saying that coronavirus symptoms and severity were highly variable, and there was no one exact progression pattern.

Glen claimed he'd got a phone call from this mythical uncle. Via message, he admitted there was no phone call. He told me he had simply forwarded on a message passed to him. In the months after, Glen regularly sent me memes of candles, for no apparent reason.

For several weeks, the uncle post was confined to relatively minor outlets. But on 27 February, Peter, an 84-year-old former art gallery owner made it go viral. He was what might be referred to as the superspreader – and he lived in Buckinghamshire. Peter's post was similar to Glen's, but again included some new information – some of which was wrong or misleading. Peter did edit the misleading parts of his post after fact checkers from Full Fact and Snopes had posted their analysis. But by then, it had been shared almost 350,000 times.

I called Peter and quizzed him on his source. He explained that he'd thought the uncle was related to this 'medical guy' who had passed on all those facts and figures. He'd just wanted to help. But it became apparent fairly quickly during our conversation that Peter just really liked all of the likes and shares. He kept detailing exactly how many the post had got – and was pretty grumpy at fact checkers who'd attempted to slow the spread.

At this time we were all stuck at home with little to do, and so I could understand why Peter might be out for some adrenaline-boosting social media interactions. Life had become very boring and very scary all at once. But when I checked in with Peter again a few months later, he was still avidly posting and attempting to dodge the fact checkers.

Soon the post wasn't just being attributed to the infamous uncle with the master's degree. He became 'a member of the Stanford hospital board' and even 'a friend's sister's friend's brother who just happens to be on the Stanford Hospital board'. Stanford University had to deny any association with the post. There was also information attributed to 'Japanese doctors' and 'Taiwanese experts' – among many other modifications. I'd be very surprised if you hadn't come across one of the versions that were out there, unless you sensibly switched your phone off in late March 2020.

The post spread far and wide, aided by celebrities – including a Ghanaian TV presenter and an American actor – but also by scores of people all over the world. At the same time, it was translated into several languages, including Arabic, Amharic, Vietnamese, French, Spanish and Italian. One new additional piece of advice suggested doing a coronavirus 'self-check' every morning by holding your breath for more than ten seconds. But there was no evidence to indicate that your ability to do this meant you didn't have the virus.

On social media, it's easier than ever for a lie to be spread all over the world. There are no official borders and boundaries, and it can be translated, turbocharged and disseminated across the globe. And in 2020, people everywhere were looking for answers about Covid-19.

This kind of viral post has a name: a copypasta.[22] It's when you repost – rather than retweeting or sharing – a block of text. Then a friend sees it on your Facebook wall or Twitter feed or on WhatsApp and thinks 'oh maybe there's something to this, it's come directly from someone I trust', copies and pastes it and so the spread continues.

The copy-and-paste technique also makes it all the more difficult for social media sites to keep track of how far one post has spread – especially its various mutations. We know that Peter's post was shared hundreds of thousands of times, but it's a colossal task to calculate how many people have seen the various copied variations of 'uncle with a master's degree' on Facebook or any of the major social media platforms.

It was the first time of many that I would contact social media sites about harmful Covid-19 misinformation – and heard them reiterating their policies to tackle this kind of content. A Facebook spokesperson told us the site had removed the posts for violating its policies – to Peter's dismay, because all of his likes disappeared. When I challenged them on this post, they set out the partnerships they had with the NHS and other official health bodies to promote accurate information. But critics would argue this happened way too slowly. The horse had already bolted – and the sites were playing catch-up.

The post was an important reminder in those early days of the pandemic that it's vital to pause before sharing. Its virality wasn't due to a complex influence operation. It was because anxious people were living through an unprecedented event online.

The most valuable lesson the post taught me was that it's crucial that people don't feel ashamed if they share disinformation, especially when it's accidental. When we are left feeling bad or silly or stupid, then we're more likely to double down. We stop holding ourselves accountable for what we're sharing or we convince ourselves that we're being censored in some way.

Sometimes when people forward these messages that are later incorrect, they also wonder, well why does it matter? Especially if that post was just a bit of a joke, or didn't really cause any harm. I'm reminded of a report I did for BBC *Newsnight* about how everyone thought Woolworths was reopening because of a fake Twitter account that even misspelled the company's name in some of its tweets. People all over – including journalists and even news sites – wrote up the story. Everyone was desperate for good news and nostalgic for better times – and Pick n Mix.

This reveals to us how disinformation works. It plays on emotions. It exploits the context and timing. If we can learn to spot lies online in all forms, then we have a better chance of quelling the worst and most harmful.

The life of a lie can be messy and chaotic. It can be planned or entirely unintentional – and the tactics used to further its spread don't have to be highly complex. There is understandable concern about AI technology turbocharging the spread of misinformation and, while the rise of convincing computer-generated images and videos certainly could make it even harder to tell truth from fiction, a lie can spread effectively in quite simple ways, too. It can be packaged up as a straightforward social media post, a viral screengrab, a copy-and-pasted message, and will spread like wildfire.

Rather than cutting-edge technology, these mistruths rely on their ability to play on all of our fears and to harness personal, shocking stories about individuals. They also rely on social media algorithms and sites that fail to halt their spread before it's too late. These lies can be spread by powerful governments, or just your next-door neighbour. But whatever their source and whatever their route, they cause real harm for the people caught up in them.

Oh, and I never did meet the uncle with the master's degree.

6

SHOCK TROOPS

It's a sunny June day, and I'm walking out of the BBC's New Broadcasting House. I'm chatting with some colleagues. The air is tinged with the possibility of the summer that lies ahead. It feels almost carefree. Only, it's not. I'm on high alert. For the past six weeks or so, a man has been living in a tent just outside the building. He has been shouting at me, and filming me, and waiting for me outside work.

He's very tall, with grey hair. He wears a fleece and a pair of combat trousers. Beside his tent are signs declaring that the BBC is complicit in protecting paedophiles. The claims he's making go a lot further than any real examples of where the BBC has failed victims – for example, of its former presenter Jimmy Savile, who was a predatory sex offender. The conspiracy theories scrawled on cardboard by this man are complex, confusing and unclear. There are pictures of people attached to them.

I saw the signs on several occasions as I walked into work, but for a few months at least this man didn't notice me. I was relieved. A lot of the conspiracy theorists I investigate believe in elite cabals of paedophiles that far surpass the reality of powerful people carrying out – and covering up – sexual abuse.

My relief, however, was somewhat short-lived. Several months in, it started. At first, it was just shouting my name. Then it was shouting and walking after me, calling me a 'disinformation agent' as I headed home from work. I'd dash away as quickly as I could, wondering if he was still following me. Next, it was waiting for me outside the revolving doors of the BBC's lobby as I headed back into the office with my lunch. He'd have his phone at the ready to film me. He'd shout and swear as I hurried inside. When this happened, I'd quicken my pace, call my editors and get away as soon as possible. He never approached me for a reasonable conversation. He would appear almost out of nowhere and shout and scream abuse.

On this sunny June day, as I'm leaving the building, he appears again. I am deliberately taking a route I thought would avoid him. He comes up close, screaming and shouting.

'Do you want to see my balls?' Then he proceeds to declare he isn't harassing me. 'Don't fucking grimace like that,' he adds. I just want to get away as quickly as I can.

I never want to be scared of the people that troll me. I am the target of particularly committed trolls who do not like me investigating the real-world consequences of disinformation, hate and algorithms. I am, however, shaken by these incidents. They're being investigated by the police, who have since removed this man from the BBC premises. They found a 'bladed item' in his tent – a flip knife, I was later told.

It doesn't stop at this, either. Weeks later, another conspiracy theorist turns up outside the BBC, desperately requesting an interview with me. They follow the BBC's director general all the way to the Tube, making their request. Security teams will later tell me they stand out on the plaza, by the doors where I work, repeatedly calling the press office and switchboard asking for me. After that, graffiti appears on the pavement outside the BBC declaring us 'Covid Liars', and a page of a conspiracy theory newspaper featuring my face is stuck up close to work. It's unclear whether this was done by the same man, or someone else entirely.

* * * *

These are stark examples of the way the hate I've experienced online seems to be spilling out into the real world. Between 1 January 2023 and the end of June that year, the BBC received 14,488 escalations regarding social media posts for 'protected assets' – often on-air presenters or people considered at risk of online abuse. Of this number, 11,771 relate to me. Those posts were escalated because they could be indicative of cyberbullying, negative sentiment, threats of physical harm and violent language, doxing, impersonations, giving personal details and more. The online abuse I experience started back in 2020, and it has continued since then, becoming increasingly committed and extreme. In my view, the escalation of online abuse in visible public forums normalizes and even encourages people to take action offline.

My offline encounters with hate first began back during the Covid-19 lockdowns, with a message scrawled in red pen on a whiteboard used for updates about mask-wearing and Covid-19 restrictions outside a Tube station close to where I work in London. It said Marianna Spring was lying about the vaccine. The note itself wasn't very offensive. What was more concerning was the message it sent: *We know where you get the Tube and where you work.* I still don't know who left that note.

After that I attended rallies where protesters told me I should be hanged for treason. Those shouts attracted other protesters, who chanted and hurled abuse. One of the people involved continued posting online about me, suggesting he would turn up at my work. Other protesters held up placards about me. One with just my name and my age on. Nothing more. Another had carefully written my name across a drawing of an extravagant red high heel.

These incidents were the real-world manifestation of narratives that were being shared on social media. Online, they said I was a silly little girl who was only in her mid-twenties and could in no way be clever enough to investigate this topic; hence the sign with my age. They claimed I was a puppet of the state, following orders. At the same time, I was apparently an evil, poisonous satanic whore who was cruelly trying to torpedo their movement as part of a cabal of nasty powerful people; hence the red high heel.

What's been happening to me is just a small part of a campaign of intimidation being waged by conspiracy activists. They have shown they are willing to act offline. And they are persistent – they're not giving up.

During the pandemic, activists turned up at the home of Chris Whitty, the chief medical officer for England, and called for him to be hanged. They harassed television and radio presenters from what they call the 'mainstream media'. They held signs showing politicians being executed. They called for doctors and nurses to be tried for committing war crimes and likened them to Nazis involved in genocide. Groups with links to the far right posted about military training for anti-vaccine activists, suggesting a level of organization to this violence. Activists took aim at the individuals they saw as complicit in these plots, pinning up 'Most Wanted' posters of journalists, media bosses and public health advisors.

The life of any online lie depends to a certain extent on 'shock troops' – the trolls deployed to defend that lie and to target anyone who disagrees with or undermines their alternative 'truth'. Understanding how trolling is tied up with disinformation is crucial. They are both 'expedient ways to manipulate public opinion'.[23] That makes hate one of the key weapons in the disinformation war. Increasingly violent rhetoric, cries of war crimes and personal threats are now posted online with ease, and seemingly pass without consequence for those who send those messages. They do have consequences, though, for the people who find themselves the targets.

These trolls are often preaching incessantly online about how they value freedom of expression and are standing up for the silenced. To me, it seems very sinister when a young female investigative reporter working in a democracy is specifically targeted with hate and abuse at her place of work. Her crime? Trying to hold conspiracy theorists and trolls, as well as powerful social media companies, to account. My way of coping with this is to investigate what's happening to me like any other case study. In this chapter, I hope, I'll help you understand why this is happening to me and to others – and how we've arrived at this point.

* * * *

One of my most memorable run-ins with the troll army came when I had just finished an investigation for BBC *Panorama* into whether Twitter could protect users under Elon Musk's ownership. The resulting article and documentary was titled 'Twitter insiders: We can't protect users from trolling under Musk' – so it came as no surprise when Musk himself tweeted about it.

'Sorry for turning Twitter from nurturing paradise into a place that has… trolls,' he said in one tweet, posting a screengrab of the report, which had a photo of me at the top. According to Twitter's own data, that tweet was seen by more than 30 million profiles.

'Trolls are kinda fun,' Musk said in another reply.

The investigation made clear that while Twitter was never perfect, hate was thriving under Musk's ownership. Twitter insiders who had spoken to me felt like Musk had used this to de-prioritize protecting users from harm altogether. They told me the site could no longer protect users from trolling and state-coordinated disinformation, following lay-offs and other changes under Musk.

Specifically, they told me how features intended to protect Twitter users from trolling and harassment were proving really difficult to maintain amid what they described as a chaotic working environment in which Musk was shadowed by bodyguards at all times. I spoke to dozens of insiders, with several going on the record for the first time.

Features that just don't seem to be working in the way they did before include nudges that ask people if they want to post a tweet that could be hateful, and a safety mode that automatically blocks followers for some accounts. Since then, Musk has even floated the idea of removing the block button altogether.

These allegations were backed up by data too, which indicated that trolls had become emboldened and harassment was intensifying. New research from the Institute for Strategic Dialogue also shows a spike in accounts following misogynistic and abusive profiles.[24]

I had approached Elon Musk as part of my *Panorama* investigation, but he hadn't responded to my requests. Instead, as I described before, he decided to share his reaction to his (then) 130 million followers.

His tweets unleashed a torrent of abuse. There were hundreds of posts, many including misogynistic slurs and abusive language. There were also threatening messages, including depictions of kidnap and hanging. Then Musk posted again, responding to one tweet that was critical of the BBC investigation – writing 'roflmao' (rolling on [the] floor laughing my ass off).

But I certainly wasn't rolling on the floor laughing. I was wading through hateful messages sent from accounts predominantly based in the US and UK. More proof to back up the investigation's conclusion that hate on Twitter was thriving.

The majority of these messages were directed at me. Now, abuse on Twitter is nothing new. After all, I'm a reporter who shares my coverage of disinformation, conspiracy theories and hate there. But in the wake of Musk's tweets about me, the International Center for Journalists and the University of Sheffield confirmed that the hate I was receiving had increased to the highest levels in a year. And the tools they used could not even pick up all the abuse. Some of it didn't use my name directly, or was in response to Musk's original tweet, which attracted more than 14,000 replies. Others were private messages – including a video of a woman being tied up and held at gunpoint, and another showing hangings. Some talked about my time ending 'in a horrible way' and said I should 'burn in hell'. Many combined misogynistic slurs with abusive and sexualized language. I was repeatedly called a bitch and much nastier insults. Most of the messages were received on Twitter, with a small number sent to me on other sites.

Many of the accounts had become more active since Musk's takeover, and several openly rejoiced at how their profiles had returned since Musk bought the platform. Some were prominent conspiracy theorists. Several had the new paid-for blue 'verified' ticks.

I approached Elon Musk and Twitter several times to ask about his vision for the social media site. They did not respond. Online, they claim that protecting the user's voice remains a priority for Twitter. Since then, the social media company has reiterated on several occasions its commitment to freedom of expression, and elevating users' voices. It has introduced new features like 'Community Notes', where it's possible for people to add additional context to posts. When this was all happening, Twitter's press office was automatically sending out poo emojis in response to requests. This is unprecedented from a social media company's press office. They are usually quick to respond and share a somewhat formulaic response, detailing how they tackle issues like hate and disinformation. The fact that there was no serious communication from Twitter's team was totally bizarre, but perhaps to be expected since huge numbers of staff had been laid off.

This raises questions about the role shock troops can play in curbing freedom of expression and pushing disinformation, especially when the most powerful people – the ones running these platforms – can deploy them at will. When trolling seems to be fair game and even journalists looking to hold social media companies to account become the targets, we can no longer dismiss this as a problem limited to the fringes of the internet.

* * * *

Better understanding my own trolls, to some extent, offers answers to a question that social media experts and psychologists have endeavoured to answer: 'Why do people troll?'

My trolls have left me in tears a few times. In general, I block the worst and most relentless accounts. But there was one time when I cried because a troll blocked me.

Mando Ricks was a Tottenham Hotspur fan, just like me. I figured this out from his Twitter profile, from which he messaged me to tell me I was a 'fucking slag cunt'. Nothing like several slurs in a row to really get your point across. He was also an ardent anti-vax activist. I hoped I might be able to confront him.

This was part of my attempts to talk to my trolls, many of whom had sent hate to other women. I wanted to understand, and hold to account, some of the people sending me some of the worst hate. I tend to find that calling out the abuse, and speaking to the people who send it – or even meeting them – humanizes us both. We're real people as opposed to online avatars.

Interrogating a selection of abusive accounts, I quickly concluded the majority – like Mando Ricks – were real people. There have been a whole range of accounts that bombard me with gender-based slurs again and again – everything from calling me a 'daft cow' and telling me I needed to 'get laid' to threatening to come and find me and violently or sexually attack me.

Let me give you just a taste of the direct messages I've received: 'I'm going to… ring my friends and ask them to rape you'… 'You dirty zionist-controlled bitch, I bet you rape and kill kids… you need beheading'. Misogynistic slurs were a frequent occurrence, referring to me as a whore, bitch, slut, slag – often replacing the letter 'l' with the number '1', most likely in an attempt to avoid automatic moderation from the social media sites.

The hate I find most difficult involves threats suggesting the trolls will come and get me, or track me down in person. From looking at some of their accounts, I can see that lots seem to be normal people. These trolls are also football fans, grandparents, vegan-cooking fans. There was even one who gave away his location by tweeting at delivery service Ocado, complaining it didn't deliver to his postcode in Great Yarmouth.

That Spurs fan Mando Ricks was one of the first that I tried to message. I was really hoping – because I like the same football team, because he seemed to do normal things as well as trolling – that he might have the guts to respond. Within minutes, I was blocked. I burst into tears.

How was it fair that he could run away when, because of messages like his, I sometimes feel unsafe? I have to think about how I leave the office, how I walk home. I don't like it when people walk up close behind me on the pavement. I double-check that no one is following me. And I take precautions when I am at home on my own.

I didn't do any of those things before I started receiving threatening messages. Now I'm targeted all the time. I like to think I'm indestructible, but after one of my trolls blocked me, I didn't feel it.

So I tried another. He was a man in his twenties or thirties. A quick bit of googling had revealed how he was a healthcare assistant in a nursing home in the South West of England, and he loved vegan cooking. His Instagram account – where he had told me that 'all of you vile horrible people will get what you deserve, cunt' – appeared to be using his real name. Another quick scour of the internet for his pictures – using the reverse image search tool – and I was happy, if that's the right word, to confirm that this man was actually using his real identity to troll.

I can never decide whether that makes it better – or worse. On the one hand, he seemed to think what he was doing was so acceptable there was no need to hide it. It's like he didn't realize the pain caused by each spiteful message. I couldn't help wondering, when he was helping put his elderly patients to bed or bringing them a cup of tea, did they have any idea that – in his spare time – he was messaging young women on Instagram with angry hate.

After some more digging I found that there wasn't just one Instagram profile. This man had multiple accounts that he clearly hopped between whenever he was suspended. It was like whack-a-troll. I messaged each of the accounts and he finally replied on one. He couldn't even remember what message he'd sent me. Did he send out hate that often? His profile showed that Serena Williams and Greta Thunberg were targets for his abuse. He agreed to a call. But each time I phoned him – no answer. It's like it was all a game. In the end, he didn't even have the guts – or maybe care – to answer.

* * * *

I was close to concluding that talking to any of my trolls might be an impossible task. And then, finally, a man called Steve agreed to speak to me on the phone. The messages he'd sent me were less offensive than most of the abuse I receive. He'd sent them over several weeks.

A quick look at his Facebook profile offered some answers. He seemed to be based in the Midlands. He looked like he was in his sixties or seventies. Like lots of account holders who send me hate, he was deep into online conspiracy theories. He'd even set up a Facebook group dedicated to them.

In his profile picture, he had short white hair, dark eyebrows and was wearing glasses. He had on a brown jacket and zip-up fleece. He just looked like an average person. One of his photo albums featured a picture of a cliff walk exclaiming 'Paradise in Cornwall'. His photos didn't really feature any family or friends. They gave the impression of a pretty solitary life.

His messages to me focused on how I was a nasty woman who didn't know what I was talking about. He revealed to me later that there were other female BBC journalists he'd targeted with hate. He hated the BBC in general – that was a theme of his posts.

When I first messaged him on Facebook, I told him I'd found his earlier messages offensive. In his reply he told me that he got 'frustrated' at the BBC and described it as a 'cesspit of corruption and disinformation'. He mentioned real examples of BBC failings relating to Jimmy Savile. But he also shared links pushing false claims about the Covid-19 vaccines and climate change.

I wasn't that surprised when he agreed to speak on the phone. I think he most likely wanted to catch my attention, and for me to listen to what he had to say. I imagine at this point he likely didn't see any problem with those messages he'd sent me.

True to all of that, when he answered the phone, he was polite. At first he told me he didn't think his messages were that bad, and I explained they were just some of many punctuated with abuse streaming into my inbox.

Then he seemed to double down, pointing out that he actually received online hate himself from 'people who believe in global warming and that 9/11 happened'. They were responding to the conspiracy theories he was sharing on social media. I tried to talk him through how that hate was a bit different from the abuse targeting me.

He also revealed to me the much more personal place some of this seemed to come from. 'When I was at grammar school, I suffered for years from a lot of bullying. Mostly mental, but some physical – which caused me to fail most of my exams.' He described leaving school at sixteen and not even bothering to pick up his results. He said one of the bullies chucked them in the canal, and they ended up in very good jobs, while his 'self-esteem was shattered for many years'.

'Maybe it helped me look at life differently and not go along with the crowd,' he said. 'I know it was wrong to call you those words, but it was nothing compared to the hell I endured at school.'

His messages seemed to be emblematic of a wider disdain and distrust in the institutions he blamed for the hard times he'd experienced. Having been bullied, he thought it was his time to be the bully instead of expressing that disdain in a reasonable way.

One of the most memorable moments of our conversation was towards the end of the phone call. As the connection dropped a little, in a muffled tone he told me he didn't always like using social media. Steve was, like those he was messaging – but in a very different way – a victim of social media too. He had become addicted to it and it was bringing out his darker side. That didn't excuse the hurt he'd caused with the hate he had sent, but he'd also been sucked into a nasty world.

I think by the end of our conversation he was coming around to the idea that sending out online hate was not the solution. 'I probably made a mistake [in sending those messages]. I'm a pretty fair bloke,' he eventually admitted.

After we spoke, Steve unsent the more abusive messages that had come my way. He did continue to message me a fair amount, but with dubious links about vaccines, the pandemic and the war in Ukraine, rather than abuse. I've come across him in other circles on social media and noticed that he is still a member of some of the groups pushing conspiracy theories.

But I've not seen him direct abuse aimed at other women on his public profiles either.

* * * *

Steve isn't the only troll I've spoken to directly. I've also spent time tracking down the people who post conspiracy theories and hate about the victims of the most horrific violence. One of those was a man who went by the name Professor Wolfie.

On Telegram, he posted that Sarah Everard – who was kidnapped and murdered by a serving police officer back in 2021 – was not real and that the attack hadn't happened. He believed it was part of an elaborate plot to increase policing powers, which was ironic given it did the opposite and provoked an outcry at the Metropolitan Police in London. His conspiracy theories were some of the most disturbing I'd encountered.

I wanted to understand why he was saying these things – and figure out how this man had arrived here. He claimed to be 'senior in the aviation industry' and he agreed to speak to me on the phone. Within minutes, he jumped between conspiracies about Sarah Everard, the 1996 Dunblane massacre, a woman who had died during the Capitol riots in the US, and more.

In his eyes, all of these events were fabricated. He kept referring to that elusive 'they' – the people who were pulling all the strings, but who he couldn't name. 'They' is also often a cover for discriminatory beliefs – especially antisemitic ones. The 'they' is more often than not a powerful, rich Jewish person or family, who in this conspiracy theorist's version of events has god-like powers.

'It's not really the government, because they're only puppets. It's only an illusion of democracy. Really. It's the oligarchs,' 'Wolfie' told me matter-of-factly, when I asked who would be capable of pulling off the plans he was describing.

He told me how, as a child, he had found school boring and difficult. He became obsessed with reading the Bible, and religious scriptures appeared to be his gateway into a conspiratorial way of looking at the world. He didn't believe people had died of Covid-19. He told me about his dad falling very ill with Covid and being in a coma for four weeks. To me, it sounded like conspiracy theories had helped him make sense of a very traumatic time in his life.

Finally, I asked him about the harm caused by the conspiracies he was promoting about Sarah Everard. Did he realize how painful those lies were to those who cared about her? There was ample evidence she was real – and what had happened was horrific. It's a question I often ask those deep into disinformation. Will at least some understanding of those they are affecting cause them to reflect on what they're doing?

For Wolfie this did seem to be the case. He was so obsessed with the conspiracy theories he'd come up with and encountered online that he hadn't really thought properly about their consequences. In a very perverse way, he believed he was somehow helping. Waking everyone up to the truth. In reality, he was hurting people after they'd lived through the worst days of their lives.

'I don't want to upset anybody. You know, that's not my game. I need to open people's minds. That's more important,' he said. But how could he not realize that these views would upset Sarah's friends and family?

When we finally met in person, months later, he had climbed down a little. Don't get me wrong, he was still deep in the conspiracy world. He did seem more self-aware, though. When I asked him about the conspiracy theories he'd shared, he admitted he wasn't actually sure if they were true – and said that they were just speculation he'd entertained, like he did all the time. It felt a little like he regretted those comments about Sarah Everard. I reckon that slight change of heart probably had something to do with our phone call. Perhaps our conversation had triggered a realization – that he wasn't operating in a bubble. He was living in a world populated by others, both online and off.

* * * *

Around the time of the general election in 2019, I was covering online hate targeting politicians and political activists. This was directed at both sides, and it was hate that went beyond just criticism – death threats, calls for hangings, and other violent rhetoric. A lot of the anger had spilt over after the 2016 Brexit referendum. Online abuse targeting politicians is nothing new, of course, but several have spoken out in recent years on how it's become so much worse. British female MPs including Nicky Morgan, Louise Ellman, Amber Rudd and Heidi Allen all decided to stand down – and cited online abuse as a factor.

Gina Miller had become a prominent activist after the referendum. She challenged the UK government over its authority to trigger Article 50 without parliamentary approval, and when the Supreme Court ruled in her favour in January 2017, some people who supported Brexit were very angry with her. Two years later, I saw how again and again, in Facebook groups and posts, some very nasty hate was coming her way.

There was one profile in particular that was targeting her with racist hate and online abuse. 'Deport the Cunt ffs,' one of its comments stated.

Another declared: 'One deluded fat fuck. Go away now. You lost. Johnson's got the majority. All you can do is piss and moan.'

And a third: 'Scum sucking cunts. They can all suck on my bloater. Talentless, traitorous – they are for the drop with a rope to break their fall.'

These messages were shared by a man called Alan. I got in contact with him, and he agreed to meet Gina to talk. So I headed down to Alan's flat in the South East of the UK to speak to him before he and Gina came face-to-face.

Alan spoke of his love of music, gesturing to the guitar displayed in his small but cosy living room. He also spoke very proudly of his then-teenage son. He explained to me that he hadn't really cared about politics before 2016. What he was seeing on social media had got him increasingly fired up.

'It was just literally because of Brexit,' he told me as we sat together on his sofa. 'I figured, there's no point in me sitting back and being passive. Everybody's got to do their bit. If you want to come out of Europe in a year, you have got to fight your corner.'

Quite quickly, our conversation turned to his own personal difficulties. He described people like him – 'white single fathers' who now felt 'disenfranchised'. He described feeling let down by politicians attempting to thwart the Brexit vote that he believed would improve his life. 'I get nothing from nobody. It just angered me to a point where I'm willing to stand up and say something 'cos I can't do with sitting and being passive about it.'

I have found time and time again that acute difficulties at home can leave someone more vulnerable to being drawn into a world of hate and abuse that preys on unhappiness and distrust. Alan had been doing some temporary work, but otherwise jobs hadn't been easy to come by. It seemed to me that this frustration was spilling over into his comments online. I challenged him on them.

'I don't regret it, but it could have been put in a much more grown-up type, viable argument,' he said. For him, it was a way of getting his point across.

But, contrary to his online presence, Alan was also welcoming and open. He was more than happy to have a civilized conversation in person. It gave me hope that face-to-face with Gina he would be able to reflect on what he'd posted.

For Gina, though, this had all been more serious. With threats online spilling over into abuse on the streets – Gina had to have security 24/7 for her and her family. 'In the beginning, I thought it was just words on social media, but then there were people actually trying to take out a bounty on my head,' she said.

She described being out with her daughter, who was going to have her eyes tested at the optician. 'This car stopped. The window rolled down and they were shouting, "Black bitch, you should be hung and killed, traitor." You know, "Dying is too good for you." And I'm standing there holding my daughter's hand.'

Gina and I met with Alan at a restaurant in central London. I could tell Alan was nervous. He'd told me he wanted to look like his musical idols, The Beatles, and was dressed in a smart velvet jacket. While Alan's online comments were hateful and offensive, it did take courage to come and speak about them face-to-face. I wondered why he hadn't backed out of doing this.

'I [don't] want to leave a bit of hate around in the world. If I could do something to clear it up then I'll talk to anybody to clear it up. It's not my place to make anybody feel like that,' he replied.

Gina immediately made clear to Alan that she was a real person – one who he had never met before and really didn't know much about. I was especially struck by her courage. It takes guts to talk to your troll in this way – one who has sent abusive and racist messages at you.

'What I find really frustrating is people think they know me because of what's in the media and what's in the papers, and I often think who is this woman because I don't recognize myself,' she explained to Alan.

Gina then told Alan about difficult experiences she'd gone through earlier in her life, including fleeing an abusive partner. Alan said he had also escaped a toxic relationship. They realized they'd both had to sleep in their cars to get away from something that was happening to them. They both cared deeply about their children too.

They also addressed the hateful messages. Gina made it clear the abuse had become very personal. 'I've noticed a lot of the anger I was getting before was about Brexit, but now Brexit is over, it's changed. It's now about me being an immigrant, a woman of colour, looking like an ape. I actually get told worse things now than before.'

'People need something to hang all their frustration on – and sadly you're getting all that abuse,' said Alan. 'They need a focal point to vent at. I don't agree with what's going on. That's absolutely out of order.'

Despite Alan previously telling Gina to 'go back home', I think it really started to sink in for him that Gina was a real person with kids and a life – just like him. Real people aren't two-dimensional. I decided to read the comments Alan had directed at Gina aloud to them both. Alan said he felt 'terrible' now that he'd met Gina. He described social media as 'poison', and Gina said it was a 'medium dedicated to hatred'.

Before this meeting I had spoken to Alan for several months. It felt like a real journey, and one that had a positive outcome. He now seemed to have a much greater understanding of the impact of his remarks. Gina forgave Alan, and the two tried to stay in contact afterwards.

I was struck by just how different the conversation was offline versus on social media. It was refreshing. The hatred had vanished almost immediately, and there was a real contrast even with the chat I'd had with Alan the day before. His bravado had disappeared. When we sit in a room and just talk to each other, we realize we're just human beings.

When I told cyber-psychologist Linda Kaye about that interaction between Gina and Alan, she described the difference between communication in the online and offline worlds. Politics on social media is very polarized – and it's possible to 'clearly display your political affiliations' in a way you can't in the real world. That means when you encounter or talk about someone from an opposing faction, you very much develop an 'us versus them' mentality. 'But in person, it's possible to realize – all right, we're not part of the same group but we have other communalities,' she said.

Conversation on social media limited to one topic reduces the scope for understanding more about who the other person might be and what you might share. After they'd met in person and talked, Alan saw Gina as a person he could relate to.

Since then, I've watched Alan's Facebook jump from British politics to anti-vax conspiracies and then disinformation about the war in Ukraine. He might be knee-deep in the so-called UK truth movements, but he does appear to have learned his lesson about social media hate. I've not spotted another abusive comment about Gina.

* * * *

This gallery of trolls reveals two things. First, how real human interaction is one of the most powerful antidotes to online hate – whether that's meeting in person or speaking on the phone. It's the most effective tool in opening someone's eyes to what they're doing and how it affects others, but it's not easy to facilitate and requires courage on all parts.

Second, that all of these trolls had quite clearly been drawn into an online world that was harming them. Linda Kaye is adamant that, without becoming embroiled in these increasingly polarized virtual communities, these people would be unlikely to target others with hate in this way. The distance that social media creates is part of what leads to this behaviour. Trolls like this aren't scary, but rather sad and troubled. Social media has given them a very unhealthy outlet for their anger.

With that in mind – does social media create these trolls? Are these platforms just housing these accounts – or are they making it all worse? From what I heard from Steve, Professor 'Wolfie' and Alan – and also Dr Kaye – it seems that their algorithms could be actively driving vulnerable users towards more hateful content.

I wanted to see what trolls – like my own – might be seeing on their social media feeds that normalized their behaviour. But social media sites are notoriously secretive about their algorithms – and so it's very difficult to see what they recommend to different people. I enlisted the advice of social media expert Chloe Colliver from the Institute for Strategic Dialogue, who said that the only way of really seeing what a troll like this might be exposed to is by setting up an undercover account.

I created a fictional character, and signed 'him' up to the five most popular social media platforms in the UK. I called him Barry. On these accounts, I copied the activities of my trolls – liking the pages they liked, following similar accounts, and watching and liking posts and videos on themes they engaged with. That included lots of content opposing Covid-19 restrictions and vaccination requirements, but also posts about a variety of hobbies, from football to gardening, and those in the local area I'd chosen for him in the UK. Like my trolls, Barry also engaged in a small amount of misogyny, liking pages that shared sexist comments about women getting back in the kitchen – and I copied some the abuse I'd been sent onto his profiles. Gendered slurs, for example.

I kept the account private so it didn't affect other users or proactively pollute social media sites with more hate. For days, I popped my troll hat on and had a scroll. It did make me wonder whether I risked becoming one myself.

Two weeks later, the results were in. First, the winners. At that time back in 2021, Barry's TikTok account contained nothing abusive – and his Twitter profile suggested only a handful of accounts posting anti-women content. Then, the losers. YouTube had suggested our account watch further videos with misogynistic content – and the dummy Instagram and Facebook accounts were suggested predominantly misogynistic pages and accounts, which became more extreme. They included posts mocking and condoning rape and sexual harassment, and content containing links to the incel movement – an internet subculture that encourages men to blame women for the problems in their lives. It's been linked to countless acts of violence – including a shooting in Plymouth in 2021.

Imagine logging on day in, day out and seeing these kinds of posts. Not only does it possibly tap into and exacerbate your own fears and concerns, but it normalizes them. You think that others are seeing this. The social media sites are actively sending you towards more of this content. Surely that makes it all fine?

Chloe Colliver fears this increases the risk not only that the user cements and evolves those misogynistic views, but is emboldened to send out more hate. After all, they are under the impression that it's acceptable for these views to spread from their feeds.

But why would the social media sites be directing Barry's profile to more content that promotes harmful ideologies?

For Chloe, it ultimately comes down to profit. If you send users towards content they might have an interest in, however horrible, they're more likely to stay logged on and spend longer viewing that content. The more extreme the content becomes, the higher the chances that their interaction and time on the platform will increase. 'Sensational, extreme or anger-inducing content keeps your attention longer, makes you engage more with the content on the site, and therefore allows them to sell more adverts because you are spending more time on the service.'

According to Statista, an online platform that specializes in market and consumer data, Facebook made around $53.53 per user in the US and Canada[25] – and more for the hyper-engaged accounts that spend a lot of time online. Meta, which owns Facebook and Instagram, told us it tries not to recommend content that breaks its rules, and is improving its technology 'to find and remove abuse more quickly'. It also said 'protecting' its community is 'more important than maximizing profits'. Meanwhile YouTube said it has 'strict policies' on hate and 'quickly' removes content that breaks its rules. Neither social media site agreed to an interview with me. But after I reached out about the investigation, Meta announced new measures to tackle sexualized hate targeting journalists, politicians and celebrities on its sites.

Both companies pointed towards the measures they already had in place to protect women from abuse. Those include suspending, restricting or even shutting down accounts sending hate. But my experience suggests it doesn't always work that way in practice. I reported an account sending rape threats and gendered slurs to me to Facebook when I received them. Months later, the account remained on platform, as did tens of Instagram and Twitter accounts that were sending me abuse. And my experience isn't unusual. New research by the Centre for Countering Digital Hate has shown how 97 per cent of accounts sending misogynistic abuse on Twitter and Instagram remain on the site after being reported.[26]

* * * *

What about the women on the receiving end of the abuse from the real accounts? From global politicians to doctors on the front lines, I've heard from dozens who have been subjected to hate just for doing their jobs. And their experiences all follow a pattern.

A woman, often in public life but not always, puts her head above the parapet. She decides to post on social media and then the trolls descend, parroting abusive slurs. Often, one or two push it further, sending a rape or death threat. The woman in question isn't sure what to do. She finds the response of the social media platforms does little to quell the hate. She doesn't want to worry her family and friends. She isn't sure whether to call it out or not, and in the end she decides to speak to someone like me because she's decided enough is enough. She might also have experienced racist or homophobic abuse, depending on who she is. I'm fortunate to never experience this kind of hate myself.

I wanted to test in real-time how abuse is directed at women versus men in the online world. Ellen Judson, from the think tank Demos, suggested reality TV was the place to start comparing online hate for two main reasons: it often neatly splits contestants by gender and includes those from different demographics – plus it invites online comments from people about who they do and don't like. Enlisting the help of Demos, I took a look at contestants from two shows with an equal gender split – *Love Island* and *Married at First Sight* in 2021. The think tank then trawled through over 90,000 online posts and comments on Reddit and Twitter.

They found the female contestants were disproportionately targeted on social media – and that the hate was frequently rooted in misogyny. On Twitter, 26 per cent of posts about female contestants were abusive, versus 14 per cent of those directed at men. The abuse directed at women was much more focused on gender than the abuse directed at male contestants, talking about sex acts, using gendered slurs and focusing on gender-based tropes. Women were described as sneaky, manipulative and evil – as well as sexual and stupid. The hate intensified for women who were black and Asian – and they also received racist abuse.

Online abuse can seem uniquely bad when it comes to reality TV. After all, the format encourages viewers to comment about programmes on social media and contestants' Instagram followings skyrocket. So often, though, remarks online go beyond criticism or challenge. Racist and misogynistic hate isn't something anyone should be experiencing while they attempt to do what is effectively their job.

There's another debate that arises around online abuse. Does tackling it pose a risk to freedom of expression? Some argue that by tackling trolls on social media – taking down hate they post, suspending the accounts sending out abuse – we are censoring conversation. Their view is that this abuse is just an accepted part of the social media world and that it would happen offline anyway.

I disagree. Having investigated the impact this hate can have on its targets, the testimony from those affected suggests online hate stifles their right to express themselves. Women have told me how they are fearful of posting. Sharing their opinion or thoughts or even just a picture isn't worth it, because of the hate they will experience in return. They post less – or decide to log off altogether. Doing something about it is actually a way of protecting their ability to speak without fear.

That, of course, does ultimately limit the ability of trolls, or anyone, to share exactly what they want to say on social media – but only when it's abusive. When I've spoken to people who have worked at different social media sites tasked with dealing with this issue, they readily admit that there is a trade-off between protecting users and allowing people to share anything they want. Do we really want an online world where anything is fair game? After all, in person, freedom of expression has its limits too. The majority of people wouldn't defend your right to walk up to someone in the street screaming a rape threat – and it likely wouldn't pass without consequence.

In 2012, Julia Gillard, then Australia's prime minister, made a monumental speech about misogyny directed at the opposition leader Tony Abbott, stating 'If he wants to know what misogyny looks like in modern Australia, he doesn't need a motion in the House of Representatives, he needs a mirror.' When she finished talking, there was silence, followed by cheers.

That speech resonated beyond the four walls of Australia's parliament building with women of all ages and political stripes. And it still resonates today – so much so that it recently spread to a new audience on TikTok. Young women lip-sync the words to her speech as they put on their make-up. For them, her argument feels relevant more than a decade later.

When I met Julia to talk to her about how online hate deters women from entering public life, it was hard to get that speech out of my head.

'I think [online hate] is designed to exclude, to intimidate women out of the public square,' Julia said, recalling years of sexist abuse. She fears that it is putting women off becoming politicians – or entering public life at all.

Demos analysed comments on online forums in which women revealed they were logging off social media or being put off doing certain jobs over fears of online abuse. They examined eighty-seven posts referring to misogynistic hate – which was by no means a representative sample, but presented 'a cross-section of how women speak about their experiences of abuse online', according to Ellen Judson, who led the research.

In the eighty-seven posts they found, women shared the negative impact of social media on their mental health. Several said they planned to leave specific platforms altogether. They said things like 'at the moment, it makes me want to quit everything I do online'. Several women also detailed the hate they'd experienced, including being calling a 'hideous fucking slut' and a 'stupid bitch'.

I've thought on several occasions about quitting specific social media sites, especially since my abuse on Twitter seems to have skyrocketed. I never want the trolls to win, though, and often my best tips for the investigations I do come from people who get in touch with me on these platforms.

The online abuse I've been talking about so far has unfolded in places with democratically elected governments and that – at least in theory – protect freedom of expression. Online abuse in autocracies brings a whole new level of risk, especially in terms of the offline violence connected to online hate.

These are often people who have dedicated their lives to fighting for freedom of expression. Take for example Nobel Peace Prize winner Maria Ressa. The online abuse and offline harassment she experiences was studied extensively by a team from the International Center for Journalists for UNESCO and deemed one of the most extreme they'd ever encountered.

Maria and her team of journalists at the news website Rappler in the Philippines have found themselves constantly targeted for their reporting on then president Rodrigo Duterte's 'war on drugs'. Under his leadership, those connected to drugs were brutally killed, with serious repercussions for their families and communities.

Powerful politicians and supporters of Duterte went into overdrive, targeting Maria with false allegations and very personal hate. Those online lies made her doubt herself, doubt her reporting, think that she might have made a mistake. They also, in her view, created an artificial reality, which made others more inclined to believe the misleading claims about her. It's a bandwagon effect. As she has said, 'a lie told a million times becomes a fact'.

'Sixty per cent of the posts [online] were tearing down my credibility. The other 40 per cent were meant to tear down my spirit. It's all about how you look [and] how you sound,' she told me.

It's there every day when you wake up, she explained. And I agree. I hate the way online abuse follows me right up to bedtime and then greets me first thing in the morning. But unlike for me, the risk of violence is incredibly acute for Maria. Those online narratives manifest themselves very directly with offline behaviour and action carried out by supporters of the former president.

Maria and her team wear bulletproof vests when out in Manila, the capital of the Philippines, because they fear the repercussions of this online opposition. 'When the hate started coming in, we had supporters of the president come to the office. They dox us, ask people to attack us, behead us.' She talked me through all the tips and techniques, all of the security advice and resources she has to follow just to keep herself and her team alive and safe. These are measures they have to take just so they can keep doing their jobs.

According to the Center for Media Freedom and Responsibility, by the end of 2020 nineteen journalists had been killed under Duterte's administration. On top of that, between June 2016 and April 2020 there were more than 170 cases where journalists – like Maria – were threatened or attacked.[27]

Maria, who has spent a lot of time investigating disinformation tactics used by the government, is uniquely equipped to analyse the barrage of abuse she's experienced that employs many of those techniques. She told me it had been both 'a blessing and a curse' to be at the heart of this, though her colleagues sometimes wonder why she keeps on looking at the hate.

In her view, the responsibility for the online hate aimed at her and female journalists all over the world lies not just with the individuals encouraging and partaking in it, but with the social media sites that host it. 'This isn't about freedom of speech, it's about freedom of reach. Algorithms amplify lies laced with anger and hate.'

* * * *

What's the solution to hate on social media that targets women in particular? That's a question I've asked a range of activists and policymakers who are campaigning for social media sites to better protect women online. In their eyes, defending women's freedom of expression is vital for a healthy and functioning democracy and society. Abuse in the online world is diminishing hard-won women's rights. Things will only improve drastically when there are major structural and cultural changes at the social media companies themselves, Dr Julie Posetti from the International Center for Journalists explains. That requires both the companies and the policymakers to take this issue seriously.

'We would like to see gender-based online violence treated at least as seriously as disinformation has been during the pandemic by the platforms,' explains Dr Posetti. While it seemed to take social media sites longer to get to grips with disinformation in those early months of the pandemic, they did introduce new measures to remove content and ban accounts sharing false and potentially harmful claims about health-related issues. But since then, there's been some controversy about how they decided who and what to suspend, ban and remove – and what power the social media sites should be allowed in order to deal with this kind of content.

Several social media sites now try to de-prioritize anti-vaccine or conspiracy content so it's not pushed proactively by their algorithms. But the undercover troll account I set up under the name Barry suggests that content hostile towards women is still being actively promoted.

Dr Posetti and her team have also called for social media sites to introduce labels for accounts that have previously sent abuse, and any other accounts the user creates. Think back to the healthcare worker who loved vegan cooking and sending me online hate. His many accounts could be visibly flagged to other users if that happened.

They want to see human moderators making the decisions about offensive material, rather than automated software. For example, threatening photographs hinting at your location but which don't feature violent language would not necessarily be removed under current rules. It's hard for a computer to differentiate between a menacing post and an innocent photograph of a front door. Dr Posetti has also suggested an early warning system for users if they think online abuse could escalate into real-world harm.

Ultimately, though, these new tools to protect women would just be a Band-Aid to put over a larger problem with the way algorithms work and the content social media sites reward.

I have previously given evidence to a parliamentary committee in the UK about the findings of my investigations on this topic. They've been working on new legislation – the Online Safety Bill – that would force social media companies to share commitments to protecting users with the British regulator Ofcom, and then share the evidence that it has upheld those commitments. At that time, big questions remained about whether social media sites will have to demonstrate they are protecting women – not just children –

children – from hate and abuse on their platforms, and whether they'll have a duty to make sure their algorithms are keeping people safe. The first step in Dr Posetti's eyes, though, is having a public conversation about online hate that puts pressure on everyone to do more.

* * * *

The sinking feeling in my stomach when England missed those three penalties in the Euro 2021 final against Italy was not just because England's hopes were dashed. It was because I thought almost immediately about how those players were going to receive a lot of racist hate online.

Marcus Rashford, Jadon Sancho and Bukayo Saka all subsequently found themselves the targets of a barrage of abuse on social media. Monkey emojis and abusive slurs soon began popping up the night of the match – often shared in public comments and tweets. You could only begin to imagine the messages that must have been shared via direct message. And it spilled out onto the streets too. A mural that honoured Rashford in Withington, the suburb of Manchester where he'd grown up, was defaced.

The only relief was the wave of love that followed. That mural was decorated with Post-it notes and letters. And online there was an outpouring of support from fans who were disgusted to see that racist hate happen. The majority of people, including celebrities and politicians, came out in condemnation of the abuse.

There wasn't just love, support and outrage. There was action, too. Accounts were flagged and social media sites swooped in to remove the worst of it. Police arrested eleven people in a hate crimes investigation, and the UK Football Policing Unit received 600 reports of racist comments directed at England players. At least three have since been charged, receiving prison sentences and fines.

Almost exactly a year before this happened, I'd been hearing from a young man around the same age as these players. He'd also been on the receiving end of racist hate online, though nothing had been done at all to protect him. His name is Momo.

For Momo, the hate didn't start with a missed penalty. One day he received a confusing message from a journalist on Instagram, in which they were asking him whether he was the protester captured on video atop the Cenotaph war memorial in London, seemingly trying to burn a Union Jack. He had no idea what it was all about, so at first he ignored the message. But soon a friend sent him a Facebook post featuring Momo's photo and a caption. Threats and abuse dominated the comments. 'He should be hanged, drawn and quartered!' and 'Go back to your country!' were two of the first that greeted him. Others were much, much worse.

Suddenly, he put two and two together. This had all started when he'd joined the peaceful anti-racism protests happening in London on 3 June. The murder of George Floyd – a 46-year-old black man who'd died after being arrested outside a shop in Minneapolis, Minnesota, the previous month – had moved him and others to action. Footage of Floyd's arrest showed a white police officer, Derek Chauvin, kneeling on his neck while he was pinned to the floor. Chauvin has since been convincted of murder.

Momo had wanted to highlight the roots of racism in the UK as well. He'd donned a red, white and blue anorak and headed out into the drizzle with a few friends, carrying a sign that read 'The UK invented racism'. They'd marched and chanted, and a few hours later Momo returned home.

He'd deliberated for a few days about posting the photo of himself protesting on his social media accounts, but eventually did on the following Monday, 8 June. In the image, he is wearing that distinct jacket and showing his sign.

Unbeknownst to him, something significant had happened in between. The previous day, another anti-racism protest had been held in central London. Although mostly peaceful, it was marred in the evening by a smaller, violent group. Twelve arrests were made and eight police officers were injured, following similar scenes the day before. The Cenotaph Flag incident happened in the middle of the melee. Pictures and news reports clearly showed a woman atop the monument's plinth. Like Momo three days before, she was wearing a red, white and blue anorak.

That's where the similarity ends, however. Momo bears little resemblance to the woman pictured on the monument. They have different face shapes and builds, and if you look closely, the pattern on their anoraks is clearly different. But there is one thing they do have in common: they are both black. 'It's become clear to me that this isn't about naming and shaming the person who set fire to the flag. Instead it's about targeting a black person with abuse,' Momo explained.

At the time, the Metropolitan Police said that a twenty-year-old woman was arrested on suspicion of criminal damage in connection with the incident at the Cenotaph. She was bailed to a later date in July. Still, that police report did nothing to stop the trolls.

This was clearly a case of mistaken identity – obvious to anyone who bothered to do even the most cursory check. But more and more accounts started publishing Momo's real name and sharing his image alongside the false allegations. Momo didn't panic until his brother noticed one particular tweet. His picture had been shared by a Twitter account which had previously posted messages opposing the Black Lives Matter movement and supporting US President Donald Trump. 'This is the scumbag who thought it was a good idea to set the Union Jack on fire on Whitehall,' the account wrote. 'I hope he is proud of himself, the filthy rat.'

Although the account didn't have a huge following, thousands of people retweeted and commented on the post. It triggered outrage from certain social media users, and the replies were littered with racist abuse. I messaged the account to tell them they were wrong, and so did Momo and his friends. But there was no response. Momo's picture then made its way onto Facebook and Reddit. In one group, the poster declared:

'Let's make this scumbag famous.' That post racked up 1,500 shares and hundreds of comments.

Momo decided not to remove the original photo from his social media accounts. He didn't want to have to censor himself online because of the harassment. And while some friends messaged him in shock about what was happening, chipping in to help report posts and accounts, Momo wasn't surprised at all.

'This whole situation really highlights the dehumanization of black people online,' he told me, exhausted after hours of speaking to the police and family. 'People just see a picture, people just see a face. People don't see a human with a family.'

At the time, Facebook did remove the posts promoting false information about Momo – and explained to me how they don't tolerate bullying. In contrast, Twitter told me that 'users cannot promote violence against, threaten or harass other people on the basis of race, ethnicity or other protected groups'. But the company also said that the original, viral false tweet was not in violation of its rules.

The failure to remove the posts sparked outrage. England footballer Rio Ferdinand was one of many who tweeted about my report concerning Momo's story. Still, social media sites took little in the way of effective action.

It reminded me of a question I am often asked when people get in touch about online trolling. If action is possible – why doesn't it feel like everyone, not just the well-known, are entitled to it? Social media sites would argue that's not the case, but from reporting on this for many years it's clear to me that public pressure is linked to action.

Social media experts – like Chloe Colliver from the Institute for Strategic Dialogue – point towards the risk posed to the companies when they deal with hate. Employing more staff who can identify hate, which is often complex in nature, and investing in more software costs money. Removing the accounts of trolls, who are often active users, costs money. The only time this tends to be trumped is when the risk to their reputation – and therefore financial risk – is higher, as happened when famous footballers were the target. Social media sites are in the spotlight, and if they're not seen to doing enough there can be repercussions from policymakers and advertisers worried about their own reputations.

That makes a case for speaking out about online abuse, and not just suffering in silence. Victims point out, though, that the onus shouldn't be on them to enact real change. They want everyone to be protected on social media – not just the rich and famous.

* * * *

When it comes to violence and aggression, both online and off, it's not just social media sites which have the power to do something. Under the Malicious Communications Act in the UK – in theory, at least – law enforcement can do something too.

I decided to report some of the hate I was receiving to the police back in 2021. I chose the most extreme abuse – including death threats, rape threats, and harassment riddled with hateful language and misogynistic slurs. Rather than offering any reassurance or some kind of a solution, though, I was left feeling frustrated. Conversations with several different officers left me with a bad taste in my mouth – this feeling that I was overreacting to online abuse and because I was 'resilient' it was just something I was expected to endure. It's often fallen to me to interrogate the trolls, find out more about their identities, and then inform the police.

When I first gathered together and reported a whole bunch of screengrabs and accounts to send over as evidence, I was assigned to officers who had no specialist knowledge and who told me they didn't know how to use some of the social media sites in question. They asked me to go back through the very abusive messages to label exactly which social media site each screengrab was from. I can assure you that wasn't a very fun task.

When I raised concerns that people sending me hate might turn up at my work, I was just told to call 999 if I felt in danger. Months and months went by with few updates – and by the time I exposed all of this via a documentary for BBC *Panorama* there had been little progress, even though I believe the messages I'd been subjected to were in breach of the Malicious Communications Act.

Since that investigation, the Metropolitan Police has been caught up in scandal after scandal – often relating to misogyny. There's been increased pressure to tackle violence against women after the killings of Sarah Everard and Sabina Nessa, and damning reports pointing out institutional sexism. Seeing the hateful messages about women exchanged between officers revealed in other cases related to misconduct, my own experience with the Met seemed even less surprising. In response to the *Panorama* investigation, the Met told me that they took online hate very seriously and that my case was under active investigation.

After I revealed my experience with the police in some of my reporting, there was a flurry of interest again from officers but with no real consequence. On one occasion, an officer turned up to find out more information about my case, forgot to take a statement and then asked me to show her 'something cool at the BBC'. The trolls largely remain online, the online hate continues. I'm just more used to it now. The police have taken the incidents of offline abuse more seriously since.

I dread to think about what it's like for women who don't have the support of an organization or colleagues who understand this, like I do. I'm unusual in having so much support. Many of those I've spoken to have nowhere to turn. They don't feel like anyone has been paying attention to even the most violent hate they receive.

We've accepted online hate as part of the fabric of our society, as though it's just something that we should expect now social media exists. As a consequence, the onus falls on the individual to call out and battle these trolls. For far too long we've been encouraged to ignore them, and in a way people are right to point out that indulging the trolls can often inflame the hate. It gives them the attention they often crave. There's no point in getting in arguments with individual accounts sharing abuse. The trolls as a collective, though, are more than random people who decide to express their anger and views in an unacceptable way online. Trolling is a tool used to silence and intimidate. It has a goal.

The reality is that if we do not highlight the issue of violent rhetoric and abuse online, those who can do something about it are let off the hook. From footballers, journalists and reality TV stars to librarians and female firefighters, some have bravely taken a stand. In return, social media sites, policymakers and the authorities have been urged to do more.

There has already been offline harassment directly linked to trolls or conspiracy theory activists, and from those I speak to – whether victims targeted or experts embedded in the social media underbelly – there remain concerns about how this could evolve. Based on the trolls in my direct messages, it seems the committed minority who use hate to target the people they disagree with are becoming more radical in both the severity of the threats they send and their intensity.

This escalation in online abuse has normalized aggression offline to such an extent that I really think that it would only require one person deciding to take it that much further for a really terrible act to unfold on UK soil. The responsibility lies with authorities and social media companies to do what they can about how trolling works – and the very real impact it has. In the meantime, I just continue to long for the day that I don't look over one shoulder as I walk home.

7

BOT OR NOT? HOW STATE-SPONSORED DISINFORMATION WORKS

Trolls are not only members of online conspiracy movements or abusive fans – they are also used as part of wider state disinformation campaigns. This chapter is about just how complicated disinformation and influence operations sponsored by governments and bad actors have become.

I want to start by telling you the story of two 4-year-old boys. Omar Bilal al-Banna and Omer Siman-Tov lived roughly 23 kilometres apart, on either side of the Israel-Gaza perimeter fence. They never met, but both loved playing outside with their siblings.

The faces of these little boys appeared on my social media feed as the war began to unfold between Israel and Hamas in October 2023. They were both killed in the violence, only the posts I was seeing were not what I expected. Accounts on social media were denying their deaths. I tracked down family, friends and witnesses. In both cases they told a tragic story. Omer Siman-Tov was killed when Hamas attacked his home in Kibbutz Nir Oz on 7 October. Omar Bilal al-Banna was killed four days later, following an Israeli airstrike on Zeitoun, east of Gaza City.

The denial of both of their deaths online is symbolic of how information battles are waged in parallel with fighting on the ground; a battle often waged or led by the powerful in a bid to control – and at times distort – the online conversation. The most brazen state-backed disinformation I've encountered has been attempts to downplay or deny violence committed against innocent civilians – often children, which shock and distress the family, friends and witnesses who know what really happened.

The first online post I saw about Omar al-Banna's death was from a pro-Israeli account on Twitter/X. It included a video, featuring a man in a grey polo shirt holding a small child's body, wrapped in a white blanket or cloth. In the accompanying caption, the person who shared the clip declared: 'Hamas is desperate!' They added falsely that the group – classified as a terrorist organisation by Israel, the UK and other powers – had 'released a video showing a dead Palestinian baby. But wait for the catch. It's not a real baby; it's a doll'.

This user said it 'exposes how hard the lying and slanderous propaganda arm of Hamas and the Palestinians works'. They suggested Hamas accounts had shared and then deleted the video because it wasn't real. According to Twitter, that post containing the video and false claims has been seen 3.8 million times. The allegations it made were then amplified by the State of Israel's official account on Twitter. It shared a new post, this time featuring that same video of the child in the white blanket

– and then a still from the same video, circling the child's face. In the caption, the account wrote: 'Hamas accidentally posted a video of a doll (yes a doll) suggesting that it was a part of casualties caused by an IDF [Israel Defense Forces] attack.'

In the hours that followed, other official accounts on Twitter – including profiles belonging to Israel's embassies in France and Austria – repeated the claims. Before long, they were being spread by pro-Israel and anti-Hamas accounts based in Israel, as well as several that seemed to be based in India. Each time, the posts would say the child was a doll. I have watched the extended footage myself, and it's clear from the video that this is a real person.

I tracked the original video back to the Instagram page of a Palestinian photographer, Moamen El Halabi. He filmed the clip of the man in the grey shirt holding Omar, and I got in touch with him. I also made contact with another photojournalist, Mohammed Abed – who works for the AFP news agency – who was there at the same time. He took a photograph of the same man holding what appears to be the same child, wrapped in the white sheet.

Both photojournalists provided me with further details to corroborate that the video and the photo had been taken at Al-Shifa hospital, outside the mortuary on 12 October 2023. The details included information about the situation at the hospital that day, and the man in the grey shirt, who was a relative of Omar's. They both told me, categorically, that the child pictured had not been a doll, but a real little boy – Omar.

They also shared additional images, which I have matched up with Moamen El Halabi's original video footage to verify the child's identity.

After we spoke, Mohammed Abed then posted an Instagram story with the photo he took. He declares in the caption: 'This picture [is] not a doll, its [one] I took at Al-Shifa hospital and it's the very truth.' It seems that part of what made people think what they saw was a doll, rather than a child, was the colour of Omar's skin in the photograph. But Mohammed said he had photographed several children killed in strikes in Gaza and their skin looked similar.

'The candle of my life' is how Omar Bilal al-Banna's mother Yasmeen describes her children on Instagram. The two photographers put me in touch with her, and I matched up her profiles on social media with the details available to me to confirm her identity as Omar's mother. I found it hard to hold back tears as I watched montages she'd shared of her children with cuddly toys; images from more peaceful times.

Omar had been playing outside with his older brother Majd when he was killed. I've seen footage where Majd confirms this, describing how the strike hit their neighbour's house, and then rubble fell on Omar. Majd was wounded too. In the footage, he seemed to be in shock. His eyes were wide and the colour had drained from his face. His leg was wrapped in a bandage.

Omar's mother Yasmeen confirmed all of this, adding that lies about the 'killing of children and innocent people are untrue and fake'. 'They have no right to say he is a doll,' she said, 'They [the Israeli government] are lying and evading their crimes and massacres.' I reached out to the Israeli embassy in the UK and their spokesperson did not comment directly on these social media posts or on the circumstances of Omar's death. They told the BBC that 'it is very important to review instances of disinformation' but also accused the BBC of spreading misinformation. I didn't hear back from Twitter when I put these allegations to them.

Then, there's the story of Omer Siman-Tov. The photo of him that appeared on my social media feed showed him smiling, surrounded by his parents and sisters. This image was shared by the Israeli government's account on Twitter, the post describing them as 'an entire family wiped out by Hamas terrorists. There are no words. May their memory be a blessing'. It was also shared by the former Israeli prime minister, Naftali Bennett. But when I read the comments below these posts and others – while there were many speaking of the terrible shock and offering support – there were dozens I had not expected to find.

Several accounts that supported Hamas claimed that Omer had been a 'paid actor' because Hamas 'didn't kill kids'. Others said this was 'Jewish propaganda at its finest', declaring that neither Omer, nor his sisters, had been killed. One wrote 'there's no evidence' they were dead and asked to 'stop the lying'. Some suggested that he and his sisters had been 'crisis actors' – the term you're probably well acquainted with by now used to describe people paid to act out a tragedy.

I wanted to figure out more about the profiles behind the comments. Many of them appeared to be real people based around the world. Several actively supported Hamas, and a couple appeared to be based in the occupied West Bank. These were not accounts with huge followings. However, the cumulative effect of their posts seemed to bolster wider, viral social media narratives trying to suggest that Hamas had not killed or attacked any children, in spite of widespread evidence of this violence. Other untrue comments I spotted suggested that the murders had been real, but that Hamas gunmen had not been responsible. One user wrote, 'I guess it's Israel themselves' who killed these children and the Israelis were 'trying to blame Hamas'.

'Omer was just an angel. He was so, so beautiful and cute and pure. He was very close to his sisters. They were always playing together and they were so kind to him,' Mor Lacob, a friend of the Siman-Tov family, told me.

She messaged them on WhatsApp on the sunny Saturday morning when Hamas gunmen broke through the Gaza perimeter fence and attacked their kibbutz. She told me they confirmed to her that they had managed to get into their shelter, but that was the last she heard. Further messages sent to her friends were left unread. Mor Lacob later found out that Omer's parents, Tamar and Yonatan, had been shot dead. Their three children – Omer plus his older sisters Shachar and Arbel – were killed when their home was set on fire. Their deaths have been covered in the media. Speaking to me from her home in Sydney,

Australia, Mor Lacob said the comments on social media had caused her extra distress at a time when she was grieving her friends. She described this kind of disinformation as 'evil and cruel'.

'I just want the world to remember and to know what happened. To deal with their death is hard enough, and all these comments make it even worse,' she told me. 'How can I respond to that? I need to prove they died? Why did five graves need to be filled with their beautiful bodies?'

When I told her how Palestinian children too, like Omar, had had their deaths denied and questioned on social media as well, she became upset again. 'My heart goes out to every single innocent [person] who got murdered and killed because of Hamas's actions,' she said. 'It's not fair.'

The stories of Omar and Omer expose the way that governments and political groups can share shocking examples of disinformation when it bolsters an existing narrative. The seed can be planted, or watered, by the posts and claims coming from the mouths and social media profiles of those in charge, and then all it takes is some real people who believe them – or in some cases what could be fake accounts – to spread the message.

Rather than this chapter focusing on the regimented armies of bots alone, it's instead about the messy online landscape that state-sponsored disinformation now inhabits. It is populated by real people – from world leaders to the average account, as well as what we'd call inauthentic activity. The murkier this world becomes, the harder it is to investigate – and its consequences are huge. Not only for families enduring personal grief during war, but for everyone trying to figure out what's really happening during battles of both violence and words. For Omer and Omar, it's really important we all understand the tactics at play, why this matters – and the responsibility both those in charge and social media companies have for how this plays out.

* * * *

To give you a bit of a crash course in how state-sponsored disinformation campaigns work, I'll tell you some more about a conversation I had with a man who was on the front line of tackling them.

He worked for Twitter. I rarely get the chance to speak one-to-one with those who work for the big social media companies, but mass lay-offs and resignations at Twitter after Elon Musk's takeover meant people were more willing to speak to me about their work and expertise than I'd experienced before.

I met Ray Serrato in a glamorous flat in San Francisco. At first Ray was reluctant to do an interview on the record, but he decided to speak out over his fears that, under new ownership, these influence operations can run amok. Twitter might not be the biggest of the social media sites, but it is the one most populated by world leaders and journalists, making it a prime target for these kinds of campaigns. Ray worked as part of a team that specialized in dealing with influence operations, having spent a lot of his career working for NGOs and the UN before he joined the social media site. The campaigns he usually dealt with were ones backed by states themselves, and which sought to undermine faith in democracy or to target dissidents and journalists.

'The most prominent examples of influence operations that a lot of people have probably heard about are the operation by Russia's Internet Research Agency to influence the 2016 elections in the US [and] the Myanmar military's influence operation, which was waged against the Rohingya,' Ray explained.

The operations that Ray sought to identify – and remove – often deployed inauthentic accounts to target other users or amplify certain messages. These kinds of accounts are often referred to as 'bots'. They're used to manipulate the conversation on social media by repeatedly pushing the same idea or counter-idea around a certain issue. They can also be used to bombard an individual with hate.

'These are accounts which purport often to be someone or a group of people located somewhere when in fact they're not,' Ray said. These bots can be increasingly convincing – and sometimes 'menacing', to such an extent they endanger not just online ecosystems but wider society too.[28]

Many accounts pushing the same idea online can give the impression that multiple people think the same thing – and therefore bots can 'distort representation of pluralism within the public sphere'.[29] That's beneficial to hostile states as it can undermine democratic discourse – sowing division in another nation.

Twitter invested specifically in teams to tackle this type of manipulation of the platform. Once an influence operation was identified, the accounts involved would be suspended, or the visibility of their posts would be reduced. Ray told me they would identify suspicious activity including employing fake accounts like this 'daily'. After Musk's takeover, however, his two-dozen-strong team was 'decimated' – it still existed, but in a 'minimized capacity'. Ray left the company in November 2021 because he felt there wasn't a clear vision of how to protect users.

'Twitter might have been the refuge where journalists would go out and have their voice heard and be critical of the government. But I'm not sure that's going to be the case anymore,' he told me. 'There are a number of key experts that are no longer in that team that would have covered special regions, or threat actors, from Russia to China.' This was all happening in the context of increasingly heightened tensions between the US and countries – like Russia and China – that had been previously accused of using influence operations to distort narratives and sow division.

The focus of this chapter will be Russian disinformation tactics, but the playbook they've employed is one used by states and governments all around the world. Russia just seems to be the leader at this.

* * * *

How likely are you to come across an influence operation or be affected by one? These days it can be hard to figure out, but perhaps by applying some of Ray's advice we can begin to spot the more complicated ones.

These sorts of operations really entered the public consciousness back at the time of the 2016 election in the US, and since then social media sites have been in a race to keep up.

That year a company called the Internet Research Agency, which specialized in carrying out online influence operations benefitting Russia's political and business interests, was accused by the US intelligence community of using troll farms to support Donald Trump in his run to become president. Based in St Petersburg and linked to Russian oligarch Yevgeny Prigozhin, the company was associated with networks of inauthentic accounts that seemed to share divisive content around key issues, triggering argument and outrage among social media users who disagreed with each other and the post at hand.

Their goal appeared to be to destabilize rival Western democracies by fuelling division and encouraging distrust in institutions. Troll farms also appeared to support Russia's military actions in Ukraine following the invasion of Crimea, and in the Middle East too. Essentially, they would distort the conversation, so that both Russian people and those in the West were under the impression there was widespread support for these actions – and as a consequence, real users were encouraged to show their support too.

People became much savvier and better at spotting these original bots, who would often steal other people's photos and use broken English. For that reason, tactics became more sophisticated. Let's look at a couple of examples of possible influence operations, and figure out whether they really are or not.

* * * *

Ultimately, it's hard for me to ever know whether these accounts were part of a more coordinated network or not. Only the social media sites, and intelligence agencies, hold that information, which they don't share widely. However, spotting when accounts are looking to capitalize on division and use it to push a particular narrative is a very effective way of figuring out whether some kind of influence operation might be playing out.

There's evidence, too, that people can unwittingly find themselves recruited to serve influence operations.

Around the time of the 2020 US election, Facebook revealed how it had dismantled a smaller network of accounts and pages that were part of an operation run by the Internet Research Agency. It was linked to the site Peace Data, which pushed opinion pieces in English and Arabic. Real writers and bloggers had been recruited by fake LinkedIn accounts to produce polarizing pieces on opposite extremes of the political spectrum. Realistic identities, AI-generated photographs and good English meant US bloggers who found themselves writing for the site were none the wiser at the time about the people in Russia who were falsely posing as editors and commissioning them to write for the site. The success of this network was limited, since the operation was identified fairly early on, before its articles really succeeded in sowing division or inflaming tensions. However, it raised serious questions about the interactions between real people and influence operations.

That was something I found myself thinking about when I was in Berlin in May 2023. I was there to meet a man called Markus, who used to write for a conspiracy theory newspaper.

We chatted in a radio and music studio in downtown Berlin. Markus was dressed smartly in a light blue shirt. A lawyer and activist, he felt energized by the issues that had come up during the pandemic – opposing the then-possible introduction of mandatory vaccinations, and lockdown restrictions.

Markus had attended anti-lockdown rallies, first across Germany and then in Spain, Italy, Austria and Belgium. It was at one of these rallies he met the editor of a conspiracy theory newspaper that had started in Germany called *Demokratischer Widerstand* or *Democratic Resistance*.

The reason Markus had decided to speak to me was over his fears that this conspiracy theory newspaper had become more extreme – both in its pages and on social media. 'The newspaper went more radical and there were some polls in the Telegram channel,' he told me, describing votes calling for the death penalty and the beating of people they saw complicit in the pandemic. 'You cannot ask the question is it OK to beat people wearing masks, and later is it OK to get a death penalty for those who made these Covid measures? What are you doing?'

He decided he didn't want to write for the paper anymore. And he couldn't understand why others didn't take more of a stand. 'You cannot say, OK, on Twitter, I'm nice. And on Telegram I say kill them all. This doesn't work, and then you have to say, OK, stop. I won't give my name for that newspaper.'

Markus and another whistle-blower I spoke to suggested that there is a link between the *Democratic Resistance* paper and the Reichsbürger group. According to them, writers from the paper and one of its key donors met with members of the group. Some of those they met were later arrested and charged over the alleged coup attempt in the country in December 2022.

At the time, the group's members said they were prepared to kill to install a new leader in Germany – and prosecutors said the group was extremely dangerous. Multiple sources have also told me how the paper promotes far-right groups, posting about them on Telegram and attending rallies with them. That includes right-wing group Freie Sachsen and the National Democratic Party of Germany, described as a far-right neo-Nazi political party.

I tried to reach out to the paper's editor, Anselm Lenz, to arrange an interview, but he refused. In his email response, he said I was 'a highly paid Nato and BBC Propagandist' and that I was a threat to him and his family.

Though he was denouncing the paper to me, Markus was still somewhat part of the wider conspiracy theory movement. I quizzed him on the muddling of legitimate concerns with more extreme conspiracy theories and disinformation. He told me that members of the movement did have 'real concerns about man-made climate change and about 9/11'.

'Sometimes the conspiracy theories are true. Like the Iraq war, there were no weapons of mass destruction. If we had had this interview in 2005, then I would have been a conspiracy theorist,' he said. 'George Bush used this [claim] to make the war, which killed a lot of people. And that's my problem with big parts of mainstream media. You have the one story. You try to frame people.'

In his view, the media promoted the idea that 'our Western society is always good and the others are always bad'. He believed the truth lay somewhere in the middle.

Since he was still on the inside of the conspiracy theory movement and connected to various key people, there was more he could tell me. According to Markus, Kremlin-linked figures in Russia had offered support – including financial help – to members of the wider conspiracy theory movement in Germany, so that they could continue to push divisive and pro-Russian disinformation, especially about the war in Ukraine.

This came as no surprise to me at all. As Russian tanks rolled over the border into Ukraine in that freezing February of 2022, those who had taken to pushing the idea that the pandemic and vaccines were part of a sinister plot started to say the same about the war. It was a hoax. Putin was somehow a saviour. I've interviewed multiple people who believe this here in the UK too, using terms like 'crisis actors' to deny the reality of what's going on.

If you're running a state-sponsored disinformation campaign, these movements are hugely useful for you. The pandemic – a moment of huge disruption, fear and uncertainty – brought with it this online movement in the Western world devoted to undermining facts and science. One fuelled by conspiracy theories that have tapped into genuine distrust and political criticism. These seemingly organic groups on social media are a secret weapon for the likes of Russia. While the exact role of hostile states in fanning the flames of these grass-roots movements is very hard to know, it is clear they are beneficial. They work in the same way as bot networks, pushing pro-Russian ideas.

* * * *

It's important to remember too that sometimes it's not a case of an influence operation at all. There are relentless allegations about so-called bot networks, but many of them are without evidence. Every time accounts copy and paste the same message – whether in support of a British prime minister or particular political cause – I receive endless messages asking me whether it's bots. In some ways, those constant calls that any kind of manipulation online must be state-backed and coming out of a basement in St Petersburg – like the Internet Research Agency – helps to fulfil the goals of those who set up networks like this in the first place. Debate over what's a fake account and what isn't divides us. It diverts everyone's attention away from other disinformation campaigns worthy of investigation.

One morning during the depths of the pandemic I woke to find my phone pinging relentlessly. Message after message from people asking me to investigate a new bot network that had been uncovered. One man had shared an image of a Twitter profile. He claimed that the Department of Health was behind a network of accounts posing as NHS staff. This main account was posting pro-government content praising its handling of the pandemic in a very simplistic way. The account and its posts went viral, hopping over from Twitter to Facebook. At a time of heightened government criticism it was the perfect storm. The cries about influence operations came thick and fast.

I set out to try to investigate the main account, which this person claimed was part of a wider network. The first hurdle I stumbled upon in this case was locating the account itself. It didn't appear to exist anymore. There was only a single screengrab of one of the fake accounts, and the cache of tweets posted under the Twitter handle.

The account used the name 'NHS Susan' – and claimed to belong to a junior doctor. The red flags almost immediately started to show. The photo attached to the account was of a real NHS nurse, who had a different name. I used a reverse image search to find the original picture, which she'd shared months before along with other pictures of her, which confirmed her identity. The account didn't belong to her.

The description in the fake account's bio said she was 'transitioning in 2020' and 'fighting COVID on behalf of all LGBTQ & non-binary people'. 'Susan' was also said to be deaf. Several tweets expressed similar sentiments. The clues were pointing towards the profile being satire – or an attempt to provoke a reaction. And the account had absolutely succeeded in doing that.

Posts triggering emotional reactions are much more likely to go viral. Those sharing disinformation often use and abuse emotion 'to foster audience's attention, engagement, and willingness to share content'.[30] After all, when something makes us feel upset, excited or angry, we're much more inclined to engage with it and even pass it on.

To this day, I'm unsure who was behind this account. Twitter did tell me they 'remove any pockets of smaller coordinated attempts to distort or inorganically influence the conversation' – and that they'd seen zero evidence linking the government to this network of fake accounts. The Department of Health and Social Care – which had been accused of running this network – said this allegation was 'categorically false'. Let's face it, I'm not sure whether their capacity at the height of that first lockdown really stretched to running NHS Susan's account. My guess is that, if this was part of any kind of influence operation, it would be wiser to look at who would benefit from creating accounts that cause disruption and division, rather than just flatly supporting government policy. By sparking outcry about the possibility of a UK state-run bot campaign, this single account without having to really post much at all had inflamed tensions and undermined faith in authority.

The man who shared the screengrab of NHS Susan's account with me repeatedly discussed handing over more details about this network of accounts, but that never came to fruition. NHS Susan disappeared like all of those early pandemic fads – loo-roll hoarding, sanitizing everything in sight, and being told off for sitting down on a park bench to eat a packet of crisps.

The answer doesn't have to be sinister state actors; it's possible it was just people in the UK looking to cause trouble. But in some ways, their willingness to play on the notion of bot networks inadvertently supports the aims of other nations looking to sow division, whether they're linked to those networks or not.

* * * *

Of course, there are the far more obvious forms of state-sponsored disinformation. Recently, the invasion of Ukraine by Russia in particular has highlighted just how complex state misinformation has become. Lies like those targeting Marianna, the pregnant woman who escaped from the hospital in Mariupol, have been brazen and explicitly endorsed by those at the very top.

Here Russia was building on the playbook it had used to deny the reality of the civil war in Syria years before. In that case, the Kremlin denied attacks on civilians despite evidence on the ground that linked them to harm caused to the Syrian people. They would also target groups, like the White Helmets, who contradicted their version of reality. Along with pro-Assad Syrian personalities, they accused the volunteer group, set up during the war to support civilians in danger, of taking sides in the fighting – carrying arms and supporting proscribed terrorist groups.

The truth-tellers fighting Russian propaganda have found themselves subject to similar tactics. One of them is Sergei Buntman. When I sat across from Sergei in his flat in Moscow, I was in awe of his courage. By then he was no longer working at the offices of the radio station – Echo of Moscow – that he'd founded after he had left university. He'd been taken off air.

Sergei has long been attempting to tell Russians the truth about their country, even if it costs him his freedom. He spent decades on the airwaves as part of Moscow's first Russian independent radio station, which he set up in 1990. He and a friend had started it in those heady days of freedom after the fall of the Soviet Union, when independent rather than state-run radio stations and newspapers like this one became possible.

'Radio. It's our friend. [It's] in our head.' His mind returned to his years growing up in Moscow and the joy he'd got from the radio. At the time he set up Echo of Moscow, news and talk shows about different social and political issues filled the airwaves – and the station tried to present a range of views, including those challenging the Russian government.

Even then, there was resistance. More recently, threats came again following Russia's invasion of Crimea in 2014. Not everyone on the radio agreed with the military action.

The quiet courage of the station's journalists was put to the test in 2017, when a presenter was stabbed several times by an intruder. The attack can be seen as a result of the increasingly brazen propaganda efforts from the Kremlin that encouraged people to take action against anyone who disagreed. 'The facts became not at all important,' Sergei explained, 'and the propaganda in this society became very hard, very violent and people became more violent than before.'

It's for that reason that the latest opposition to Echo of Moscow didn't really shock Sergei. Tensions had been building over several years. When Russia invaded Ukraine in late February 2022, to his surprise the radio station was still able to broadcast for those first few days. Then, on 1 March, everything changed.

Sergei remembered being out at a bar. He was grabbing a bite to eat and having a beer. While the people of Kyiv shivered in air raid shelters and fled the life they'd known, Russia attempted to continue like normal. The crippling sanctions were only just starting to take effect.

Glancing at his phone, Sergei saw several messages:

'It's been cut.'

'The station has been taken off air.'

'It's closed.'

He dashed to the radio's office. They were given about two weeks to clear away twenty-eight years of memories. Everything had to be stuffed into boxes. The journalists and presenters were distraught, as were the technicians. Jobs were lost, lives put at risk. For Sergei, clearing out Echo of Moscow's offices was like clearing out the home of a parent after they've died. It was painful watching the life drain out of his radio station so quickly.

Russia's media watchdog says it blocked Echo of Moscow for spreading 'deliberately false information about the actions of Russian military personnel' as well as 'information calling for extremist activity' and 'violence'. Under Russia's new 'fake news' laws, you can go to prison for describing the invasion of Ukraine as a war. In Sergei's view, this was a call made by the very top.

It wasn't just his radio station that was affected either. The TV station Rain was also closed down and the newspaper *Novaya Gazeta* announced it was ceasing production until the war ended.

An important question remained – why now, when Echo of Moscow had survived so much before? In Sergei's eyes, this was Putin's final battle – one that he'd prepared for through Crimea, Georgia and more. These other conflicts weren't so crucial to Putin's survival. The gamble this time seemed greater, and it seemed to be the primary goal of years and years of state-sponsored propaganda.

The journalists weren't planning to give up so easily, though. In Soviet times, to get round censorship, people created their own publications to hand out door to door – an activity called samizdat. Having been taken off air, Sergei and his colleagues refused to stay silent. Instead they effectively created a modern version of samizdat – and turned to reaching their audience online.

Social media ended up being the radio's saviour. They set up new channels where they could reach listeners in Russia – and all over the world. There were fresh ideas as well as the old ones. Sergei's channel on YouTube was called 'Live Nail' and he started working again with Echo of Moscow's editor-in-chief Alex Venediktov.

Like with samizdat many years ago – where people reproduced censored and underground publications – this carried a significant amount of risk. But as Sergei pointed out – tongue in cheek – 'it's impossible to arrest everyone'.

He decided to stay put even as many others understandably fled Moscow. For sixty-six years he's lived in the city, a place his father had helped to build the Metro. 'I think my family made more things than the whole government of Russia,' he said, chuckling. He told me about his grandparents who had fought the Nazis – and yet he was being branded a Nazi by those who believed state narratives spun about anyone who opposed what Russia was doing in Ukraine.

'It's become very dangerous for many journalists, but it's our duty. It's our profession. We have to do it.' That's why he was continuing to try to tell Russians the truth. Even though, in his view, many had been primed to believe the opposite and choose not to seek out the facts. I asked him whether the truth was easy to find in a media landscape constructed from propaganda. He mentioned Telegram channels where there was outside information available – places online where people could turn if they so chose.

Sergei said that, now, when he walked around the streets of the city he loved, he felt as though he didn't recognize the people around him. They were living in another reality he desperately wanted to wake them from. It hurt him that they didn't want to prove to their Ukrainian friends and relatives that they would not stand for war like this.

Echo of Moscow had been replaced on the airwaves by the state-sponsored Sputnik radio. Sergei didn't plan to be tuning in any time soon. But he also saw no merit in sitting at home frightened. He had things to do. Threats, in his eyes, just got in the way.

A few months later, I caught up with Sergei again. I was relieved to learn he was still broadcasting to Russians on YouTube, attempting to tell them the truth. His greatest fear was not being arrested or fined or punished, it was lying – and being complicit in the horror by refusing to counter mistruths.

Sergei is a reminder of how the most dangerous influence operations can be those waged by a government on their own people. It's not just about unsettling Western democracies, but about convincing entire nations of alternative realities.

* * * *

Russia is by no means the only nation guilty of pushing propaganda. All governments do it to some extent, and those disinformation campaigns are especially valuable in autocracies. While it's important we investigate and expose bot networks and tackle the most brazen lies head-on, we have to accept that disinformation campaigns tend to be much messier and more complex than we'd like to think, especially when it comes to twenty-first-century warfare. Disinformation doesn't just operate in neat silos, waged with fake accounts and far away from real people. And there's one story in particular that exemplifies this for me.

In March 2022 I was on the phone to a woman named Tetiana, talking about the war. She told me loved Ukraine, but she was critical of those in power. She would have made an excellent president, she explained to me. Better than any man. The line crackled. She was speaking to me all the way from central Ukraine.

In the early days of the war, Tetiana found her family thrust into the limelight when her son Roman, who she described as 'an ordinary guy from an ordinary family', did an extraordinary thing. The 32-year-old was working as a guard on Snake Island, a small island off the coast of Ukraine in the Black Sea. Roman had become a border guard as a young man, joining a group of thirteen posted to the island. Snake Island is of particular strategic military importance to Ukraine – and is used to defend its territories and waters. That's why the Russian warship *Moskva* turned up so quickly on the first day of war.

Those on board the *Moskva* suggested via radio communication that the border guards on Snake Island surrender. Laying down their weapons was the best way to avoid bloodshed and casualties, they advised. The alternative was to be bombed. The response from one of the border guards was not what they'd anticipated.

'Go fuck yourself.'

The exchange was recorded and shared widely across social media. Those three words had been uttered by Roman, Tetiana's son. In that moment, he became a kind of hero, emblematic of the defiance and bravery and stoicism of ordinary people. He raised spirits, Tetiana told me, and had become a Ukrainian legend at a time when the country most needed it – and that made her very proud.

After that, Russian forces captured the island and the Ukrainian government announced that all of those border guards – Roman included – had been killed. President Zelensky's broadcast reached Tetiana at home, where she was all on her own. They'd be awarded medals, he said – but that was little consolation. Tetiana believed she'd lost her only son.

'I'm sorry, Marianna, but without him, my life just doesn't make sense,' she said to me. 'I call him my diamond. That's all I have in this life. So when he disappeared and there was no news at all, I just didn't want to live. I wouldn't [want] a day on this earth without him.'

Tetiana was fifty-five at the time I spoke to her. She'd wanted to be an English translator, but her late teens had been marred with tragedy and that dream became impossible. Her mum had died, and she'd had to look after her sister. 'My childhood was very difficult because of this hardship – that's what made me such a tough and courageous woman. Even some men can't compare in endurance and their mental strength. And that's how I am as a mother.'

She described Roman's message to the crew of the *Moskva* as 'a cry from the heart and one of courage – one of a person with no way out'. I can't imagine hearing those words from your son broadcast all over the world, thinking that was the last thing he said. Friends and family attempted to console her. They reminded her of her courage and strength.

Then Roman suddenly appeared on Russian TV. He was alive, though apparently he'd been taken prisoner.

The story of Snake Island – which had initially been a powerful nationalist story for Ukraine – now began to be weaponized by the Russians. They attempted to show that the Ukrainian government had lied about the fate of the soldiers in order to make Russia look even worse. Russian senators and politicians deplored the distress it must have caused for relatives and friends. This narrative captured the attention of Russian people – and I've heard many times since how it was proof of the Ukrainian government lying.

In the fog of war, it can be hard to tell what is a concerted effort to mislead – i.e. war strategy and propaganda – and what can just be put down to confusion. While the allegation that the border guards on Snake Island had all died did make them the ultimate martyrs – and Russia the ultimate aggressor – that it turned out not to be true seems more about the chaos of the early days of the conflict than deliberate disinformation.

In the days that followed the attack, Ukrainian authorities tried to get to the bottom of what had happened. A Ukrainian search and rescue ship, *Sapphire*, went to the island on 26 February, but it was swiftly captured by the Russian navy. And when the Ukrainian authorities did finally find out what happened, they were quick to correct the record and show that the soldiers had in fact survived.

For Tetiana, Russia wanted to make the most out of the confusion of what had happened to her son to avoid accountability. But amidst the war of words around the border guards from both countries' governments and media, Tetiana still didn't know when she'd get to see her son again. The information war has its own casualties.

She heard whispers of prisoner exchanges, but was reluctant to get her hopes up. Then, her phone rang: an unrecognized number. Roman's voice greeted her on the other end of the line. A small hello – a 'mum' she thought she might never hear again.

'I was afraid I almost fainted. The ground fell away beneath me, the earth from under my feet,' Tetiana recalled. Roman returned as a celebrity. He received a medal. There was even a postage stamp printed in his honour, showing a soldier raising his middle finger to that ship. Videos of him crying out 'Glory to Ukraine' were shared far and wide on social media.

Roman has messaged me since I reported on his story. His newfound celebrity status has settled down a little. Tetiana is still fiercely proud of the hope he inspired.

Snake Island continued to be a focus of fighting, though the *Moskva* was sunk in April 2022. Ukrainian officials said that their forces damaged the ship with missiles, leading to a fire on board. It was the largest Russian warship sunk since the end of World War Two.

At the time, Russia flatly denied it. That provoked a whole wave of new lies, and the parents of the crew – just like Tetiana – were left with no news of what had happened to their sons. Some were told their children hadn't died, but were given no evidence they were alive. I read numerous posts on the Russian social media site VKontakte from one dad who was desperate for news about his son. He believed he was being lied to by the authorities about what had happened.

When I talked to Tetiana about this, it was hard for her to empathize. After all, Russia had invaded Ukraine – not the other way round. But it's a stark reminder that the misinformation that proliferates during war – whether intentionally or not – breaks families too. Lies are painful wounds that are hard to recover from. Unpicking the various state disinformation tactics – and keeping up with their evolution and complexity – is vital to protecting the very real people who find themselves pawns in an information war fought by the most powerful.

8

VIRTUAL IS NOW REAL

Social media touches every aspect of our daily lives, from how we vote in elections to how we interact with other people. And there's no one it touches more than the generation who have grown up with it as an integral part of their lives. The dangers posed by social media for children and teenagers can be even more acute. They are young, often impressionable – and hyper-exposed to the pitfalls of the online world, including bullying, violence and so much more. There's so much at stake for these digital natives.

It's important to remember that teenagers and kids are the future of social media. If you're a teenager reading this, it makes me feel a bit old writing that. They are the audience the social media companies rely on for the continued success of their platforms. And that means keeping them as engaged as possible. It's likely why Meta launched the Metaverse. They describe it as 'a set of digital spaces to socialise, learn, play and more'. It's entering a virtual world, which you'd imagine might appeal to teenagers who are fans of gaming.

I hear time and time again from parents about how difficult it can be to keep children safe online. But unlike when there's a problem at school and there are teachers on hand to discuss parents' concerns, there isn't a direct line of communication with these social media giants.

The story of thirteen-year-old Olly Stephens is one of the most shocking examples of the harm that social media can do when it comes to the youngest and most vulnerable people in society. It highlights the parallel world of violence and hate that can rage in a teenager's phone, the consequences that world can have, and the struggle of parents to hold these big companies to account.

Stuart Stephens first messaged me on Instagram. He told me about how his son, Olly, was murdered – and asked if I could look into the role that social media had played in what happened to him. He described himself as a tech dinosaur. His message was accompanied by three emojis: a rose, a rainbow and a heart. They'd become Olly's special sign-off.

Amanda and Stuart Stephens had lived on the outskirts of Reading for nineteen years. They described it as social, friendly, safe. At least, it used to feel safe. When Olly left the house one day in January 2021, he told Amanda that he loved her. He reassured her he had his phone location switched on, so she'd know where he was. It felt like a normal Sunday after Christmas, with the family preparing to go back to work and school the next day.

Amanda and Stuart watched from separate windows as Olly wandered over to Bugs Bottom, a field opposite their house. Olly had his sliders on his feet, his mobile phone in his hand.

About fifteen minutes later, there was a knock on the door. Amanda was surprised Olly was home so quickly, but when she opened the door, it wasn't Olly. Another boy they knew told her Olly had been stabbed. Having overheard the conversation, Stuart came running down the stairs with Olly's older sister. He didn't bother putting his shoes on, and dashed out to the field where Olly lay wounded. He fell to his knees, crying out, 'My boy, my boy, no.' Olly had turned pale and his feet were jutting off at strange angles. He lay in a pool of blood. Friends, neighbours, dog walkers – they all tried to help. Stuart held Olly's hand and asked him not to leave. But it was too late.

In Olly's room, his bed is still made up with his favourite duvet cover, and his cuddly toy called Tarzan lies on his pillow. Cards, bunting, and presents from all over the world line his shelves, sent after his story made headlines internationally. There's also a car he was building with his dad at Christmas, just before he was murdered. A patterned bike seat sits on his bed. It was a fourteenth birthday present Amanda bought for him after he was killed. When Amanda hoovers Olly's room – something he used to hate – she still mutters to Olly, 'I'll only be a minute.' Producer Alys Cummings and I struggled to hold back tears as Amanda let us into this special place – a bedroom frozen in time.

Just before he was murdered, Olly was diagnosed with autism. He'd struggled at school, and his parents fear this left him more vulnerable. It might have made it more difficult for him to detect the warning signs about what was happening.

Far from his parents' gaze, a whole other social media world was unfolding on Olly's phone that looked very different to the reality he was living at both home and school. It was filled with profiles of kids he knew dressed in balaclavas, evidence of bullying, and the sharing of violent videos featuring knives. It was only the night after they lost Olly, looking through social media with their daughter, that Stuart and Amanda began to realize the role it had played in Olly's death – and that it was key to understanding how it had happened. Amanda described it as 'this secret world where you can do and say exactly what you want.'

Later, it would be revealed how Olly was stabbed to death by two teenage boys, after they recruited a girl online to lure him there. The entire attack had been planned on social media and triggered by a dispute in an online chat group. Digital evidence helped the police piece together exactly how this shocking murder had unfolded.

* * * *

It was DCI Howard at Thames Valley Police who had been tasked with investigating the world inside Olly's phone. For him, this was a very unusual case. There was a mountain of digital evidence in a way he'd never seen before – 90 per cent of the evidence came from mobile phones. Police forces are often reluctant to call teenage witnesses to the stand because of the impact it can have on them. It's hard to recount a story like this reliably, and difficult to convince them to come forward in the first place. For this case, though, the huge amount of digital evidence meant they didn't have to call any young witnesses at all.

The police had pieced it together like a jigsaw. A spreadsheet that ran on for pages featured countless voice notes, images, screengrabs and videos, all from teenagers' phones. I was shocked by the sheer number of messages and posts and calls – conversations that had been happening almost constantly in the days leading up to Olly's death.

That evidence was eventually used to convict two boys – aged thirteen and fourteen – of murder. A thirteen-year-old girl, who had led him to the park where he was stabbed, was convicted of manslaughter in November 2021.

The chain of events that led to Olly losing his life had started with a Snapchat video showing an attack. Videos of physical or verbal violence like this are shared on social media to humiliate the person they feature. It's a form of bullying. In the weeks before he was killed, Olly had seen a video of a younger boy being humiliated and tried to alert the boy's older brother, who he knew from school. When two boys who were in a Snapchat group with Olly became aware he had passed it on, they were furious.

DCI Howard told me those boys thought Olly was 'snitching, grassing on them' – and that had led to the fallout. It was clear to the police how quickly these relationships forged online could splinter and fracture. They were volatile. At least two of those involved in Olly's murder had not met in real life until that day.

The most disturbing part was listening to a few of the hundreds of Snapchat voice notes from the two boys and girl who fell out with Olly, seemingly planning the action they were going to take. In the four days leading up to the murder alone, there were 1,980 relevant to Olly and the three defendants. They continued right throughout the night and morning of the day Olly was murdered.

The language they use is shocking. Comments including 'you're going to die tomorrow Olly' and 'I'll just give him bangs or stab him'. In one voice note, the female defendant says, '[Male 1] wants me to set him up so then [Male 2] is gonna bang him and pattern him and shit. I'm so excited you don't understand.'

None of these voice notes appear to have been flagged to Snapchat, meaning that they were not moderated. When I spoke to Olly's mum, she kept telling me that if someone had heard these kids talking about weapons and attacks in the playground, they would have stepped in. But they didn't, because there didn't seem to be any adults who were aware of these online conversations. The recordings continued to be made, even after Olly was dead. Voice notes talk about destroying the evidence, and being on the run from police. 'We got chased by armed feds around the whole of Reading so now we're kind of wanted,' one says.

This evidence gathered by the police was just the information required to prosecute – and DCI Howard fears they only just scratched the surface. In his view, it's likely those involved were regularly exposed to violent content – and desensitized to it.

A study from the University of Huddersfield commissioned by the West Yorkshire Police and Crime Commissioner's Office shared exclusively with the BBC backs up that idea. Their research reveals how social media use was found to be a decisive driving factor in nearly one in four – 23.4 per cent – of youth offences sampled from West Yorkshire's caseloads. The majority were acts of violence, typically disputes beginning in a virtual space that spilt out into real violence on the street.

Quantifying the connection between social media and violent offences committed by young people is no easy task, as records aren't systematically kept at the moment. Instead, the team working for the University of Huddersfield had to rely on social media evidence being recorded or officers discussing social media with the offenders. That line of questioning, they found, often doesn't happen. For that reason, those who led the research also anticipate these findings underestimate the true extent to which problematic social media use actively drives offending in young people.

What really struck me as I discovered more about the digital evidence in the Olly Stephens case was just how at odds the image these thirteen- and fourteen-year-olds were presenting online was with the reality they were living. By all accounts, these were children who lived like most teenagers in the leafy suburb of Reading. They went to school, had tea with their families and did their homework.

That's not the impression I got, though, from several images DCI Howard described to me. There were videos of knives and acts of violence, which he said were being shared 'openly and very regularly' on Instagram and Snapchat. In his view, this represented 'a very unhealthy attraction' to filming quite serious violence. It all builds up a picture of the world these kids inhabited – one where a simple online dispute could unexpectedly trigger a murder.

This isn't just an issue affecting the UK. When my BBC *Panorama* investigation into the case aired, I was surprised by how popular it proved to be in other countries, from Brazil to Nigeria. Wherever you are, it's quite likely you know a teenager who uses social media regularly. Families all over the world fear what happened to Olly happening to their own children.

Olly's mum and dad worry that social media sites want to keep kids like Olly on their platforms at whatever cost – and that they just don't take responsibility for the harm caused by their sites. 'Those bosses in Silicon Valley, they weren't in the field when our son died,' Stuart told me.

They want more transparency too about what the sites are doing to protect young users, especially in terms of what algorithms recommend to children and teenagers. And they want the UK's regulator Ofcom to have greater powers to fine and punish social media sites when they don't uphold those commitments.

* * * *

The social media sites' algorithms were something I really wanted to interrogate as part of this investigation. I wanted to find out exactly how kids are exposed to violent content, so I registered an account as a thirteen-year-old across five major social media platforms: Instagram, Snapchat, TikTok, Facebook and YouTube.

The profile picture I used was AI-generated – and the accounts were all set to private. There were no followers, subscribers or friends. I ran them from a separate phone, so that my own online activity didn't interfere with the results in any way. I'd like and follow different content that was suggested to my fictional thirteen-year-old – as well as finding new groups and posts relevant to his interests.

I enlisted one of Olly's best friends, Ben, to help me set the accounts up. He was twelve years old when Olly was murdered. As we sat in his living room, his mum Shelley watched on from the sofa.

Ben started using social media from the age of around ten or eleven – and all of Olly's friends I spoke to admitted to signing up to social media sites way before they turned thirteen, the age you have to be to have an account on most of the platforms. They all said there were no attempts to verify their ages. Olly's parents told me he also opened some of his accounts before he was thirteen.

Ben helped me to follow the kinds of content he likes on social media. He's a big rugby fan so that's where we started. Then we followed pages about football, funny memes, wrestling, bikes, gaming – and some tribute pages to Olly. I also followed some pages about things that other thirteen-year-olds seemed to follow on their accounts – including drill music (a subgenre of hip-hop), cars and pages against knife crime.

After running the dummy accounts for two weeks – and liking posts to do with the range of interests I'd started with, as well as content suggested across the social media sites – the results were striking. On Instagram, YouTube and Facebook, our thirteen-year-old's account was recommended content such as people showing off knives, knives for sale, and posts glorifying violence. The account was registered to a user who was thirteen years old and was actually trying to seek out anti-knife crime content, using search terms like 'no to knives' and 'anti-knives'. But in the process the account was being exposed to pro-knife groups and videos selling and glorifying blades.

On Instagram, the 'shop' – with products for sale tailored according to what the site thinks you'd be interested in buying – was full of knives. Several of the posts on the Explore page, where the site suggests content from other popular users you could be interested in, presented the gang-style imagery that Olly's parents and the police had described seeing on the accounts of the teenagers convicted of his murder, including posing with swords.

On Facebook, groups glorifying knives had been recommended, as well as several pages promoting and endorsing guns, cannabis, pornography and gang culture. On YouTube, the teenage profile was repeatedly recommended videos glorifying gang killings and stabbings, featuring violent language and weapons, as well as those showing off knives. In contrast, on Snapchat and TikTok, while drill music showing artists in balaclavas did feature, posts showing violence and knives were not recommended to the account.

Only once was the account told that a YouTube video was restricted access for under-18s. Otherwise, across all of the social media sites, I wasn't restricted from accessing or watching any of the content. All of these sites say in their own guidelines that they protect teenage users from harmful content – and Meta says it doesn't recommend content featuring blades to under-18s. So far, this undercover account seemed to show that wasn't happening in practice.

I wanted to take it a step further. Since various images and videos of knives promoted to the account shared similarities with those on the phones of the defendants, I also wanted to test what happens when a thirteen-year-old shares a post like that on social media. Since the accounts were all private, no one could see the image or video of the knife except for the social media sites themselves. But no action was taken after a post showing off a knife was shared on Instagram, Facebook, YouTube and Snapchat. None of those sites removed or labelled the post – or even flagged it.

TikTok, however, did remove the video for violating its guidelines on dangerous acts – and the account was warned it was close to being suspended. Ultimately, this suggests that it is possible to detect and remove this kind of content if a social media site commits to stricter guidelines – and maintains them.

And there was one final surprise in store from the experiment. The adverts being promoted to this thirteen-year-old – predominantly on YouTube, but also on Facebook and Instagram – were often based on his interests, pushing computer-coding and football courses aimed at teenagers. That suggests in some cases the data from young users is being used to target them with adverts for profit, but not to protect them.

When I showed Olly's parents these results, they were deeply frustrated that more isn't being done. They feel as though the safety of teenagers online is secondary to the financial success of these social media companies. The role of algorithms in shaping the world that teenagers in particular are exposed to cannot be ignored.

Joe Caluori, who heads up a think tank called Crest looking at the role of social media in violent crime, examined Olly's case. He fears social media has played a far bigger role in youth violence over recent years – and it's only because of cases like Olly's, where there is a very obvious link to what's happening online, that people are beginning to realize that.

When I reached out to them, all of the social media sites expressed their sympathies to Olly's family. Meta said that they 'don't allow content that threatens, encourages or coordinates violence' and have 'a well-established process to support police investigations' – as they did in Olly's case. They said they would 'urgently investigate the examples raised in this investigation'.

YouTube stated it has 'strict existing policies in place to ensure that our platform is not used to incite violence'. TikTok said 'there is no such thing as "job done" when it comes to protecting our users, particularly young people' and it would 'continue to build policies and tools' to help teens and their parents stay safe online. Snapchat said they 'strictly prohibit bullying, harassment and any illegal activity' and 'provide confidential in-app reporting tools' on their platform.

These are the sorts of responses I often receive from social media sites. They are practically interchangeable, and often describe policies that my reporting contradicts or reveals to be inadequately enforced. That's why, at the time, I wanted to match up what my fictional thirteen-year-old's account revealed with the experience of real teenagers. It was sitting on Olly's memorial bench on the very spot where he was killed with his friends that I had the chance to do that.

I was with Poppy, Patrick, Izzy and Jacob. Plus Ben – who helped us set up the undercover account in the first place. They were all now fourteen or fifteen. The experience of sitting in the place where Olly was killed was painful for them all.

I showed them several screengrabs from the accounts I'd set up, without exposing them to too much of the content we'd been recommended. But they weren't shocked by the results at all and admitted they see knives and violence regularly on their feeds. They told me they'd seen bigger knives than those I'd been recommended – and posts of people showing off weapons. They describe machetes, Rambo knives, butterfly blades – and the gang-like image people their age try to portray. People swinging knives around, threatening people.

These posts were just part of using social media for them. So was cyberbullying. Videos showing someone's humiliation – like the one that triggered the dispute between Olly and the defendants – were commonplace.

Their relationship with social media remained bittersweet. The obsession with documenting and sharing everything online had left them feeling on edge and could cause arguments. But they also cherished all of the memories they'd filmed. Izzy and Poppy showed me videos of Olly trying to climb into a yoga swing, sunbathing in the shade, and trying to get a coin out of a toaster. There were montages with music and lots of laughing and dancing. I saw the kids' faces light up as they watched. They also shared special moments away from their phones. Stargazing, talking about the future...

For Olly's parents, seeing his friends at his bench – chatting, enjoying themselves – meant a lot. But there was someone who would always be missing.

* * * *

It's not just parents like Stuart and Amanda who have told me about a different world that exists inside teenagers' phones – and the risk it poses. I've heard from several teachers who are also concerned about how the situation is escalating and leading to increasingly extreme behaviour offline from kids who might never have gotten involved with it before.

When I was at school, I set up a Facebook account without my mum's permission – and then one on Instagram, too. She was fuming. Back then, to me it felt like the most serious harm was fallouts with friends online. The sleepover you weren't invited to, or an online spat. My mum was worried about online predators. Still, it felt less all-encompassing than it does now. You took your phone to school with you, but it didn't bleed so directly into the everyday.

In February 2023, a protest at Rainford High School in Merseyside about checking the length of girls' skirts was posted on TikTok. Within three days, students at over sixty schools had held and filmed their own version of the protest. Within a week, there were over a hundred schools where protests had been held.

But these rallies weren't just kids exercising their right to protest and oppose uniform rules that people were asking legitimate questions about. Windows were smashed, trees were set on fire and teachers were assaulted. I was shocked to see how a significant number of students seemed to be behaving in an unusually extreme way. Some schools were even forced to get the police involved. Then the protests spread to different issues. Kids began to oppose asking to go to the toilet – and the school's decision to lock the loos in reaction to that as well. Again, though there were legitimate concerns, in some places it escalated into something more extreme, with toilets vandalized in several cases.

Videos of the protests spread at breakneck speed on TikTok in particular, which seemed to embolden other kids to get involved and share their own videos to rack up views and likes. Several I messaged confirmed this was the case. According to TikTok, most of the videos showed pupils engaging in peaceful demonstrations – but teachers and students I spoke to were concerned about the cumulative effect.

I decided I wanted to set up another undercover account, this time one purporting to be a fifteen-year-old, to understand more about how teenagers were encountering this type of content – and whether it could be connected to the more extreme behaviour occurring at these rallies. TikTok seemed to be the key vector, and so that was where I set up the account.

It only liked and viewed videos, rather than commenting on them or messaging accounts. I selected interests like football, and the first few videos I was recommended were about this and gaming. After viewing those videos, the fourth post that came up as I began to scroll through the For You page was from a 25-year-old influencer called Adrian Markovac. As well as promoting self-improvement, some of his videos encourage rebellion against school rules on uniform, homework and asking to go to the toilet, and suggested calling teachers offensive names. Over the next few days, the algorithm drove more and more of his content to my feed.

I started to look at the comments under his videos, which were mainly from teenage boys based in the UK. They suggested some of them were changing their behaviour after watching these TikToks. One read: 'Thank you brother, I've just been suspended'. Another user declared: 'I've been excluded for that'.

Others said: 'I will show my teacher and see what they do' and 'Almost got [isolation] going to the toilet without permission'. Some commenters pushed back, having noticed the behaviour of their friends and the anxiety it was causing teachers.

For these teenagers, the social media world seemed to be very directly informing their real-world behaviour and distorting what they considered to be socially acceptable. After all, we take our cues for what we consider 'normal' from the people around us. If videos are recommended to us and liked and viewed by millions of others, this validates their position and warps what we consider OK or not OK. It's even more the case when you're impressionable, young and trying to figure out how to fit in.

Markovac told me he encourages young people to 'rebel against ridiculous rules' but he said he could not be held responsible for the poor decisions of a minority of viewers. TikTok reiterated to me how its 'algorithm brings together communities while prioritizing safety' and that it has tens of thousands of safety professionals using technology to moderate content.

* * * *

The riot at the US Capitol in January 2021 is one of the starkest examples of how what unfolds on our social media feeds can affect the way people react and behave in the real world. Conspiracy theories about the US election, including those from the QAnon community, spread like wildfire on social media. They left a committed minority of Trump supporters suspecting that everything was rigged against Trump.

The riot came as a huge shock to people all over the world, mainly because they weren't living inside the social media feeds of the people who were caught up in this. As someone who's spent a fair amount of time exploring the Conspiracyland some of those in attendance were residents of, I was less shocked. They were living in an alternative reality that had bled into the real world, constantly bolstered and validated by the other people who were a part of it.

Looking ahead to the next election, I decided to again deploy undercover accounts – this time for the BBC's *Americast* podcast. I wanted to be able to track the build-up on social media in real-time. I created social media profiles belonging to five fictional characters, reflecting views from across the political spectrum in the US. They each had accounts across the five major platforms: Facebook, Instagram, YouTube, TikTok and Twitter.

From the start, their social media feeds reflected what was happening in the world at the time. Throughout the course of 2023, that included the indictments of former president Donald Trump over allegations of business fraud, falsifying documents related to hush money paid to porn star Stormy Daniels, and of conspiring to overturn the result of the 2020 election.

Aside from Trump, the feeds also included debates about gun rights triggered by numerous shootings, including those in Nashville and Uvalde where young children were murdered. Campaigning for abortion rights also dominated the US social media world, after the *Roe v Wade* ruling was overturned by the US Supreme Court in June 2022, leaving abortion policies and reproductive rights in the hands of each US state.

Social media feeds, though, do more than just reflect what's happening. It's also about what they recommend, target and suggest to users – content they might not have seen before or seen in such high volumes.

The idea to create these undercover characters and profiles was – in part – sparked by a conversation with former Facebook employee turned whistle-blower Frances Haugen, who I'd reached out to when I was looking at the role of social media in the murder of Olly Stephens.

Haugen had worked as a product manager on the civic integrity team at Facebook. In 2021, she left the company out of fear that it was prioritizing 'growth over safety'. But before she left Facebook, Haugen took screengrabs and photos of various internal documents. They were disclosed to the US Securities and Exchange Commission, and provided to Congress in redacted form by Frances Haugen's legal counsel. Meta, Facebook's parent company, quickly shot down the leaks as misleading.

I was able to look at the files themselves. In some of the pictures you can see her reflection. Several memos from 2019 and 2020 reveal attempts by Facebook to reduce the costs of tackling hate speech, concerns that policies around misinformation were not being applied fairly to different accounts – and a lack of action over users who repeatedly spread falsehoods.

Facebook has repeatedly said it's committed to tackling disinformation and hate speech. But the discussions between employees seen in the leak suggest concerns about the harm caused by both of these, something that has been raised and researched internally, is not being adequately reflected in policy decisions.

The leaked documents show that Facebook employees feared that policies to remove misleading harmful content were being applied differently to right-wing media accounts. In some memos, Facebook admitted it hadn't done enough to tackle the accounts spreading misleading information – concentrating instead on the individual posts.

A memo shared in 2019 described how 'hate speech is the most expensive problem' for the social media site – and laid out a rethink of how to use artificial intelligence to delete potential hate without the intervention of human moderators. Without access to internal memos and documents from within social media companies it's tricky to figure out what other users are being exposed to.

When I finally came face-to-face with Haugen in a studio in East London, she described the way we only ever get a glimpse of a much larger social media world through our own feeds. That's part of the problem – the total lack of transparency. The main goal of her leak was to force the social media companies to have to reveal more about how they operate and what people are being exposed to.

In the early days of the internet, predictive algorithms were developed so that sites could detect patterns of use and 'steer users' aesthetic and thematic predilections'.[31] That's good for social media sites. You're driven towards content you're more likely to be interested in, and you stay logged on for longer.

We know these computer systems are able to track what we like based on how we interact with different content, but exactly how those algorithms decide our interests and the data they use is not always clear. Because what the algorithm pushes to users is personalized to each of our interests, it's essentially impossible to monitor what different people are recommended online without them sharing that information with us. That's why I wanted to create my five different online personas – so I could inhabit these subjective online universes and track in real time what they were recommending.

According to research from Pew, around seven in ten Americans use social media.[32] While creating my undercover accounts on the various sites wouldn't offer an exhaustive insight into what every US voter could be seeing on social media, it could give me a snapshot into what different types of voters across the political spectrum were being exposed to on their phones.

I chose the Pew Research Center to inform my online characters, too – after conducting a wide-ranging survey of more than 10,000 randomly selected US adults in 2021, Pew defined nine different typologies of US voters who sit along the political spectrum.[33] They asked participants for their opinions on everything from guns, immigration and abortion rights to their economic situation and where they turn to for information.

'The gulf between the two major political parties in the US – the Republicans and the Democrats – is a seemingly unalterable condition of American politics,' Jocelyn Kiley – part of the team behind this research – explained to me. 'But a focus on partisan polarization can obscure the divisions and diversity of views that exist within both partisan coalitions. Many Americans hold views that diverge from the orthodoxy of either party.'

Pew's research aims to analyse the variety within the electorate and the nuances that exist across the political spectrum. Our tendency is to put people in boxes, and social media aids us in doing that. But most people I speak to don't fall into neat boxes; their views are less regimented and predictable.

I selected five of the nine types defined by Pew, and based my characters on data on demographic, age, interests, and opinions on different political issues. The Democrat-leaning and Republican-leaning characters would offer an insight into what the greatest proportion of active voters would be exposed to online. The more apolitical type represented less of the electorate.

After choosing my types, I then went on to flesh out mini biographies – and social media interests – for each.

Larry, my Faith and Flag character, is a seventy-five-year-old insurance broker. The group he represents – the most conservative of those defined by Pew's research – is all about patriotism and religious, conservative values. This group has the oldest voters according to Pew's research – with a third aged 65+. This group is also the least diverse, with the highest proportion of non-Hispanic white voters, as well as the highest share of male voters.

What would Larry be like on social media? He has very conservative values and follows and likes pages that are pro-gun and supportive of the Second Amendment. He is loyal first and foremost to the Republican Party and whoever represents them. Fox News is the main place this voter group goes to for news.

For Larry, religion is very important in public life. He is an evangelical Protestant who is married to a woman and has grown-up children. He follows several anti-abortion pages and groups. He doesn't think the federal government should have too much power. He likes lots of groups and pages about his local area and community in Oneonta, Alabama, as well as several US Army-related pages.

Britney, fifty years old, is the part of the Populist Right. She votes Republican, but unlike Larry she's much more critical of big business. She likes some posts on social media opposing billionaires and supporting higher taxes for big corporations. She also follows pages about unfounded conspiracy theories like the Great Reset and New World Order. She is very supportive of Trump – and wants him to be President again in 2024. Her loyalties lie with him rather than the Republican Party itself.

The Populist Right group is overwhelmingly white – but 54 per cent of the voters who fall into this group are female. It is also one of the least highly educated groups, with just two in ten graduating from college. Recently divorced Britney and her children live in Houston, Texas, where she works as a school secretary and takes part in parent groups online.

Half of this group opposes Covid-19 vaccines – so Britney likes and follows some anti-mask and anti-vaccine content on social media. Like Larry, she is also religious and follows many anti-abortion accounts and pages. Fox News is also where she gets her news – and it's the outlet she was recommended on Twitter when she signed up.

Gabriela, forty-four years old, is a floating voter – and Pew's research dubs this group the Stressed Sideliner. This typology is the most apolitical of those defined by Pew. These are people who tend not to vote and don't really identify with any of the political groups, but still care about issues that affect their lives – hence the 'stressed' descriptor.

Gabriela's views vary and she is much more into hobbies. She likes music, dance, fashion – and topics that are generally apolitical. This group is 56 per cent women – and has the highest share of Hispanic voters compared to all the other groups. Gabriela lives with her husband and children in Miami, Florida, and likes and follows pages about her local area as well as the Hispanic community there.

About one in four Stressed Sideliners live in lower-income households. Gabriela has liked lots of groups and pages about saving money on monthly shopping. She is a nanny, so has also joined lots of parent groups and others advertising work. Her views on social issues vary. According to Pew's research, on abortion, banning guns, legalizing marijuana and making university free, Stressed Sideliners align with Democrats. But they're more conservative when it comes to the death penalty and they're supportive of the police. Gabriela has liked some pro-choice content.

Michael, sixty-one years old, is part of the Democratic Mainstay group. This group is staunchly in support of the Democratic Party – and is the most diverse group, with the highest proportion of black voters at 26 per cent. Three-quarters of this group are religious – and it has the highest proportion of black Protestant voters. Michael really values faith and family. He's interested in pages linked to churches in his local area, as well as US and black history.

He's been a committed Democrat for years. He likes lots of pages, groups and accounts linked to the party, as well as popular politicians like Joe Biden, Kamala Harris and Barack Obama. Democratic Mainstays are slightly older and have less formal education than other Democrat-leaning groups. Michael is a teacher in Milwaukee, Wisconsin – where he lives with his wife and kids. He is economically more liberal. On social media he follows various teaching unions and charities that help families make ends meet. But he is more moderate on other social issues and is pro-military. He prefers left-leaning news outlets, including CNN.

Emma, twenty-five years old, is my Progressive Left character – the most liberal of all the types. According to Pew's data, 48 per cent of this group has received a university degree, and most of them are white. Emma attended university and lives in New York City with her girlfriend, where she is a graphic designer. The creative arts are very important to this group, and Emma follows accounts about art and film. This group is made up of younger voters – with a third under thirty. They are also the least religious of all of the groups, and Emma is an atheist. These voters are likely to get their political news from NPR and the *New York Times* – which are pages Emma follows.

Progressive Left voters are very passionate about racial and gender equality – 88 per cent judge there to be serious discrimination against black people. Emma follows lots of accounts in support of the Black Lives Matter movement. She is also pro-choice and passionate about the environment. Emma likes a variety of pages about intersectional feminism, women's marches and LGBTQ+ rights, including those supporting the transgender community. She follows environmental activists and she supports the legalization of marijuana, liking several pages that promote this.

Emma and Larry would be the most politically engaged, according to Pew's research. These groups voted at the highest rate in the 2020 presidential election, they post about politics online and they donate to campaigns too. I tried to reflect that when I was running their various social media accounts. I logged on regularly for a similar period of time to like the kinds of posts they would, check what they'd been recommended and see where the social media algorithms had taken them. I had a different phone for each character, and used a VPN so my location could be set to the US. I could usually be found carting round multiple phones and forgetting whether I was Marianna or a fifty-year-old Texan called Britney.

I know I've written this several times now, but I'll say it again very loudly for the trolls at the back who tend to deliberately misunderstand these undercover accounts: I made a conscious effort not to further pollute the online world, so the accounts were all private and there was no interaction with anyone real. It was just about liking, following, joining – according to their interests and recommendations. That didn't, however, stop Donald Trump Jr tweeting about my undercover voters not long after they were launched. 'And still some question if fake news exists. The BBC just admitted it created fake profiles across social media,' he wrote. I'm still waiting for an opportunity to explain to him who the undercover voters really are.

It didn't take long for their feeds to get interesting. After little more than a week, the account belonging to Populist Right Britney was recommended pages on Instagram and Facebook promoting disinformation that Trump really won the 2020 election – the same narratives that played a part in triggering the riots at the Capitol in 2021. Rather than specific allegations about rigging in different states, these were more generic accusations that the election was fraudulent in some way. Britney came across similar content on TikTok.

False claims were sometimes accompanied by violent rhetoric in reference to Trump's opponents. On Britney's feed, anything that happened to Donald Trump was woven into the narrative that an evil cabal in government was out to get him, and this confirmed he'd really been victorious in the election. Several of these pages opted for phrases like 'Trump won' rather than 'stop the steal', the term used on social media ahead of the Capitol riots.

My experiment was suggesting that, far from disappearing after the 2020 election, the same false claims about 'ballot mules' and 'ballot trafficking' were continuing to spread online. It wasn't just about fraudulent voting, either. They tied into whole range of other conspiracies – punctuated by antisemitic claims about sinister global plots.

When I reached out to the social media site about what I'd found so far, TikTok and Meta emphasized their commitments and responsibility to protecting election integrity and combating misinformation around the midterms. They described well-staffed teams in place to deal with the unfolding narratives, but the evidence I was seeing on Britney's feed suggested the same old narratives were still able to spread, even if only among some committed Trump supporters.

I wasn't seeing this stuff through my other undercover voter feeds. Larry – the Faith and Flag conservative whose loyalty lay with the Republican Party and his very conservative values – was recommended content criticizing the raid on Trump's property Mar-a-Lago over allegations he was storing classified documents with national secrets from when he was president. He was also repeatedly recommended pages promoting guns and other weapons. The content he – or rather, I – saw did not tip into conspiracy so readily. In contrast, the accounts belonging to Democratic Mainstay Michael and Progressive Left Emma were pushed memes celebrating the investigation into Trump and quizzing why this hadn't happened sooner.

At first, Gabriela – our undecided voter – didn't see much politics at all. Her profiles were generally apolitical and so her social media feeds were dominated instead by posts about her home town of Miami, fashion, dance and saving money during the cost-of-living crisis. But then there was a shift. The spikiest posts following speeches from President Biden and Donald Trump cut through. On the left, cries that Trump needed to just accept that he'd lost the 2020 election. On the right, shouts that the threat to the US was not to do with MAGA pro-Trump Republicans – but rather anti-fascist and Black Lives Matter groups. I was left questioning how possible it is now to remain apolitical on social media.

When US voters finally headed to the polls to vote in the midterms in 2022 – two months after I'd set up the undercover voter accounts – it was Britney's profile that was the greatest cause for concern, as it was exposed most frequently to hate and disinformation. Just days before the election, I opened up her Instagram account and clicked on an account that had been recommended in her feed. I was greeted by a meme falsely declaring that President Joe Biden never really won the 2020 election, and several others targeting named female politicians with misogynistic comments and abusive language.

Instagram also showed her conspiracy theories contradicting the police account of what happened when Paul Pelosi, the husband of US House of Representatives speaker Nancy Pelosi, was violently attacked in their home with a hammer just before the midterms. Paul Pelosi's injuries were serious, including a fractured skull that required surgery.

Forty-two-year-old David DePape was arrested at the scene. In posts online he had promoted conspiracy theories linked to QAnon and far-right ideas. He'd posted videos suggesting the 2020 election was stolen, as well as Covid-19 misinformation and false claims about the murder of George Floyd.

Posts on accounts recommended to my undercover profiles made light of the violence, and continued to push disinformation about what had happened, alluding to some kind of affair between Pelosi and DePape, even though all of the evidence available at the time suggested the two were not known to each other.

The most frequent targets for the misogynistic posts were Nancy Pelosi, Kamala Harris, Alexandria Ocasio-Cortez, Michelle Obama and Hillary Clinton. There were comments about them performing sex acts, and slurs about their appearances, alongside criticism of their politics. While posts often spoke about Joe Biden and Donald Trump in hateful terms, they were not subject to the same sexualized language.

Larry was exposed to posts featuring misleading claims about the 2020 election and abusive language directed at politicians, while Emma was also recommended several pages using abusive language aimed at supporters of Donald Trump and Supreme Court justices, but nothing on the scale of what Britney was seeing. Gabriela was also increasingly recommended right-leaning content on social media, often about inflation and the cost-of-living crisis, but it stopped short of the more extreme disinformation and hate that Britney encountered.

Findings from the Institute for Strategic Dialogue, which tracks extremism and disinformation worldwide, backed up what I was seeing on her feed. They revealed how election conspiracy claims and abusive language aimed at politicians online intensified in the run-up to the midterms in 2022.

Their research also expressed concerns that the major social media companies are not taking election denials seriously. Meta, TikTok and other social media sites reiterated they had bolstered their teams and had robust measures to combat misinformation, including partnerships with fact-checking organizations.

* * * *

After the first year of running these undercover accounts, I understood more about what different voters would be recommended and exposed to. What I was yet to see was whether the content that was appearing on people's feeds actually affected their views about who they wanted to be the next US president.

I finally got my chance in August 2023, in a bar in Milwaukee, Wisconsin – known for its cheese curds and beer. The city was hosting the first debate between Republicans hoping to be the party's nominee in 2024.

I'd gathered together five different voters, with a range of political views. Working with the *Americast* team, I'd found them on Facebook groups, on Telegram channels – and one or two joined in since they were already at the bar where we were recording. We perched on stools around a high table, podcast equipment recording and cameras surrounding us. I could tell they were perplexed by the many old phones I had with me, screengrabs at the ready to gauge their reaction to the content these undercover accounts had been recommended. I was especially interested in how social media feeds were shaping their views of President Joe Biden, former president Donald Trump and the election process – as posts about those three topics tended to dominate the feeds.

Everyone agreed that memes of Donald Trump were inescapable. Sometimes he'd be dressed like a superhero, and sometimes there were computer-generated pictures of him in an orange jail uniform. These images were funny, according to Andrew, who said he didn't feel represented by mainstream political figures anymore and used social media as his main source of news. He was in his thirties, with a long ginger beard.

Well, it's funny to a degree, he added. There were times when he realized that politics was actually serious, that these people are in charge and he was losing trust in them.

The memes seemed to have solidified in his mind the image of Trump as someone who was a winner. But, like several of the other voters on my makeshift panel, the oversaturation of Trump-related content was turning him off the former president. Andrew was animated as he said, 'Everybody cares about Trump and Biden. They don't care about anything else in this country. It's like "which one of these two is more screwed up?"'

Ken agreed. In his sixties, he was a professor of justice and public policy at Concordia University Wisconsin, as well as a retired Milwaukee police lieutenant. He said he was tired of the constant battle on social media and the way memes pitted candidates against each other. 'I'm seeing the same vitriol on both sides, and for the first time in my life I'm tired of politics.'

Posts about President Joe Biden, who would be running again in 2024, also came up a lot. Videos frequently commented on Biden's age, and showed examples of where he'd lost his footing or slurred his words. He was branded as 'Sleepy Joe', a nickname Trump had given him. That image really resonated with all of the panel. They all said they'd seen this kind of content, and their main criticism of Biden was his age.

The memes were a little exaggerated but there was some truth to them, said Mary, originally from Wisconsin but now living in Florida in retirement. 'I mean, Joe Biden is old and sleepy. He hasn't done a lot of positive things for the country. He needs to move on. And Donald Trump did some great things for the country when he was president. But Donald Trump has probably had his time as well.'

Other posts describe Biden as 'Dark Brandon', depicting him with bright red eyes like an evil mastermind. It's an image Biden's own campaign have attempted to capitalize on. After all, you'd probably rather be evil, competent Joe than old, useless Joe.

There are positive images as well online, presenting Biden as efficient and on top of the economy, often accompanied by bar charts and animations. Amanda, who was born and raised in Milwaukee, was more aligned to the Democrats and tended to see good things about Biden on her feed. 'I think he is old and slow. But I think he's doing the best he can, given his age.'

By this point, Trump had been charged by prosecutors in Washington and in Georgia with trying to subvert the results of the 2020 election, which he'd lost to Biden. Most of the panel in Milwaukee condemned the posts they had seen that falsely suggested the election was stolen. They described Trump as a 'sore loser'.

Andrew, however, was not so sure. The content he'd seen online suggesting the election was rigged appeared to have undermined his faith in democracy. 'There's a lot of distrust in government,' he says. 'Maybe Trump is a sore loser. Maybe we [Republicans] lost. Maybe they cheated and maybe he didn't. How am I suppose to tell?'

Despite being unsure if the election was rigged, he still planned to vote in the next one, but feared his vote might just 'go in the trash'.

Ken, the retired police officer, pushed back. 'I think there needs to be more transparency, right? I've worked polls, I've been a chief poll inspector for Milwaukee during an election.' If people like Andrew understood more about how the process worked, said Ken, maybe they would be able to trust the process.

My main takeaway from our chat was that they all appreciated having a positive conversation in person, free from the polarization they encountered online. 'I don't think people are nearly as divided as they make it seem like,' said Andrew. 'I feel like at the end of the day, the five of us would all kind of agree on something similar.'

Amanda said she found it really hard to even post about politics anymore. 'Sometimes I'll post one thing and then all of a sudden I get a lot of hate and I'm like, "Okay, I wasn't trying to have an argument."'

That division, in Ken's mind, can be blamed on social media and its recommendation systems, which reinforce opinions on both sides. 'I wish we spent more time getting to know people different from us here in Wisconsin than bothering with who the next president is going to be.'

* * * *

I have no doubt these five undercover voters will expose every-thing from disinformation campaigns to possible influence operations affecting the democratic process, whether home-grown or foreign interference. But already, just having seen up close how other people might experience events through these varying social media prisms has been revealing. By comparing different people's experiences so directly we can see how deeply intertwined social media is with what we experience in the wider world.

It's not just about harmful content either. Undercover accounts are not simply a tool to expose and interrogate the bad bits of the online world, but a way of showing how social media pushes us to see the world through a particular lens. If we step out of our own echo chamber, we can better understand the tactics – especially used by politicians and activists – to target us and change the way we think.

This level of social media literacy is increasingly valuable, not least in terms of safeguarding democracy. Looking ahead to the UK's next general election, undercover voters will again be critical for revealing how voters are targeted and what they're being exposed to. As social media sites are not – and to some extent cannot be – transparent about exactly what their algorithms suggest to different users, undercover accounts can be an invaluable way of investigating online spaces, a very modern iteration of what undercover journalists have been doing for years to get to the truth of what's really going on.

9

WHAT NEXT?

We're almost at the end of our journey. Together we've encountered some of the victims – and perpetrators – of disinformation, trolling and harmful social media content. I suspect that in a decade we'll look back and wonder how this all happened. Likely by the time this goes to print, another online frenzy connected to harmful behaviour, or a disinformation battle that harms real people, will have occurred. Now it's time to look at where the phenomena covered in this book are going – and where the solutions lie.

There are all kinds of worries on the horizon. Will AI technology – computer-generated photos, videos and sound – make it harder to spot disinformation? Will it make it easier to create hateful, misleading videos – or to catch them? What will social media sites do with the increasing amount of data they have on us?

My answer to those first two questions is that AI is something to worry about. But at the time of writing, as this book has revealed, the somewhat old-fashioned tactics used to spread disinformation and hate – from memes to newspapers – are proving just as effective.

That last question in particular has been raised by politicians across the world in relation to Chinese-owned TikTok. Often it's in relation to how information about us can be used in some kind of warfare, but I think the bigger worry is how it can inform algorithms that are distorting the world right under our noses.

TikTok has boomed since the pandemic, with over 1.5 billion users as of 2023 and a young captive audience. It's famed for its addictiveness and the sensitivity of its recommendations system, which drives you to content you like within seconds. Videos are short and snappy. I'd spotted that ability to drive frenzies when looking at the videos about the disappearance of Nicola Bulley and the school protests. But those actually weren't the first times I'd noticed it happening.

In November 2022, four students from the University of Idaho were murdered in their bedrooms while their two surviving housemates slept. Speculation around who had committed the murders gripped TikTok, without any evidence to back it up. I had never heard of the town Moscow in Idaho, before, but the murders quickly flooded my feed in a way that wasn't happening on the other social media sites. Within a few days, I was seeing nothing else.

The murders seemed to be turning up on the feeds of users who had never heard about them before either – just like what was happening to me. Accounts based in Australia, the UK and South Africa were all remarking on how speculation about the town of Moscow, Idaho, was all over their For You page.

I discovered that TikTok was uniquely obsessed with the

case. Looking at the Idaho4 hashtag, I found that TikToks about the murders racked up 2 billion views between November 2022 until August 2023 – compared to far fewer on the other social media sites over the same time period.

The witch hunts had started on TikTok, too. The target of one of the main ones in this case was someone called Jack Showalter. He seemed to be the person featured in footage of two of the victims taken at a food truck the night of the murders, he was dubbed 'hoodie guy' by TikTokers. They made videos forensically unpicking the footage as well as photos from his social media accounts, levelling serious claims against him – saying that he owned a knife similar to the murder weapon, accusing him of fleeing the country and suggesting his family had political connections that were protecting him.

Police confirmed that the person in that video had been ruled out of the investigation, but the false claims continued. According to all the evidence available, the students' deaths had nothing to do with Jack, and those close to him were forced to deny the false rumours spreading. Jack's sister posted online about the harm this had caused, condemning the 'threats and harassment' that her family and Jack 'didn't deserve'. A man called Bryan Kohberger has since been arrested and charged with the murders. It seems the students' deaths had nothing to do with Jack.

I found one TikToker, Olivia, who had taken it a step further and decided to visit the scene. Some of her posts were racking up over 20 million views. 'There was something that really drew me to it,' she told me. 'I felt this need to go out there and dig for answers and see if I can help out in any way.'

She flew over six hours from her home in Florida to Idaho to look into the case. For her TikTok videos, she spoke to neighbours and students. She told me the reaction on the ground was usually 'positive', but it wasn't always that way.

Unlike other TikTok users, Olivia did not so explicitly level false accusations at people, but she did acknowledge that she would 'post controversial videos of things that are not yet really confirmed'. While some were gripped by her videos, others were more critical and asked her to stop relentlessly speculating about the case or turning up at the scene.

'The [TikTok] content that I make where I am actually at the scene of something does much better versus if I was just at home sitting somewhere and talking about a case,' she explained. 'I feel a lot of people will accuse me of or say that I sensationalize these stories and that it's bad, but I don't see it as sensationalizing it. It's just the way that I edit.'

Olivia's behaviour struck me as unusual, and I was taken aback by how far she was willing to take this. 'I think that TikTok does encourage people to participate more than other apps because of the engagement, and it makes it more relatable because you can just be sitting on your couch and make a video and then reach tons of people,' she pointed out. 'One video on Tik Tok could get millions of plays – versus if I post the same video on Instagram, it'll get like two hundred views. And it's just the algorithm of TikTok.'

Olivia described this as the Wild West – a new 'frontier' for journalism. But, unlike me, she isn't subject to journalistic codes of practice. Alarm bells rang in my mind. Citizen journalism has enriched the media landscape; it makes the industry more inclusive and diverse, and vitally it expands the audience. But where are we headed if what I've just described to you is seen as journalism, where clicks matter more than waiting to get to the truth of what's unfolding?

As we saw in earlier chapters, frenzies have popped up all over the place, and as well as being linked to innocent people being accused of murder, they can be connected to vandalism in schools, riots and interference in police investigations.

From speaking to users and former employees of the company, it seems to be that TikTok is the product of a social media arms race to create the most engaging platform yet. That comes with positives – like people joining new niche communities talking about books, pottery or other shared interests or experiences – and lots of money for TikTok, too. But it also comes with negatives, like these events I'm describing.

Following my investigation into this issue, police leaders and teachers' unions in the UK have been quick to warn that TikTok frenzies that encourage antisocial behaviour are putting a strain on public services. From various conversations I've had with police commissioners, constables and teachers, it seems to me that these people are finding it difficult to cope with the real impact a very rich tech company is having on their schools or serious cases they're investigating.

While TikTok may prove more effective than some other social media sites at dealing with more traditionally harmful content – racism, hate and child abuse, for instance – it seems to struggle with the unpredictable situations its algorithm is pushing content about. This evolving threat poses possibly the greatest problem for social media companies. Quicker moderation and de-prioritizing content like this before a frenzy starts seem to be the only solution. But would any social media site ever fundamentally overhaul their very successful model? And what comes next in this arms race for views and clicks? When I put all of this to TikTok a spokesperson made clear again that its 'algorithm brings together communities while prioritizing safety'. They also described how the social media site looks to interrupt repetitive patterns by recommending different types of content, removing harmful misinformation and reducing the reach of videos from unverified information. They also described how 'prioritizing safety is not only the right thing to do, it makes business sense'. They did not agree to an interview with me about any of this.

* * * *

These social media companies are often impenetrable and unaccountable, with rich bosses and headquarters outside of the UK. As you've seen throughout this book, at times I'm sent bland statements with details of how they are taking action and cherry-picked examples of how it's working, but that just bypasses the evidence and the very real experiences people are having.

The companies have fought hard to avoid government regulation and demonstrate they can keep on top of hate and disinformation. Elon Musk's acquisition of Twitter could have marked a new era in how social media companies counteract these issues, but that certainly hasn't come to pass so far. In fact, it's gone in what seems to be the opposite direction.

Musk openly rejected the commitment to tackle harmful content, instead seeing Twitter's ultimate role as allowing freedom of speech. That has become even more apparent since the conversation I detailed with Ray at the start of Chapter 7. Those watching on were no longer under the pretence that Twitter intended to devote its time and resources to policing itself. It highlighted just how much power one person at the helm of a social media site can have, and the danger posed when they don't even pretend to play ball.

There's one conversation I had with a former Twitter employee that really spoke to that point – and where solutions to trolling might lie when it comes to social media policy and innovation. Lisa Jennings Young was once Twitter's head of content design. Before she left the company, she was part of the team tasked with introducing features to protect users from hate. Twitter was a hotbed for trolling long before Musk took over, but she says her team had made good headway at limiting this. 'It was not at all perfect. But we were trying, and we were making things better all the time.'

Lisa's team worked on several new features – including safety mode, which can automatically block abusive accounts.

They also designed labels to apply to misleading tweets, and something called the 'harmful reply nudge'. The nudge alerts users before they send a tweet in which AI technology has detected trigger words or harmful language. The research again backed up the idea that these tools were effective. 'Overall 60 per cent of users deleted or edited their reply when given a chance through the nudge,' Lisa told me. 'But what was more interesting, is that after we nudged people once, they composed 11 per cent fewer harmful replies in the future.'

These safety features were being implemented around the time my abuse on Twitter seemed to reduce, according to data collated by the University of Sheffield and International Center for Journalists. It's impossible to directly correlate the two, but given what the evidence tells us about the efficacy of these measures, it's possible to draw a link.

Lisa's entire team was laid off in late October 2022 – and as the boss, she was the only one left. She herself chose to leave in late November. I asked Lisa what had happened to features like the harmful reply nudge. 'There's no one there to work on that at this time,' she replied. She had no idea what had happened to her former projects. So, we tried an experiment. She suggested a tweet that she would have expected to trigger a nudge: 'Twitter employees are lazy losers, jump off the Golden Gate bridge and die.' I shared it on a private profile in response to one of her tweets, but to Lisa's surprise, no nudge was sent. Another tweet with offensive language we shared was picked up – but Lisa says the nudge should have picked up a message wishing death on a user, not just swear words. It didn't seem to be working as it was designed to.

There were others still on the inside who were able to give me some more information about what was happening. One engineer – who was responsible for Twitter's computer code – told me that while the façade looked fine, the site was like 'a building where all the pieces are on fire'. As he was still working at Twitter, he gave the interview anonymously. I'll call him Sam. He was taking a huge risk speaking out while at the company.

'I can see that nothing is working. All the plumbing is broken, all the faucets, everything,' he explained to me. He attributed the chaos to the huge disruption in staffing. People from other teams had had to shift their focus. 'A totally new person, without the expertise, is doing what used to be done by more than twenty people. That leaves room for much more risk, many more possibilities of things that can go wrong.'

He said previous features still existed, but those who'd designed and maintained them had left – he thought they were now left unmanned. 'There are so many things broken and there's nobody taking care of it… you see this inconsistent behaviour.'

The level of disarray, in his view, is because Musk doesn't trust Twitter employees. He describes Musk bringing in engineers from his other company – electric car manufacturer Tesla – and asking them to evaluate engineers' code over just a few days before deciding who to sack. Code like that would take 'months' to understand, Sam said.

He believes this lack of trust was betrayed by the level of security Musk surrounded himself with. 'Wherever he goes in the office, there are at least two bodyguards – very bulky, tall, Hollywood movie-[style] bodyguards. Even when [he goes] to the restroom.'

Sam thought that for Musk it's about money. He told me cleaning and catering staff were all sacked – and that Musk even tried to sell the office plants to employees.

Ultimately, it's the users that pay the price for this. Those like Ellie Wilson, a young woman from Glasgow who posted about her experience of being raped. She wanted to raise awareness for survivors of sexual assault and violence. Back in the summer of 2022, she received a supportive response from other users on Twitter.

But when she tweeted about her attacker in January 2023, after he was sentenced and following Musk's takeover, she was subject to a wave of hateful messages. She received abusive and misogynistic replies – with some even telling her she deserved to be raped.

Her Twitter following was smaller before the takeover, but when I looked into the accounts targeting her with hate, I noticed her trolls' profiles were more active since Musk had been at the helm, suggesting they'd been suspended previously and recently reinstated.

Some of the accounts had only been set up around the time of the takeover. They appeared to be dedicated to sending out hate, and were without profile pictures or identifying details.

Several followed and interacted with content from popular accounts accused of promoting misogyny and hate – also reinstated on Twitter after Musk decided to restore thousands of suspended accounts, including that of controversial influencer Andrew Tate.

'By allowing those people a platform, you're empowering them. And you're saying, "This is OK, you can do that,"' Ellie told me. Several of the accounts had targeted other rape survivors she was in contact with. I reached out to Andrew Tate's team, but was met with no response. Musk and Twitter never responded to the investigation either, except for those tweets directed at me that I mentioned in Chapter 6. What does it mean for user safety when the person in charge isn't even willing to share their commitment to protecting people like Ellie? Since then, her fears have continued to be affirmed.

Like Ellie, I've thought several times about quitting Twitter. I only use it to investigate tip-offs and share my podcasts or documentaries. I'm greeted with more trolls than ever now. But what a world where the BBC's disinformation and social media correspondent – who investigates the online world for a living – doesn't feel like she can be on a particular site because of the hate it triggers.

In its publicly available guidelines online, Twitter continues to say that 'respecting the user's voice' remains one of its 'core values'. Musk has defended the decisions he has made at the social media site on several occasions. Back in December 2022, he released internal documents called the 'Twitter Files' to explain why he believed the company hadn't been fairly applying its moderation and suspension policies under the old leadership.

* * * *

It's for all of the above reasons that policymakers around the world are increasingly considering the option that social media sites can't be trusted to self-regulate, especially as tackling harm tends to impact their profits.

Parents – like Olly Stephens's mum and dad – have campaigned tirelessly for politicians to force the sites to do more to protect their users, especially young children. Ian Russell is one of the people who has lobbied for tougher rules to ensure the companies are liable if they don't protect their users. Ian's fourteen-year-old daughter Molly ended her life in 2017 after viewing suicide and self-harm content online. The coroner who looked into her case actually wrote to the social media companies and the government with recommendations – including separating the sites accessible to kids from those accessible to adults, and reviewing just how the algorithms work. In Molly's case, she seemed to have been pushed more and more of this kind of content in the build-up to her death.

The government and MPs have for several years been looking into legislation that would give the UK regulator Ofcom the power to regulate social media companies. The bill in its current form mandates that social media companies make commitments to protecting users – especially kids – and share those with

Ofcom. If they don't then share how they've honoured those commitments, they risk fines and other punishments. That legislation was passed in the second half of 2023, around the time of Olly Stephens' sixteenth birthday, and was welcomed by his mum and dad who felt like the government was finally putting measures in place to stop this happening to another family. The Technology Secretary for the British government at this time, Michelle Donelan, told me the legislation was part of 'decisive action to prevent social media content from spiraling out of control and putting people at risk'. She said the bill would take 'a common-sense approach to reigning in the Wild West of social media'.

But questions remain about how – and whether – that can work in practice. It's sparked a huge amount of debate about balancing user safety with freedom of expression, which is the main dilemma when it comes to any kind of social media regulation. There are wider questions, too. Is this legislation trying to do too much all at once? And if it's too general, will the social media sites be able to wiggle around it?

I spoke to an insider at the UK's regulator who has knowledge about the dilemmas the bill faces. On the whole, there has been widespread political support for the bill's attempt to protect kids online from both illegal activity and legal but harmful content and behaviour.

But there's been much more opposition when it comes to efforts to limit adults' exposure to harmful content. That poses a problem because – as this source points out – a two-tiered internet for children and adults is highly complicated. It would require age-verification tools and technologies to be applied broadly across large and small tech platforms. In reality, that just looks very difficult to do.

What this legislation requires of the social media sites, in their view, is 'potentially game-changing'. That includes forcing companies to be more transparent about how they operate. They will have to think about risk before rather than after they launch new policies and products.

That's one of the key themes that's come through in the reporting I've done so far: that harm is exposed, and only then do policies attempt to tackle it after the fact. But the victims are already affected. It's too late for them.

In addition to those points about transparency, the UK's regulator Ofcom will also have significant hard enforcement powers to sanction companies that don't comply with the new laws. All of that said, my insider made clear that, in their eyes, limitations remain. 'The bill is huge, veering on the unwieldy in places. It contains an enormous number of not always coherent demands on the regulator and on platforms,' my source explained.

When it comes to the victims of disinformation, hate and all things social media you've encountered in this book, it's unclear how the online safety bill will protect them in practice. The social media insiders I've discussed this with don't trust that the social media sites will do anything – and don't trust that the legislation will really deter the trolls and conspiracy theorists either. They'll just see it as a part of this plan to censor what they have to say.

It's for that reason that some of those affected by disinformation and hate are turning to the law for solutions instead, after losing faith in their own government or the social media sites to do anything to help them. Think of the court case involving Alex Jones, or Martin Hibbert, the survivor of the Manchester Arena bombing who filed a landmark legal action against conspiracy theorist Richard D. Hall.

While people have taken trolls to court for criminal proceedings, including for stalking, a conspiracy theorist has never been taken to court for tracking down survivors to see if their injuries are real and promoting false ideas they could be faking their injuries. Martin's lawyer Neil Hudgell recognizes how complex this issue can be to deal with. 'I think where we are, in broad terms, is this interplay between the right to free speech and the ability to express your opinion on a range of matters, and where that crosses the line into areas of privacy, harassment and infringement of individuals' rights,' he explained as we chatted on the phone. 'I think we have an obvious example here of where we do cross that line.'

It doesn't stop there, though. These legal cases have extended beyond this phenomenon of 'disaster trolling' to wider conspiracy theories. I covered one such situation that had unfolded in Dublin.

At the end of 2022, a woman called Edel Campbell called up a radio programme on the Irish broadcaster RTÉ and was telling them about her eighteen-year-old son, Diego. He'd taken his own life in August of that year.

'He loved his family so much, didn't cause any grief to anybody,' she said, her voice shaking. 'Everywhere you went people would say what a mild-mannered wee boy. Always saying hello and polite. We miss him very much.'

She described how he had bought a new PlayStation the day he died. 'We didn't know he was suffering. We didn't know there was anything wrong. If I'd had known I wouldn't have hung up the phone call, I would have done a million and one things differently. Nothing is going to take him back.'

Just over a year after he died, Diego's picture was included among forty-two photos of people on the front page of a conspiracy theory newspaper called the *Irish Light*. The headline read: 'Died Suddenly' and the article falsely suggested Diego's death was connected to the Covid-19 vaccine. 'Died Suddenly' is a trend used by conspiracy theory activists to suggest that the unexpected deaths of young people are actually related to the Covid-19 vaccine.

'For people to be saying died suddenly, it's just torn my life completely upside down to think that anybody could do this,' Edel said.

The conspiracy theory paper in question, the *Irish Light*, was edited at the time by a journalist, Gemma O'Doherty. Edel said O'Doherty never contacted her and that she'd 'ripped the heart clean out' of her.

The *Irish Light*'s front page is very similar to that of *The*

Light, the conspiracy theory publication I introduced you to in Chapter Two. They have the same branding and the articles are also a mix of more run-of-the-mill feature pieces and others based on disinformation. Headlines such as 'Pfizer knew the vaccine would kill', 'Why manmade climate change is a fraud' and 'Irish to become a minority' populate its pages.

The editor of the UK *Light* told me he does not have editorial control over what the Irish paper publishes, so I decided to take a closer look at the Irish paper's editor. O'Doherty worked as a journalist on mainstream newspapers for years. She was sacked from the *Irish Independent* in 2013, but won cases for defamation against the paper and unfair dismissal against its parent company. She later founded the political group Anti-Corruption Ireland, which has been described as a far-right group by the Global Project Against Hate and Extremism.

In the article that featured Diego's picture, the paper claimed that the establishment was not questioning the 'mysterious deaths' of young people because 'they know exactly what it is: the untested and dangerous injection they forced into the Irish people'. It also pointed the finger at harm caused by lockdown measures, but the overriding allegation of this piece and the 'Died Suddenly' trend it employed was that the loss of these young people's lives was connected to the Covid-19 jab.

There have been a small number of deaths from the Covid-19 vaccines, but these are rare. I investigated several of the cases featured on this front page by the *Irish Light*. I was able to confirm that one of the young people featured died in a swimming pool accident, another from a head injury, another from meningitis.

It was distressing for Edel to see her son's photo in an article spreading disinformation about the Covid-19 vaccine. She pleaded for O'Doherty to take the online version down, and to never share her son's photo again. 'All I want is for her to say sorry. All I want is for her to stop using him. I don't really have many avenues left. Nobody seems to want to listen, nobody seems to care,' she said on the radio at the time.

One person who heard Edel speaking on RTÉ was solicitor Ciaran Mulholland. I met him at his office, just a few miles outside of Dublin, to talk about the case.

He was immediately very chatty and told me he'd spent time in the military before qualifying as a solicitor. The walls of his office were adorned with many awards and accolades. At that time, Ciaran was spending most of his time defending people accused of murder, but he decided he wanted to represent Edel in this case against the *Irish Light*, and it was unlike any other he'd ever worked on.

'This was a lady who was on the radio pleading for the political powers to intervene. I think there just seemed to be a reluctance to the authorities to do anything,' he told me. Ciaran was representing Edel pro bono. 'This wasn't about retribution. It wasn't about compensation. All Edel Campbell wanted was to protect the integrity of Diego, and her family as a whole. And as you can understand, [for] anyone who loses a son in such tragic circumstances, there's a ripple effect.'

The mistruths quickly unravel. According to Ciaran, Diego was never vaccinated. Ciaran thought that would make things straightforward, and he said he reached out to the *Irish Light* asking them to remove the photograph of Diego from posts available online. He tried to appeal to their humanity. At this point, there were no threats of litigation. They just hoped the paper would remove the photograph and not share it again. Instead, the request just inflamed the situation.

I was shocked that this hadn't worked, even as someone who deals with conspiracy theorists a lot. You'd think that they might change tact and seem like they're on the side of a grieving mum, while still laying blame on the vaccine and the Irish government.

'The short answer is I don't know what their logic was,' Ciaran said. 'They certainly have firm beliefs that what they're doing is right. Irrespective of the conspiracy – that they believe in and they're entitled to believe in – it has to be done in a respectful manner.'

What happened next, Ciaran described as 'nothing short of shocking'. Edel found herself subject to hateful messages on social media and more conspiracy theories were shared about her son's death. It was only then that she and her legal team decided to bring a civil case against Gemma O'Doherty and *The Irish Light* for harassment with defamation. The case is seeking damages for the emotional distress caused to Edel and the infringement of her privacy.

The legal action further inflamed the hate: there are messages online where Gemma O'Doherty's and the *Irish Light* accounts refer to a grieving mother as being involved in 'massive fraud', describe her 'outrageous lies' and accuse her of being 'mentally unstable' – as well as making extreme references to suicide.

Edel told me that the *Irish Light* has made her life hell and now she's too scared to speak out in interviews because of the further online abuse it could trigger.

'There was an increased and sustained and persistent campaign,' Ciaran explained. 'In terms of the character assassination of Edel Campbell, which made outrageous claims ranging from involvement in drug dealing and criminality, to [Edel] being responsible for the death of her son. It just snowballed from there and it continued.'

The abuse extended to her legal team, too. Ciaran said he was threatened with 'execution' and there were posts suggesting he be 'shot'. 'This has certainly had an impact upon me, because of the personal threats that have been levelled at me, and my staff in my office, to such an extent that we have had to increase security at the office, because members of staff have flagged their own personal security that they didn't feel safe.'

For Ciaran, this is emblematic of a wider problem: a lack of accountability when it comes to anonymous online trolls. 'This isn't something that's isolated to Ireland but throughout the globe – that what is said on social media, kind of what is said online, it's kind of different to what you say in person, or it doesn't seem to [come with] that same responsibility.'

I've also seen evidence that Edel made reports of harassment to the police in Ireland – the Garda – but, at the time of speaking, Ciaran told me the police were yet to contact or question Gemma O'Doherty. Garda Síochána told me that it 'does not comment on named individuals' or 'specifics of on-going investigations'. It said it continues to 'actively investigate the alleged harassment of an individual in the North Western Region' of Ireland.

A restraining order was granted to stop the *Irish Light* editor from contacting Edel. But abusive comments have continued to be shared about her online, including from the *Irish Light* Twitter account – which Gemma O'Doherty has admitted to running. Ciaran said he thinks that this online abuse deters other families affected by this front page from taking any action. 'I would probably go as far as to say a lot of these families are sitting back, [thinking] no, I will not dignify that with a response. Because of the individuals involved and given how the *Irish Light* and their supporters conduct themselves, you can understand why a lot of people were incredibly reluctant to go to [a] solicitor or correspond directly when they saw the backlash with Edel Campbell.'

This is believed to be the first time anywhere in the world that someone has taken legal action against anti-vaccine conspiracy theorists who have played a part in this 'Died Suddenly' trend. In Ciaran's mind, there's 'no doubt' this case will set a precedent, especially in terms of balancing freedom of expression with the right to privacy. He doesn't want legal action, though, to take the pressure off other people he thinks should be acting over this kind of content.

'Irrespective of the judgement, I don't believe that it deviates away from the responsibilities of government, and the responsibilities of watchdogs to ensure that social media broadcasters are subject to some form of regulation.'

Telegram, where abusive messages directed at Edel were shared, told me that the platform 'supports the right to free speech, but calls to violence are expressly forbidden by our terms of service'. Twitter has not replied to my request for comment.

When I contacted Gemma O'Doherty about an interview and put all the allegations to her, she did not respond. But on social media, the *Irish Light* says I was planning a 'character assassination' because she 'exposed the vaccine genocide'. Online, O'Doherty denies harassing Edel Campbell and her legal team – and continues to suggest Diego's death was sinister or mysterious in some way.

As I travelled home from Dublin, I kept thinking about the price of holding to account a conspiracy theory newspaper. I've faced trolling myself for investigating this topic, but the campaign of abuse mounted against Edel and her legal team is one of the most extreme I've come across.

It doesn't surprise me that the abuse that can accompany pursuing legal action could deter other people from seeking accountability. Whether that's the intention of those waging the campaign of online abuse is another question. It could just be that they truly believe these conspiracy theories, and that they're saving us all from sinister plots to cause harm.

That brings us onto ongoing questions about whether these kinds of cases could help pull those deep down the conspiracy rabbit hole out of that world. After all, in some ways the true believers – not so much the leaders – are victims in this social media mess, a point emphasized by social psychologist Dr Daniel Jolley. 'Time will tell the impact these kinds of court cases have, as they are new. Could it provoke a reflection… about the harm this causes, or will they double down and see it as part of an attempt to silence the community?'

After all, in his view conspiracies are 'rooted in someone's belief system'. Once they become part of someone's identity, it's all the more difficult to reject them. No legal case or social media regulation or legislation will be capable of changing their minds, because it won't satisfy the needs that led them there in the first place.

* * * *

I'm an investigative reporter, not a campaigner, but from speaking to victims, conspiracy theorists, trolls, social media employees, experts, politicians and more, I can see there are some solutions at their disposal. They are not quick fixes, but they do offer hope in the face of a serious risk to the future of our society, and the kids growing up in it.

First and foremost, let's start with the social media sites. They wield as much power as many governments, and the feeling of experts immersed in this online world is that the level of scrutiny and accountability they're subjected to should mirror that. Reporting on social media now is in many ways like being a political journalist, and there's a concerning lack of ability to ask the people in charge of these companies difficult questions. We need to be able to get up close, and investigate and expose all of the impact this is having.

We also need to listen to and stick up for the victims caught up in this. There's been a tendency for society to decide what will help and what won't on their behalf: just log off, don't talk about it, it doesn't really matter, it's not real. Time and time again I find the people targeted by disinformation and hate – those whose lives have been affected by social media and its algorithms – fear no one is listening to them. They want more transparency, they want more accountability, they want people to care about what's happening in the way they care about other public scandals. Just because accountability is more difficult when it comes to big social media companies, that doesn't mean their voices shouldn't be heard.

We do have to ask questions of society beyond social media. Better psychological support is a suggestion that's come up several times – including when I was giving evidence in parliament to MPs looking at the online safety bill. One politician on the committee I was talking to raised the prospect of better support for children in schools. The conspiracy theorists and trolls I have interviewed have often grappled with a sense of isolation and anxiety that has left them more vulnerable to extreme ideas on social media. Despite the damage they do, they are victims here too – and the dilemma of how or whether to tackle and prevent the root causes of some of this behaviour is one for policymakers, not reporters like me.

Then there's education. If we teach our kids how to spot what's true or false – and just more in general about how their social media feeds work – this could be less of a problem. Take Finland, for example, which appears to have had some success taking this approach. Critical thinking and media literacy have been part of the curriculum there for a very long time. From 2016, it was revised so that children would be taught how to spot misleading and fake news online. Across various subjects, including maths and art, teachers deliberately encourage that kind of critical thinking. Students are on the lookout for manipulation and understand how propaganda works.

Finland is a very high-trust society. According to an OECD report, 71 per cent of the Finnish population trust the government. The average for other countries in that report is just 41 per cent.[34] Perhaps this kind of education bolsters trust; or perhaps it's possible because citizens are more trusting of the people in charge in the first place.

That brings us to the final problem I've identified: trust. Ultimately, if the boom in online disinformation, trolling and conspiracies is linked to distrust and the (poor) health of our public discourse, can any of this ever be enough? No piece of legislation from policymakers looking to regulate the big tech companies nor repeated legal action will restore the levels of trust across society. But if institutions are held to account with rigorous investigative journalism, politicians are more truthful, and everyone is more transparent about what is going on, it helps to repair that trust.

Trolls and conspiracy theories seep through the cracks of divided communities. From everything I've uncovered and everyone I've spoken to, remedying distrust in institutions and the media, bolstering communities and offering people opportunity and hope, trying to make people happier – all of these things ought to reduce the problems that make people vulnerable to these beliefs.

Social media contributes to the fracturing of society by polarizing our world and pushing harmful content onto users – and a fractured society is more vulnerable to the harmful ideologies and activities and ideas promoted on social media. It's a bit of a vicious circle, and it seems to me that the only real remedy lies in dealing with both. I can't even begin to imagine what may have unfolded in Conspiracyland or in the online – and offline – worlds more broadly since I finished writing this book. I hope these pages will mark a moment in time and serve as a wake-up call to everyone who gets to this final line. I've been among the trolls and this disinformation war is changing the world as we know it. It's affecting every single one of us.

ACKNOWLEDGEMENTS

I want to thank my agent Trevor Dolby, editor James Pulford and all of the team at Atlantic Books who have brought *Among the Trolls* to life. I'm grateful that they were willing to navigate the world of conspiracy theories, trolls and algorithms with me. Thank you for accommodating the very busy schedule that comes with covering all of this.

I'm so grateful to all of the people who trust me to investigate their stories. I never take for granted being let into the lives of those I talk to. I appreciate the courage of those affected by this, and thank them for allowing me to bring their experiences to light. I'm grateful to everyone who lets me question them and who welcomes me into their world. I investigate this never-ending online universe that spills out into the everyday for all of these people – as well as those who watch, listen and read, like you. So, thank you.

Behind every troll hunter and disinformation and social media reporter is an army. A big thank you to my wonderful mum and dad, who have always taught me to stick up for what matters, be brave and do what I love. Thank you for all your support, even when I was eight years old reading out stories I'd written in the back of the car and you'd turn up the music so you couldn't hear me. I want to extend that thank you to all of the brilliant people in my life who I love so much and who make it possible to report on all of this day in and day out. I am choosing not to share your names here, because of – you guessed it – the trolls. Your willingness to enter this world and explore it with me, while also having your feet firmly planted on the ground, is invaluable. Thanks to Mia too, the best cat ever.

A huge thank you is owed to all the exceptional teams at the BBC who make this journalism possible. They were by my side through so many of the encounters you've read about in this book. Their talent and hard work are what allow these investigations to happen.

The team at BBC *Panorama*, the first place I was given the opportunity to really pull off investigations that mattered. Karen Wightman, who has taught me how to do right by people and have the courage to take on the bad guys. Alys Cummings, whose brilliance and brains have enabled us to investigate everyone from big social media companies to the most shocking cases of trolling and social media harm. John O'Kane, who very early on reminded me to ask: How do we know this? And why do we think it's true? Leo Telling, Tom Traies, Alice Crinnigan, Adrian Polglase, Alison Priestley, Eamonn Walsh, Diana Martin, Tom Stone, and everyone else involved in every *Panorama* I've worked on.

Also, the Radio 4 podcasts team, who have trusted me to investigate Conspiracyland in innovative and brave new ways.

Rhian Roberts, a commissioner with real spark and vision who has the guts to take a gamble on new people and ideas. Nathan Jones, whose thoughtful creativity and passion have been a driving force. Ant Adeane, whose gentle genius has brought several of these podcasts to life. Emma Close, whose wonderfully sharp mind and very kind heart have made her a valuable companion in navigating Conspiracyland. Ed Main, for his kindness, tenacity and willingness to become just as obsessed with an investigation as me. Mike Wendling and Jeremy Skeet, who backed this job ever existing in the first place, and for teaching me to beat the system. Mohit Bakaya, Phil Marzouk, Alex Portfelix, Marco Silva, the team at BBC Sounds, and everyone else who made these podcasts happen.

The team at BBC News podcasts who always have my back. Sam Bonham, thank you for indulging my sociopathic work tendencies, for always being excited about everything in these pages, and for really caring about my safety. Jonathan Aspinwall, I'm so grateful for your endless support, and your willingness to innovate and to take risks on and with me. One day, you'll be able to type just as quickly. The peerless Louisa Lewis and the ever excellent team at BBC's *Americast* – including Justin Webb, who has hopefully learnt how to use the internet after reading this.

Thanks to all of the team at BBC Three for their hard work and creativity in investigating these uncharted online worlds with me: Katie Rice, Katie O'Toole, Olivia Lace-Evans, Mike Radford, Jo Carr, and many more.

I'm also really grateful to everyone beyond those teams who makes the journalism I do possible. Thank you to Esme Wren, Stewart Maclean, Dan Clarke and the people at *Newsnight* who supported me when I first started at the BBC. In particular editorial and legal advisors Matthew Eltringham and Sarah Branthwaite, who have the best brains and judgement in the business; the brilliant Lindsay McCoy, who has the right priorities and makes the right calls; Finlo Rohrer – mostly too clever for his own good – and the team at BBC Verify and Trending; Merlyn, Kay, Olga, Reha and many other wonderfully supportive and talented colleagues; the wonderful Kathryn Westcott, whose insights about clothes are just as sharp as her invaluable advice about investigations; and everyone brilliant I work with from the BBC's online and digital teams. Deborah Turness and Fran Unsworth, who are the reason the BBC has someone investigating this beat, and Kevin Silverton (for giving this a read and battling the trolls!).

NOTES

Introduction

1   Caleb Madison, 'Trolling's Surprising Origins in Fishing', *The Atlantic*, 9 May 2022, https://www.theatlantic.com/newsletters/archive/2022/05/trollings-surprising-origins-in-fishing/629784/.

2   Brian K. Blount, *Revelation: A Commentary*, Louisville, KY, Westminster Knox Press, 2009, pp. 248–9.

3   https://journals.sagepub.com/doi/10.1177/1368430220982068.

1 True Believers

4   Van Prooijen & Douglas (2017).

5   S. Shahsavari, P. Holur, T. Wang, T. R. Tangherlini and V. Roychowdhury, 'Conspiracy in the time of corona: Automatic detection of emerging COVID-19 conspiracy theories in social media and the news', *Journal of Computational Social Science*, vol. 3, no. 2, 2020, pp. 279–317; https://www.theguardian.com/world/ng-interactive/2021/oct/26/why-people-believe-covid-conspiracy-theories-could-folklore-hold-the-answer.

6   L. Stasielowicz, 'Who believes in conspiracy theories? A meta-analysis on personality correlates', *Journal of Research in Personality*, vol. 98, 2022, p. 98, https://doi.org/10.1016/j.jrp.2022.104229.

7   Douglas (2021).

8   Ibid.

9   D. Jolley, S. Mari and K. M. Douglas, 'Consequences of Conspiracy Theories', in *Routledge Handbook of Conspiracy Theories*, ed. Michael Butter and Peter Knight, London, Routledge, 2020, pp. 231–41.

10 Ibid.

11 Douglas (2021).

12 J.-W. van Prooijen and K. M. Douglas, 'Conspiracy theories as part of history: The role of Societal Crisis Situations,' *Memory Studies*, vol. 10, no. 3, 2017, pp. 323–33.

13 Douglas (2021).

14 Joseph E. Uscinski and Joseph M. Parent, *American Conspiracy Theories*, New York, Oxford University Press, 2014, p. 99.

2 The Non-Believers

15 Jolley et al. (2020).
16 Z. Ren, E. Dimant and M. Schweitzer, 'Beyond belief: How social engagement motives influence the spread of conspiracy theories', *Journal of Experimental Social Psychology*, vol. 104, 2023, https://doi.org/10.2139/ssrn.3919364.
17 Amy Mitchell et al., 'Most Americans who have heard of QAnon conspiracy theories say they are bad for the country and that Trump seems to support people who promote them', Pew Research Center, 16 September 2020, https://www.pewresearch.org/journalism/2020/09/16/most-americans-who-have-heard-of-qanon-conspiracy-theories-say-they-are-bad-for-the-country-and-that-trump-seems-to-support-people-who-promote-them/.

4 Escaping the Rabbit Hole

18 Robertson, David G. 'Conspiracy Theories and the Study of Alternative and Emergent Religions.' 2015, https://doi.org/10.1525/nr.2015.19.2.5.

5 The Life of a Lie

19 S. Shahsavari et al. (2020).
20 Christopher Paul and Miriam Matthews, *The Russian 'Firehose of Falsehood' Propaganda Model: Why It Might Work and Options to Counter It*, Santa Monica, CA, RAND Corporation, 2016.
21 Ibid.
22 L. Nitschinsk, S. J. Tobin and E.J. Vanman, 'The disinhibiting effects of anonymity increase online trolling,' *Cyberpsychology, Behavior, and Social Networking*, vol. 25, no. 6, 2022, pp. 377–83.

6 Shock Troops

23 Hal Berghel and Daniel Berleant, 'The Online Trolling Ecosystem', *Computer*, vol. 51, 2018, pp. 44–51, https://doi.org/10.1109/MC.2018.3191256.
24 Institute for Strategic Dialogue, 'BBC Panorama research: Misogyny and abuse on Twitter before and after Elon Musk's takeover', 6 March 2023, https://www.isdglobal.org/digital_dispatches/bbc-panorama-research-misogyny-and-abuse-on-twitter-before-and-after-elon-musks-takeover/.
25 Statista, 'Facebook average revenue', July 2023, https://www.statista.com/statistics/251328/facebooks-average-revenue-per-user-by-region/.
26 Research for the BBC by the Centre for Countering Digital Hate.

27 Philippine Center for Investigative Journalism, 'State agents linked to over 100 attacks', 3 May 2021, https://pcij.org/blog/1105/state-agents-linked-to-over-100-attacks-threats-against-ph-media-under-duterte-admin.

7 Bot or Not? How State-Sponsored Disinformation Works

28 E. Ferrera et al., 'The rise of social bots', *Communications of the ACM*, vol. 59, no. 7, pp. 96–104.

29 H. Chang et al., 'Social bots and social media manipulation in 2020: the year in review', USC paper, 2021, https://arxiv.org/pdf/2102.08436.pdf.

30 N. Corbu et al., 'Fake News Going Viral: The Mediating Effect of Negative Emotions'. Media Literacy and Academic Research, vol. 4, no. 2, 2021, pp. 58–85.

8 Virtual Is Now Real

31 J. van Dijck, *The Culture of Connectivity : A Critical History of Social Media*. Oxford: Oxford University Press, 2013.

32 https://www.pewresearch.org/internet/fact-sheet/social-media/.

33 https://www.pewresearch.org/politics/2021/11/09/beyond-red-vs-blue-the-political-typology-2/.

9 What Next?

34 https://www.oecd.org/gov/gov-at-a-glance-2021-finland.pdf.

INDEX

INDEX